Why everyone (else) is a hypocrite

PRINCETON UNIVERSITY PRESS   Princeton and Oxford

Robert Kurzban

Why everyone (else) is a hypocrite

Evolution

and the

Modular

Mind

Requests for permission to reproduce material from this work
should be sent to Permissions, Princeton University Press

Published by Princeton University Press, 41 William Street, Princeton, New Jersey 08540
In the United Kingdom: Princeton University Press, 6 Oxford Street, Woodstock,
Oxfordshire OX20 1TW

press.princeton.edu

Library of Congress Cataloging-in-Publication Data

Kurzban, Robert, 1969
   Why everyone (else) is a hypocrite : evolution and the modular mind / Robert Kurzban.
     p.   cm.
   Includes bibliographical references and index.
   ISBN 978-0-691-14674-4 (hbk. : alk. paper)   1. Modularity (Psychology)
2. Evolutionary psychology.   3. Self-deception.   I. Title.
   BF311.K867 2010
   153–dc22   2010026707

British Library Cataloging-in-Publication Data is available

This book has been composed in Glypha LT with Bruno JB

Designed and composed by Tracy Baldwin

Printed on acid-free paper. ∞

Printed in the United States of America

10 9 8 7 6 5 4 3 2 1

Dedicated to all those denied liberty for pursuing happiness

contents

acknowledgments

Some time ago, I was lucky enough to attend a small workshop on "self-deception" with some of my scientific idols, including economist Thomas Schelling and biologist Robert Trivers. Surprisingly, to me anyway, the overall timbre of the conversation—and I think that the people who were there would probably agree with this characterization—was a general intellectual spinning of tires.

What struck me during and especially after the workshop was how the concept of modularity—a conceptual backbone of my graduate training in evolutionary psychology—easily unraveled the Gordian knot of self-deception. When I returned to the University of Pennsylvania after the workshop, I started work on what would eventually become two papers that I co-authored with a graduate student who was working with me at the time, Athena Aktipis. Writing the papers got me thinking about a number of issues in the literatures in psychology and economics that modularity helped clarify. For whatever reason, researchers in the social sciences have been, by and large, allergic to evolutionary explanations, and the commitment to modularity. This meant that there were large areas of research that could be usefully informed by this approach. The results of my thinking about these areas, more or less, became this book.

I want to thank the people who were kind enough to take the time to read part or all of various versions of this manuscript, including Clark Barrett, Terry Burnham, John Christner, Angela Duckworth, James Fowler, Amy Kurzban, Nina Kurzban, Steven Kurzban, Mike McCullough, Hugo Mercier, Steve Pinker, Alex Shaw, Ewa Szymanska, and Bart Wilson. Not a few of the ideas in here were developed in concert with another former graduate student of mine, Peter DeScioli. Some of the material toward the end draws heavily on the ideas of yet another former graduate student at Penn—though he was not my student—Jason Weeden, who also provided comments on an earlier draft.

Special thanks to my father, Stan Kurzban, and my sweetie, Nicole Buttermore, who bravely endured various iterations of this project and whose contributions cannot be overstated. My appreciation also to my agent, Max Brockman and, at Princeton University Press, Eric Schwartz and Debbie Tegarden, all of whom were very tolerant of me in general and my various rookie mistakes in particular during the process. I can't possibly thank Jodi Beder enough for her careful copyediting and many helpful suggestions. Any and all errors, of course, are my own.

And finally, thanks to all the people who have been subjected to the ideas in this book in classes, seminars, conferences, and even the Thanksgiving table. I appreciate the tolerance, the feedback, and the yams.

Robert Kurzban
Philadelphia, PA
March 2010

Why everyone (else) is a hypocrite

prologue

Ignorance can save your life in Philadelphia.

If, like me, you've spent some time in Southern California, then you're probably accustomed to cars stopping when you're in a crosswalk. You might even occasionally make eye contact with a driver coming your way. *I see you, you see me, so we both know you have to stop.*

This could get you killed in Philadelphia. If a driver sees that you see that he's coming, then he knows that you know that your best bet is to stay out of the street, since in the game of person versus car, person always wishes she hadn't played.

So, here's the best way to cross the street in Philadelphia. Keep your eyes away from any lanes of traffic with cars that might run you over. Cross the street looking a little lost or confused; try to "walk like a tourist."

The goal is to appear conspicuously ignorant. Because drivers will actually stop for a pedestrian who has no chance of escaping if they barrel through the intersection, your best ally is ignorance: to appear completely— blissfully—unaware. This way, the driver knows you don't know he's coming, and you're now safely categorized as someone who can't be counted on to try to escape.

He'll slow down.

Well, he'll probably slow down. If you really want to be safe, cross with other pedestrians. If you really, really want to be safe, stay in your car. Or out of Philadelphia.

Life in Philadelphia is, in many ways, very much unlike the old video game, Frogger. In the game, you had to move your frog across five lanes of traffic without getting run over by the cars or trucks speeding along the road. After you got past the road, there was a stream with logs, alligators, and turtles in it, and you had to hop on top of these, using them like stepping-stones to get to the other side, paying careful attention to the turtles, which could suddenly submerge beneath your frog, which, I guess, couldn't swim.

Unlike in Philadelphia, in Frogger, *refusing to watch for traffic won't help you.* It won't work because the cars and trucks on the screen don't care if you know they're coming. They're programmed to run you over, and that's that.

The basic point is that in Frogger, you're not playing a game against another *person*, but rather you're playing a game against *Nature*. Only cold, hard reality determines how well you do. *Being ignorant or stupid can't help you.* In contrast, in Philadelphia, you're playing a game against other people. Here, the rules are very different. Ignorance and stupidity can help.

In cases like Frogger, in which outcomes depend only on Nature, it's no use being stupid or ignorant because Nature doesn't care one way or the other. If you don't watch for cars, she runs over your frog, and you're done.

Ah, but . . . but when you play games against other people, everything changes. In cases like crossing the street in Philadelphia, in which your out-come depends on other people rather than Nature, it can be useful to be ignorant or stupid.

■ ■ ■

I'm an evolutionary psychologist, and I think a lot about how the human mind is designed. Natural selection has made us, humans, capable of wonders, and from our hands—or, really, our brains—have come spacecraft to explore the heavens, sonnets to lift the spirit, and Frogger, to consume the quarters I was supposed to use to buy lunch in my high school cafeteria.

But amid the wonder at the marvels of fine works of engineering like the human eye and our immune system, the reputation of various bits of human brains have been taking a beating. Books and headlines are filled with reports of human shortcomings and frailties, about how we make bad decisions (*Predictably Irrational*), are swayed by irrelevant information (*Nudge*), and behave poorly while driving (*Traffic*).

I'd like to say that this book will turn the tide and strike a blow for human nature, telling you that, hey, we're actually not all that bad after all . . . but it won't.

This book is, rather, an attempt to explain *why* we act the way we act, and, perhaps partly in our defense, to show that if we are wrong a lot, well, being right isn't everything.

My argument is going to be that much, or at least some, of what makes us ignorant, mind-numbingly stupid—and hypocritical—is that we evolved to play many different kinds of strategic games with others, and our brains are built to exploit the fact that being knowledgeable, right, or morally consistent is not always to our advantage. Because humans are such social creatures, while being right is still really important, it's very far from everything.

In fact, being ignorant, wrong, irrational, and hypocritical can make you much better off than being knowledgeable, correct, reasonable, and consistent.

As long as you're ignorant, wrong, irrational, and hypocritical in the right ways.

chapter 1

Consistently Inconsistent

■ *The mind consists of many different parts. These parts often "believe" differ-ent, mutually inconsistent things. Sometimes this is obvious, as illustrated in cases of brain damage and optical illusions. Other cases are less obvious, but no less interesting.* ■

Do I contradict myself?

Very well then I contradict myself,

(I am large, I contain multitudes.)

—Walt Whitman, *Song of Myself*, section 51

The very constitution of the human mind makes us massively incon-sistent. In this book, I try to persuade you that the human mind consists of many, many mental processes—think of them as little programming subrou-tines, or maybe individual iPhone applications—each operating by its own logic, designed by the inexorable process of natural selection; and, further, that what you think and what you do depends on which process is run-ning the show—your show—at any particular moment. Because which part of the mind is in charge changes over time, and because these different parts are designed to do very different things, human behavior is—and this shouldn't be a surprise—complicated.

What's worse, because so much of what goes on in our heads is inac-cessible—that is, we don't know why we think what we do, an idea recently made popular by, among others, Malcolm Gladwell in *Blink*—we are often not able to say what's really causing our behavior. If you're like me, you have often—and quite honestly—answered the question "Why did you do that?" with "I have absolutely no idea."*†

But the good news is that a fundamental insight about human psychology allows us to think more sensibly than ever before about all the different subroutines in your head and the way that they are organized. Evolutionary psychology—my discipline—focuses our attention on the idea that the different bits of our brain have *functions*. Just as some of your mind's subroutines are for seeing, some for processing language, and some for controlling muscles, the rest have functions as well, some of them having to do with choosing mates, some with making friends, and—one subject I currently study—some with morally condemning others for doing things like baking pot brownies.

This is *not*, however, just another book about how people are irrational, or why we make bad decisions. There are enough of those already.

This book also isn't about our "emotional self" and our "rational self," or about the difference between "affect" and "cognition." It's not about our right brain and our left brain. It's not about the duality of man, the duality of woman, or the triality of Freud's id, ego, and superego. As we'll see, cutting up the brain into such a small number of parts undersells, by a fair amount, just how complicated things are.

Instead, this book is about contradictions. It's about how you— OK, *I*— can, at one and the same time, want to go for a training run and also want to stay in bed on a cold November morning. It's about how you can, at one and the same time, during a severe economic downturn, both want to know how your retirement fund is doing and also not want to know how your retirement fund is doing. It's about how you can, at one and the same time, want the government to leave people alone as long as they're not hurting anyone and also very much want the government to interfere with people's lives even when they're not hurting anyone.

---

*In many ways, you're holding a book-length apology for (many) such moments. Sorry, sweetie!

†I'll use footnotes, here on the bottom of the page, for material that is important enough that you might want to read it, but not so important that it needs to go in the main text. I'll use numbered endnotes, which are at the end of the book, for references to others' work and for a small number of technical discussions. Endnotes are more or less serious, but footnotes . . . not so much.

It's also about how many, perhaps even most, contradictions in our heads go unnoticed.

The reason it sometimes feels as though we're conflicted, the reason it feels like we have multiple competing motives, and the reason we're inconsistent in the way we think and reason about fundamental issues of morality, are all explained by this important insight about the human mind. Because of the way evolution operates, the mind consists of many, many parts, and these parts have many different functions. Because they're designed to do different things, they don't always work in perfect harmony.

The large number of parts of the mind can be thought of as, in some sense, being different "selves," designed to accomplish some task. This book is about all these different selves, some of which make you run, some of which make you lazy, some of which make you smart, and some of which keep you ignorant. You're unaware of many of them. They just do what they're designed to do, out of sight and, as it were, out of mind.

This book is about how all of these different parts of mental machinery get along or, occasionally, don't get along, and it's about how thinking about the mind this way explains the large number of contradictions in human thought and behavior.

It explains why we are conflicted, inconsistent, and even hypocritical.

Understanding the whole of human behavior requires understanding all of the large number of different parts that produce it.

These parts are called *modules*.

Half-truths

To start off, I'm going to persuade you that you—yes, *you*—simultaneously believe (or, at least, "believe," with quotation marks around it) many, many things that are mutually contradictory. I'll start out by talking about some weird people, continue by talking about some weird cases, and before I'm done I'll talk a little bit about why you do weird things like locking your refrigerator door at night.*

---

*I'll explain about the refrigerator by and by.

If you know about the structure of the brain, you probably know that it is divided into two hemispheres, the left and the right. The two hemispheres are, in normal people, connected by the corpus callosum, which, roughly, allows the two halves of the brain to "talk" to each other. That is, it allows for the transmission of information from the left cerebral hemisphere to the right, and vice versa.

In some cases, this connection is surgically severed in patients with epilepsy to prevent the spread of epileptic seizure activity from one cerebral hemisphere to the other. This procedure, called a corpus callosotomy, prevents the spreading not only of seizures, but also of information that would normally move from one hemisphere to the other. People who have undergone this procedure are called "split-brain" patients for this reason.

Why am I telling you this? Because a brain in which there is limited or no direct communication between its two hemispheres illustrates a very straightforward case—albeit an unnatural case—in which a brain can have mutually inconsistent pieces of information. Suppose that the connections between the two hemispheres, under normal conditions, allow information from the two sides to be integrated and reconciled. If so, then if these connections are cut, you can wind up with information in one that is inconsistent with information in the other.

Neuroscientists Mike Gazzaniga and Joseph LeDoux performed experiments that illustrate exactly this. They took advantage of the fact that the way the nervous system is set up, it is possible to present information to one hemisphere but not the other. Further, it is also possible, in some sense, to get one hemisphere to respond to a question without involvement from the other. Split-brain patients make it easy to think about having "multiple selves" because you can communicate with each hemisphere separately.

The short (and slightly imprecise) story is this. When you present information to these patients in the right visual field (basically, stuff in front of them to the right of their nose), that information goes only to the left hemisphere, and when you present information to the left visual field it goes to the right hemisphere.

Now, because the right hemisphere controls the left hand and the left hemisphere controls the right hand, if you want to ask the right hemisphere a question, you can ask the question verbally—which goes through both ears and on to both hemispheres—and ask the patient to respond using his left hand. This tells you what the right hemisphere thinks the correct answer is.

You can also tell the patient to respond to the question verbally. Because the vocal apparatus is controlled by the left hemisphere, the answer to the question tells you what the left hemisphere "thinks" the correct answer is.

In a set of classic studies, Gazzaniga and LeDoux[1] showed a split-brain patient two pictures at once: a chicken claw, shown to the left hemisphere (in the right visual field), and a wintry scene to the right hemisphere (in the left visual field). The patient was then shown an array of cards with pictures of objects on them and asked to point, with each hand, to something related to what he saw.

Consider each hemisphere separately. The left hemisphere was being asked to use the right hand to point to something related to a chicken claw. The right hemisphere was being asked to use the left hand to point to something related to a wintry scene.

The hands—or the hemispheres—did fine. The left hand pointed to a snow shovel. The right hand pointed to a chicken.

Now consider what happens when the "patient"—really the left hemisphere—was asked to explain why his hands were pointing at those pictures. The right hemisphere, even though it heard the question, couldn't answer it, not having control of the verbal apparatus. As for the left hemisphere, what did it know? Well, it knew the question, it knew that it saw a chicken claw, and it knew—because it could now see if it looked—the left hand was pointing to a snow shovel. (It probably also knew that it was one hemisphere of a split-brain patient.) What would I do if I were asked to explain the relationship between a chicken claw and a snow shovel? I might, as the patient's left hemisphere did, say that the shovel is for cleaning up after the chicken.

If you were able to ask just the right hemisphere, which knew the question, saw a wintry scene, and—if it looked at the right hand pointing to a picture of a chicken—saw the two seemingly unrelated facts, it might have given you a very different answer.* It might even have responded, "Well, I

---

* I like to think it would be something about really cold chickens.

know that I'm a split-brain patient, so you annoying experimenters are probably messing with me. My left hemisphere controls my right hand, and who knows why my right hand is pointing to a chicken." At any rate, it seems unlikely that it would have said anything about cleaning up after a chicken.[2]

What did "the patient" think was going on? Here's the thing. *There's no such thing as "the patient."* There's no real answer to that question because "the patient" is two more or less disconnected hemispheres. You can only ask about what individual, distinct, and separated parts think. The question asking what "the patient" sees is bad, and the answer is meaningless. (Questions can be bad in many ways, for example by assuming a condition contrary to fact, like the infamous "Have you stopped beating your wife?"[3]) Here, asking what "the patient" believes assumes there's one, unitary patient who can have a belief about something. If I'm right about the ideas here, then a lot of intuitively sound questions like this one will turn out to be at best problematic and at worst incoherent.

Seeing with your brain

The cases of split-brain patients aren't the only ones in which it is easy to see that different parts of someone's brain seem to believe two mutually inconsistent things. Neuroscientist V. S. Ramachandran, among others, has written about many such cases, and among the most interesting are the mysterious-sounding instances of "phantom limb."

People who have had an arm or leg amputated frequently report that they still "feel" the limb that has been removed. (These sensations vary, but they are often sensations of pain. The neurophysiology of this is interesting, but, as I do in nearly all of the remainder of this book, I am going to ignore all the neurophysiological details.) Do patients with a phantom arm "believe" that they have both arms intact? Well, if you ask them, they can tell you that one of their arms is missing. So, no, they don't believe they have two arms.

However, the fact that there is a sensation of pain *in the missing arm* means that *some* part of the nervous system "believes" that there is an arm there. Indeed, anecdotal evidence from Ramachandran suggests that this part of the brain not only *thinks* there's an arm there, but positively *insists* on it. He reports a case in which he told a patient to reach for a cup of coffee with his phantom arm. He then yanked the cup toward himself . The patient yelled "ow" because his phantom fingers got caught in the cup's handle just as Ramachandran was moving the cup away.[4] Some part of his brain "really" believed there was an arm there.[*]

By the way—and we revisit this in more detail later—there's no reason to say that we should discount the part of his brain that thinks there's an arm there just because it disagrees with the part that talks (and because the talking part happens to be correct), as though what the person says is the only thing that matters. In the split-brain case, we don't think that the patient *only* saw the image of a chicken just because the part of the brain that talks was the part that saw it. It's a mistake to pay attention only to what comes out of the mouth when we're trying to understand what's in the mind, because there are many, many parts of the mind that can't talk.

It's easy to put special emphasis on what people can report. Ramachandran says that even though some part of the patient's brain did not know that the limb was missing, "John 'the person' is unquestionably aware of the fact."[5] Ramachandran didn't say, "the bit of John's brain that controls the vocal apparatus." I hope to have persuaded you already or, failing that, that I will have persuaded you by the time you're done with this book, that the bit of John's brain that caused him to say "ow" even though the phantom fingers couldn't really have been caught in the cup handle is as at least as entitled to—or, at least nearly as entitled to—being considered "John, the person" as is any other bit. There's nothing special about the bit of the brain that controls the vocal cords; it's just another piece of meat in your head.

Moving on. In the literature on patients with neurophysiological damage, perhaps no condition is more compelling than alien hand syndrome (AHS). Patients with AHS report that the affected hand moves without the exercise of their will.[†] Not only do they talk as though the hand is not under their control, but they also say that it is not even their hand. Patients will, in this case, literally "talk to the hand," addressing it with the second-person

---

[*]Apparently, according to the report of this incident, some part of the person's brain also thought Ramachandran was a jerk for ripping the cup out of his "hand."

[†]Think of Dr. Strangelove.

pronoun "you"—and not always politely ("Damn you!"). Patients report that the alien hand prevents them from doing various tasks. As one patient put it, it is "as though it has a mind of its own."[6] In this case, the hand would wake the patient up, interfere with eating, and un-tuck shirts previously tucked in by the other hand. In this case, "conflict" is literal: "[T]he patient's wife also observed the hands 'fighting.' "[7]

It is tempting to dismiss such patients smugly as being foolish. Who could possibly believe that the hands attached to the rest of their bodies were not under their control? Anyone who has spent a spooky evening moving the pointer around on a Ouija board convinced that some otherworldly entity was in charge shouldn't be so smug. And anyone who never believed it for a second but still somehow feels that, yeah, "it *does* seem like I'm not moving my own hands," well, you don't get to be smug either.[8]

One more illustration of seeming contradictions in patient populations before moving on to normal people: blind sight. Consider the following. A patient reports that she can't see anything—that she is completely blind. Her eyes themselves are undamaged. There is, however, damage to parts of the brain that are responsible for allowing light coming into the eye to be converted into an image of the world *out there*.

Nonetheless, you tell such a person that you are going to present X's and O's in front of her, and you want her to tell you which letter she is seeing. She protests that she would love to do this little experiment, but reminds you that she's *blind*. You insist, and, being polite, she agrees. You show her the X's and O's, and she gamely guesses, or at least tells you that she was forced to guess, reminding you that she's *blind*.*

The thing is that some patients perform statistically above chance. To be above chance, some part of their brain *must* have access to the information about whether you presented an X or an O. Further, this bit must be sending its information to a part of the brain that itself is connected to the vocal apparatus, or the patient couldn't say the correct answers aloud. But *some* part of the brain, also hooked up to the speech-production systems, doesn't seem to know all this is going on. That's the one that keeps reminding the

---

*I'm embellishing the details here, but preserving the sense. I'm just envisioning what I'd say if I were blind and someone asked me to perform a visual discrimination task. I think I'd be a little snarky about it.

experimenter that "Hey, I'm *blind*." So, one part of the brain thinks—or, really, knows—that it is seeing, and another part of the brain thinks that the first part can't see. Oddly, there is a sense in which they are both right. Again, the perverse way they can both be right is that when the patient says, "I'm blind," that "I" is tricky. Yes, the part that talks has no experience of sight. This does not mean that no part of the brain does.

A similar phenomenon has been observed with emotional expressions. One patient was shown pairs of faces: happy or angry, happy or sad, and fearful or happy. The patient didn't get them all right, but was above chance for all three pairs. Interestingly, the part of the brain involved in this task seems to be pretty specific in its function. The patient did no better than chance when presented with male and female faces and asked to guess which was which. The patient's responses were no better than chance even when presented with faces compared to jumbled faces. That is, this person was not able to distinguish a non-face from a face, but could distinguish (again, imperfectly) a happy face from an angry one.[9] Taken together, this suggests that some bits of the brain that are responsible for some parts of visual processing are working, at least a little, while others are not. These working parts have pretty narrow jobs—distinguishing facial expressions.

One patient, referred to with the initials TN, who was known to have such abilities despite being blind, was recently given the task of navigating a hallway in which various obstacles had been placed.[10] He was able to go from one end to the other without hitting anything, even though he had to change his course to do so. Reports indicated that TN was not even aware that he altered his course, let alone why he did so. This is another case in which you shouldn't "believe" that the part of the brain that talks is special. There is some sense in which, in cases like this, the talking part is wrong.

This is a profound illustration of how parts of the brain do many interesting jobs, while remaining inconspicuously out of awareness. Evidence like this has suggested to some people that the case of TN is not so unlike that of normal people. As neuroscientist Chris Frith put it, "the mark of the self in action is that we have very little experience of it. Most of the time we are not aware of the sensory consequences of our actions or of the various subtle corrections that we make during the course of goal-directed actions."[11]

Just like TN.

Seeing is disbelieving

Even if you agree that these examples illustrate that contradictory information can simultaneously be present in the same brain, perhaps you think that there's something strange about these cases, drawing as they do on people with brain damage. Well, that's fair enough. I'm suggesting that two pieces of information that are separated from one another in the brain can be in conflict, and having a split brain—or other kinds of damage—somehow seems to load the dice in my favor. So let's try some examples with normal brains.[12] Let's try yours.

Consider first an optical illusion called the "same color illusion" (figure 1.1).[13] In this picture, have a look at the squares labeled A and B. Are they the same shade or different shades? You've probably had enough experience with these sorts of things that you know that I wouldn't be asking you unless A and B, strange as it seems, are the same shade. You can verify this for yourself by covering up all the bits of the picture except the two squares in question. Without the board and the cylinder surrounding our two key squares, you'll see the shades of the two squares are identical.

Optical illusions are fun, but what's the point? First, ask yourself if it's true that some part of your brain "thinks" that the two squares are not the

Figure 1.1. The same color illusion.
The squares marked "A" and "B" are the same shade.
Copyright ©1995, Edward H. Adelson.

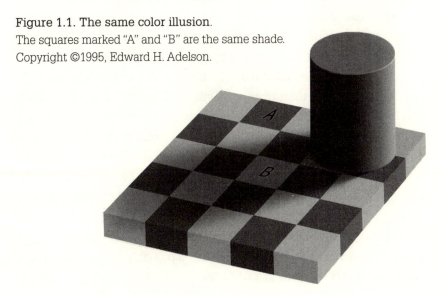

same shade. It seems to me that the answer is transparently "yes." You can only have the experience of seeing the two squares as different if they are *somehow* perceived and experienced as different by your visual system. So, roughly—and I clarify how I use words like "belief" later on—it must be true that some part of your brain—your visual system, or a part of it—"believes" that the two squares are different. If you could directly quiz that part of the visual system, as we did with individual hemispheres of split-brain patients, it would tell you that they're different.

Now, you've covered up the rest of the figure, and you've also seen that the two squares are the same shade. They appear to be different once you see the figure in its entirety again, but "you" "know"—and by that I mean something like, the information is in your head somewhere—that the two squares are the same shade. So, my claim is that this simple optical illusion is a case in which two contradictory pieces of information—same shade versus different shade—are simultaneously present in different parts of your—normal—brain.

Well, OK, you say, you'll grant that. In very strange, contrived cases, it's *possible* that the same brain can have conflicting information that is left unresolved in different bits. I'm satisfied, at this point, if you're willing to concede just that much, because the remaining arguments I'm going to advance only turn on the *possibility* of such conflicts being present in your brain, and take the question of the actual amounts of conflict—how many there are, how frequently they occur, what areas they are present in—to be something that we can only answer by looking at the relevant evidence.

But, just to push the point home, let me answer a couple of possible objections. Perhaps you think there's something funny about the visual system and, in particular, that the visual system is special in that perceptual experience can't be affected by new knowledge or new experience. That is, maybe you think perception is just too "bottom up" to be able to be changed by "high-level" information. If that's your argument, then what you want to be true is that once I show you a picture, simply telling you something about it can't change the way you perceive it.

Take a brief look at figure 1.2. Describe it. Say it out loud, so you can't cheat and say you knew it all along later. You probably said something like, "It's a bunch of black blobs in a white field." That's true as far as it goes. OK,

Figure 1.2. Black blobs on a white field. Photograph © copyright 1965 by Ronald C. James.

now look at the bottom left part of the picture, and try to see the head of a Dalmatian. She's munching something on the ground, and you can see her ear flopped over and her collar. Now how would you describe the picture? Look away, and look back, and try to see the picture as you did before, as just a bunch of blobs. Most people report that this is difficult, even impossible. Once you get the information that it's a dog, the way you see the image changes.[14]

There are any number of other optical illusions that show that the visual system has one set of "beliefs" about the world, while some other part of your brain has a different one. I'll mention just one, the Müller-Lyer illusion

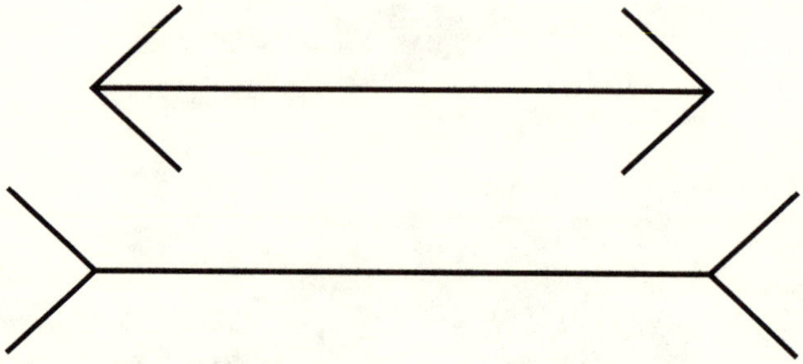

Figure 1.3. The Müller-Lyer illusion.

(figure 1.3), which consists of two equal-length lines, one right above the other. The line with the outward facing arrows appears longer than the one with the inward facing ones.[15] This is true *even if you yourself just drew the equal-length lines*. Some part of your brain, part of the perceptual system, contains the information "the lines are unequal in length," whereas another part of your brain contains the information "the lines are equal in length." Again, it's tempting to put more weight on the part that thinks they're equally long, since that feels more like "you"—and, again, that part is correct in this case—but I think that's a mistake. More about that later.

You might also be thinking that there's something funny about all of these things because they're illusions, somehow obscuring the world as it "really is." I'm not going to get into the philosophy of the reality of the world, but it's worth mentioning another effect that isn't subject to the same criticism.

Those of you old enough to remember turntables and the records they played might also remember that it was possible to play the record by spinning the turntable manually. This worked forwards as well as backwards, and for a short period of time it was popular to record material that could only be understood if the record was played backward.

Two researchers, John Vokey and Don Read, conducted a now-classic study investigating this.[16] They listened to a bunch of material, including Lewis Carroll's "Jabberwocky" and the 23rd Psalm, played backwards. In any material played backwards, it's usually possible to find some bits and pieces that sound kind of sort of like real phrases, and these researchers identified some, including, in the "Jabberwocky," the phrase "saw a girl with a weasel in her mouth." They played the recordings backwards for a group of subjects and told them particular phrases to listen for. Most subjects did indeed hear the phrases. However, they *only* reported hearing each of the phrases *after* they were told to listen for it. Their expectations caused them to hear phrases that they otherwise were oblivious to.

If you listen to this stuff yourself, once you're told what the phrase is, it's actually pretty hard *not* to hear it, just as it was hard not to see the Dalmatian once you had a hint. But, of course, unlike the Dalmatian case, you're hearing a phrase that isn't "really" there.

The "Jabberwocky" case and the Dalmatian case show that some kinds of information—that there's a Dalmatian in the picture, that someone is saying "saw a girl with a weasel in her mouth"—in one part of your head can actually change your experience. "High-level" information, such as what an experimenter tells you, can change your low-level perception, transforming dots into a dog and a mix of phonemes into a phrase. No such "feeding down" occurs in the case of the same color illusion. When you see the checkerboard with the surrounding material, your perception of it doesn't change even though some part of your brain knows that the two labeled squares are equally bright.

These relatively simple demonstrations illustrate something important about the way normal brains work. Illusions like the checkerboard show that different parts of your brain can "disagree" about what's true. Further, in some cases, information that one part of your brain "knows" to be true doesn't change, or update, the part of your brain with the discrepant information. So, just as in the cases of patients mentioned above, *normal human brains can have mutually inconsistent information in different parts*.

Moreover, these examples illustrate something about the way the brain updates information from one part to another. In some cases, updating occurs, and the expectation to hear "saw a girl with a weasel in her mouth" really does change a string of sounds into the sense that one has heard the phrase. In the checkerboard case, perception doesn't change.

This implies that, even in normal brains, *information can stay isolated in particular brain parts*. If the knowledge that the two squares were equally bright changed how the figure looked, that would be good evidence that this kind of information "fed down" into the perceptual system. It doesn't.

To link this to the technical literature in cognitive science, the philosopher Jerry Fodor, in a highly influential book called *Modularity of Mind* published in 1983, used the term "encapsulated" to refer to this aspect of information flow in the brain.[17] A system is said to be encapsulated from another part in cases like the checkerboard illusion. Here, the visual system that generates the perceptual experience is encapsulated with respect to the part of the brain that "knows" that the two squares are equally bright. This just means that the information either doesn't get into the visual system generating the perceptual experience, or it doesn't affect it.

While Fodor thought encapsulation might be limited to cases like the perceptual system, we'll explore cases that suggest that it happens in many areas of psychology.

Snack break

If inconsistencies in human brains were restricted to cases like optical illusions, then it might not be worth worrying too much about them. These are interesting and fun examples, but hardly something to get worked up over.

Some kinds of inconsistencies, however, get people very worked up. In the provocatively titled book *Why More Sex Is Safer Sex*, economist Steven Landsburg wrote: "It has always seemed to me that the two great mysteries of the Universe are 'Why is there something instead of nothing?' and 'Why do people lock their refrigerator doors?' "[18] I'm really not in a position to solve the first of those two mysteries. I think I can say a little about the second one, though.

In essence, what Landsburg is worried about here—so much so that he dubs it a Great Mystery of the Universe, is human inconsistency. He reasons that there is a very big—and mysterious—inconsistency here. People who are dieting are occasionally given advice to make getting food more difficult as part of their regime. The idea is that if it's hard to satisfy a craving for a midnight snack, you'll be less likely to indulge. But this advice carries an apparent contradiction in the sense that if people don't want to snack when they wake up in the middle of the night, then, well, they simply shouldn't snack when they wake up in the middle of the night.

Landsburg, like many other economists and probably most people in general, has a view of the mind without divisions or compartments. Here's how it works. Each person's mind has a vast store of knowledge about the world and the person's own preferences. When the mind faces a decision, it integrates all of the relevant information together and spits out the answer. Given everything that I know, and all of my preferences, what is the best course of action to take to satisfy my preferences? It doesn't matter what time it is, what room I'm in, or whether my stomach is, at that moment, empty or full—on this view, the same answer comes out each time.

If you think this is how the mind works, then if you ask it, before you go to bed, if you should snack or not snack at midnight, it'll tell you not to snack, and if you ask it at midnight, it'll say the same thing. So there's really no need to lock the refrigerator door before you go to bed.

This view of a mind without divisions reminds me of the old toy, the Magic 8-Ball. The Magic 8-Ball—"has all the answers you need!"—is a little larger than a regular 8-ball. You ask a yes/no question, concentrate really hard, shake it up, and, presto! the answer appears in a little window cut into the ball. The 8-Ball is, of course, completely random, giving one of 20 possible replies, including "It is decidedly so," or "Better not tell you now." But imagine a genuinely *Magic* 8-Ball that has all the information in the world, integrates it, and comes up with the best answer. If the mind were like a Magic 8-Ball in this sense, taking everything that one knows, and one's preferences, and integrating them all together—a process as magical as what economists refer to as "rationality"[19]—then people would behave consistently, just like the sort of person Landsburg and other economists have in mind. Shake your 8-Ball/mind up before bed or at midnight, the right thing to do is clear.

I don't think that economists literally believe that the mind works this way, that the mind has supernatural or magical abilities. What is clear is that many of them don't seem to think that the mind has important divisions within it. Rather, they think of it as more or less "unitary," the opposite of the modular view.

My hope is that by the time you finish reading this book, you'll want to demote the refrigerator door problem from a Mystery of the Universe to just one of a large number of phenomena that can be easily explained with modularity.

The morals of this story

One type of inconsistency is moral hypocrisy, which I'll take to be something like expressing moral condemnation for something and then doing exactly that thing. Hypocrisy is so easy to imagine that it might be hard to imagine anyone who *isn't* a hypocrite. So, just to give a sense of what the *absence* of hypocrisy might look like, here's a fanciful example.

Consider the android Commander Data from *Star Trek: The Next Generation*. It doesn't have to be exactly him; only someone like him. Suppose this android has to travel about in a universe full of people, and has to make various decisions, many of them having some sort of moral weight. Being an android, he has bad intuitions about morality, so he carries a notebook around with him with encyclopedic information about what is and is not immoral.

Our android is programmed to consult his list whenever he is about to pronounce judgment on whether some act is wrong or not, as in, "Lieutenant La Forge, it would be morally wrong for you to set your phaser on 'kill' and fire it at Captain Picard, intentionally causing his death." Importantly, he *also* consults his list whenever he himself is about to act. If a potential action is morally wrong, he doesn't do it.

It seems to me that our android, by and large,* can't be a hypocrite. If his list guides both moral judgment and moral action, he's going to be morally consistent. Take his list and change it from a notepad into a little hard disk that he can place somewhere in his body, and now our android has a little morality machine that will allow him—roughly—to be consistent.

---

*The hedge is here because morality is sufficiently complicated that I'm not sure this is going to work out properly in practice. What would Data do if he could only save the *Enterprise* or, heck, the entire Federation from certain destruction, by killing Captain Picard? Our own moral notebooks are unclear on this point.

Whether such an android could now or ever be built is beside the point.[20] This little thought experiment is simply to illustrate what something or someone would be like if the same sets of principles—the beliefs and rules on the notepad—guided both action and moral condemnation. Such a robot could not find itself in the position of a certain former governor of New York.* Any robot that condemned prostitution could not participate in it because if prostitution was on the list, he couldn't patronize a prostitute. If it weren't on the list, he couldn't condemn it.

Whatever one thinks of the plausibility of this robot, we, humans, are very unlike it. Without a doubt, the moral principles that people endorse clearly are not guiding their behavior, or, at least, are not the only force guiding their behavior. Our hypothetical android is very unlike the modular minds that I've been describing to this point. We have brains that seem to be divided up into different sections, with different, even mutually exclusive sets of beliefs. This situation—the architecture of human cognition—allows hypocrisy as just one kind, albeit a very important kind, of human inconsistency.

Where we're going

In this book, I present arguments and evidence that the human mind—your mind—is modular, that it consists of a large number of specialized parts, and that this has deep and profound implications for understanding human nature and human behavior. One important part of this is that modules, because they are separated from one another, can simultaneously hold different, mutually contradictory views, and there is nothing particularly odd or surprising about this. Such an idea is perfectly continuous with the material we've already visited in this chapter and, indeed, with the rest of the biological world.

The next three chapters develop this argument gradually, building on the ideas in this first chapter. Chapter 2 presents some ideas drawn from the

---

*New York Governor Eliot Spitzer resigned in 2008 after it was revealed that he had engaged the service of prostitutes. Previously, as the Attorney General for New York State, Spitzer had—visibly and vocally—overseen the prosecution of two prostitution rings. He ran for Governor in part on his record of convictions. In his inaugural address, Spitzer said, "all citizens will win when we finally get a government that puts the people's interests, openness and integrity first."

functional approach to understanding the human mind. This branch of psychology assumes that minds are useful for various things, and that thinking about what the mind is *for* might be helpful in understanding what the mind actually *does* and how, exactly, it does it.

Part of this functional approach includes the idea that in the same way computer software that is very flexible consists of a very large number of subroutines,[21] the human mind has a large number of subroutines—modules—designed for particular purposes.

An important consequence of this view is that it makes us think about the "self" in a way that is very different from how people usually understand it. In particular, it makes the very notion of a "self" something of a problem, and perhaps even quite a bit less useful than one might think.

In contrast, one idea that *is* very useful is the idea that if the mind consists of a large number of modules, then it needs one module to speak for the whole. In chapter 4, I introduce the notion that if you like the metaphor of your mind as a government, then "you"—the part of your brain that experiences the world and feels like you're in "control"—is better thought of as a press secretary than as the president.

This view helps explain certain puzzling things about human psychology. In chapter 5, I discuss why certain modules might not be designed to seek out the truth, and what the advantages are of ignorance. In chapters 6 and 7, I go beyond the value of ignorance and discuss how certain modules function *better* if they're not just ignorant, but actually wrong. Chapters 8 and 9 show how inconsistencies in the modular mind give rise to interesting phenomena surrounding "self-control" and, finally, hypocrisy.

My hope is that by the end you will come to have a fundamentally different view of human nature. Even though it might feel like there's one "you," and that "you" are in charge, in fact, just as Whitman said, you contain multitudes. The multitudes are designed to work together, but nonetheless contradict one another with some frequency.

In this lies the origins of human inconsistency, and the explanation for why everyone in the world except you is a hypocrite.

chapter 2

Evolution and the Fragmented Brain

■ *Adding "instincts" to lifelike machines makes them increasingly sophisti-cated. Thinking about how to build such machines illustrates that, just like artificial machines, natural (biological) machines—organisms—need to have very specific mechanisms on board in order to function well. The gradual accumulation of little functional bits through the process of evolution leads to both sophistication and conflict.* ■

One of my favorite little books is called *Vehicles: Experiments in Synthetic Psychology* by Valentino Braitenberg.[1] The book is even cooler than you might think from the title, consisting of a description of increasingly complex Vehicles in a series of thought experiments. In the first one, the Vehicle—think of something like a shoe-sized Matchbox car—has a sensor on the front attached to motors, which are in turn attached to the wheels. Suppose the sensor detects heat and we've hooked it up so that the more heat there is, the faster the motor driving each wheel goes—in reverse. If you watched this (imaginary) Vehicle, you might say that it "doesn't like" heat, or maybe that it "likes" cold.

Braitenberg adds more and more sensors and connections between the motors and wheels, and the Vehicles get pretty sophisticated by the end. Even the early Vehicles are pretty complicated: Vehicle 3c (out of 14) has four different kinds of sensors hooked up in various configurations to the motors; one sensor is sensitive to light, one to temperature, one to organic material, and one to the level of oxygen. Because of the way that the sensors are connected to the motors, this Vehicle has various tastes or preferences. As

Braitenberg says: "It dislikes high temperature, turns away from hot places, and at the same time seems to dislike light bulbs with even greater passion, since it turns toward them and destroys them. On the other hand it definitely seems to prefer a well-oxygenated environment and one containing many organic molecules, since it spends much of its time in such places."[2]

I'm not the only fan of Braitenberg's work, and many people have developed little simulations, programming in the relationship between the sensors, stimuli in the environment, and the connections to the motors that move the wheels. Some of them are pretty sophisticated. It's worth a Google search, if for no other reason than to see just how lifelike these relatively simple Vehicles look when they "behave."

This simple setup is just a way to take information—heat, light, etc.—and do something useful with it. The wiring basically gives the Vehicle an "instinct"[3] to get away from hot things. The combination of the sensor and the wire connecting it up to the motors can be thought of as a "heat-avoidance mechanism."

This is what I mean when I talk about modules. A module is an information-processing mechanism that is specialized to perform some function. That's it.

The word "module" might make you think of something like a Lego block. That makes sense if we're talking about physical stuff, like the furniture in the living room, in which configurations are made out of little components: loveseat plus couch equals seating area. Here, however, we're talking about brains—or anything that processes information—so we're not talking about structure, but rather *function*. An information-processing module, then, is a computational mechanism that does some job.

This is how I'll use the word "module" for the rest of the book.[4] It is very much like a subroutine in computing—a bit of computer code that performs a function—generally operating relatively independently of other parts of the code. The details of how subroutines operate—how they perform their function—are often "opaque" or "invisible" to other subroutines, an idea that, as we will see, has a direct analog in terms of the mind's modularity.

Returning to Vehicles: Adding sensors connected in some way to one or more of the motors—adding modules—increases how many different functions the Vehicle can perform. Vehicle 3c has a heat-leaving module and an oxygen-seeking module. Vehicle 3c and the ones that come after it illustrate how very complex information-processing devices—whether a human brain, a pig brain, or a complex piece of computer software—contain specialized subroutines with particular functions. Clearly, *adding modules leads to increasingly complex behavior.*

I italicized that last sentence because it's a little counterintuitive; modules seem like they're "simple" instincts, and in some ways they are. But, clearly, a*dding a lot of little specialized systems*, like the ones Braitenberg imagines, *adds flexibility* to behavior. As computer scientists, artificial intelligence researchers, and manufacturers of smartphones have recognized, the way to make one big smart machine is to bundle a large number of less smart machines together.[5]

Note that on these Vehicles, each sensor-motor connection—each module—is pretty specialized. Sensors are tuned to only one kind of thing—heat, oxygen, light, etc.—and cause the Vehicle to respond to only that kind of thing in a particular way. Now consider Vehicle 3c near some really hot organic matter. This Vehicle is in conflict because one module is driving the motors to move it *away from* the heat source while another module is driving the motors to move *toward* it. When the heat source and the organic matter are the same thing, the two modules necessarily compete. Depending on the details of the Vehicle, it is going to move either toward or away from the hot organic matter—it can't do both at the same time (though of course it could remain motionless, like the proverbial donkey caught between two equally appealing bales of hay).

Even this very simple Vehicle already demonstrates what you might think of as an issue any modular system must face. In a way that foreshadows similar conflicts we encounter later on, *this Vehicle both "likes" and "dislikes" hot organic matter.* In some sense, like Walt Whitman, it contradicts itself. Once Vehicles have different modules on board, conflict between them is a straightforward possibility.

Conflict can be resolved without any direct connection between the modules, as when two modules activate the motors to different degrees, and the result is just the sum of the influences; the modules "fight it out." One can imagine problems with this kind of solution. Letting each system move the Vehicle in combination with the other systems might prevent the

Vehicle from accomplishing anything useful, as its modules will be moving it this way and that, more or less toward and away from various things in the environment. A Vehicle that "likes" both light and heat might get stuck in between a dark, warm place and a cool, light place, having the worst of all possible outcomes. Just letting systems resolve conflicts by sending signals to the motors might not be the best way to go.

There are other possibilities. For example, one can imagine a Vehicle with connections from the organic matter sensor systems that go both to the motors and to the heat sensors. These connections might turn off the heat sensors whenever the Vehicle senses a certain concentration of hot organic matter. This Vehicle, with connections among modules, doesn't just let the two separate mechanisms fight it out, but uses the activation of one to inhibit the other. In this case, the Vehicle will approach organic matter even if it must endure high temperatures to do so.

This last possibility avoids the tug-of-war between the two instincts by building a new connection between modules. Of course, any two systems as I've described them might come into conflict. Consider conflicts between the heat-avoiding module and the other three modules on the last Vehicle. To avoid having to fight it out with each of these systems, the module needs three new sets of connections, one to each of the other systems. Clearly, as Vehicles get more complicated, setting up all the possible links among all modules is likely to get very cumbersome. If you add a new sensor to a Vehicle with a bunch of preexisting modules, you'll have to build many additional connections to deal with potential conflicts. As Vehicles get more complicated, letting the different modules fight it out is more appealing than building new connections among them.

In general, is it better to let systems on Vehicles fight for control or build comprehensive links among all the systems on a Vehicle to deal with and potentially avoid conflicts among the instincts? If you do build connections among the modules, how do you decide which to give priority?

Well, it depends. What's your Vehicle for?

[R]evolutionary psychology

We'll return to Vehicles, but first I need to introduce a few basic ideas from my field, evolutionary psychology (hereafter EP). This is an important interlude because it answers the question at the end of the last section: What are the information-processing modules that compose the human mind for?

Excellent accounts of the evolutionary approach to human behavior can be found elsewhere—Steve Pinker's *How the Mind Works*[6] is arguably the best and most thorough—so I'll just highlight the key ideas and assumptions here.

First, EP has much in common with other areas of psychology. First and foremost, it's a scientific endeavor, committed to the usual principles of hypothesis generation, falsification, and so on. I mention this here because ill-informed but vocal critics seem to have missed this.*

Second, EP, like cognitive science, assumes that what brains do is process information. The field endorses the "computational theory of mind." In this sense, EP is just like cognitive psychology and, roughly, entails the idea that you can think of the mind as a machine that processes information. Research in the field is aimed at figuring out the details: what programs the brain is running.

Third, EP is committed to the idea that there is at present only one natural explanation for organized functional complexity: Darwin's theory of evolution by natural selection, including subsequent additions and refinements to the theory. This topic has been discussed in many places at length, so, again, I won't belabor the issue. The basic point is that organisms are wildly improbably organized bits of matter. They got that way as a result of the process of evolution, which causes genes that lead to their own replication to persist at the expense of other candidate genes. Richard Dawkins's *The Selfish Gene*[7] remains one of the most accessible treatments of this material.

The ideas that brains process information and that evolution sculpted them are not particularly controversial. That is not to say that the discipline hasn't generated some animated discussion. Jerry Fodor's cleverly titled

---

*You know who you are.

The Mind Doesn't Work That Way,[8] a response to Pinker's book, gives you a sense that there is less than full agreement out there.

Fourth, EP, like evolutionary biology, assumes that because of the way evolution works, our minds have the design that they do as a result of how the genes that build them fared in the *past*. Because the genes we have are the ones that did well when they built our ancestors' brains and bodies, novelty can be a problem.

Now, novelty isn't an absolute thing. Any given penguin isn't facing the *particular* sea lions the penguin's ancestors faced; it's facing novel ones. Modern penguins have adaptations designed to cope with individual instances (philosophers like to use the word "tokens" here) of the general category ("types"). Evolution can give rise to mechanisms to deal with any number of tokens of predators, prey, and so on, because the organism is well designed to deal with the types.

But that's all. Natural selection can't act on *future* threats and opportunities. So, members of any given species are designed to solve the adaptive problems faced by their ancestors, something as true for humans as for anyone else.[9] Further, because selection is slow, and many, many genetic changes are required to make large changes to complex parts of the organism, there is a potential time lag.[10] It takes many, many generations for complex adaptations to be sculpted by natural selection. Humans have adaptations designed for our hunter-gatherer past (though of course there have been recent genetic changes), about which so much has already been written that I'll pass over it here.[11] The lesson is that human adaptations are designed to work in a world that in some ways—though not, of course, all ways—is different from the modern world.

Many organisms find themselves in environments that contain elements their ancestors didn't face. Some of this, though not all, has to do with human activity, which has drastically changed many of these environments. To take just one example, in the environments in which fish evolved, most small, wriggly things in the water were a source of a safe meal, and so fish who consumed them did just fine. In modern environments, any number of small wriggly things are attached to sharp hooks, which are in turn attached to fishing poles, which in turn are wielded by tool-using bipedal primates. This is all to the good for the primate with the pole, but fish are taken in because they have adaptations designed to cause them to try to eat things that wriggle, a fact that fisherpeople exploit to attract them.[12]

This principle has many applications. Most bits of food over the course of the mouse's evolutionary history have not been sitting on top of mouse-traps. Most bird calls have been made by birds, rather than by hunters imitating bird calls. Humans have been able to exploit otherwise quite sensibly functional adaptations for their own gain because of our facility with artifacts and our ability to plan.[13]

To give Nature her due, we're not the only ones to exploit adaptations in this way. One of my favorite examples is the angler fish (*Lophius piscatorius*), which also lures small fish into its predation range with a structure that wriggles in a way that resembles a prey item. This is just one of many connections between human engineering and natural engineering, a topic that is fascinating in its own right.[14]

The claim here is not that we—and other organisms, for that matter—can't cope because the modern world is so different from that of the past. Not at all. Birds open milk bottles and humans play chess, in both cases using adaptations designed for some other purpose to accomplish something novel. There is nothing mysterious about this, certainly no more mysterious than the fact that penguins evade individual sea lions who never before existed and therefore, in and of themselves, could not have driven selection for sea lion evasion.

Differences between human ancestral environments and modern environments generate many interesting phenomena, many of which have been discussed at length elsewhere.[15] To give a sense of the problem, consider that we're designed to find dense calorie packages, such as ripe fruit, appealing to eat, which is why these things taste sweet to us. Now, all sorts of things can be produced to take advantage of this appetite, including anything from a Mars bar to a carbonated beverage with Splenda in it to a marshmallow Peep. Our appetite for sugars has a very different effect on our health in the current world than it did in the world in which the only sweet things around were fruits. The mismatch between the past and the present—the transition from a world of scarcity to a world of plenty - undermines the function of human adaptations as much as the adaptations of the fish eating a baited hook.

Still, many things that were true in the past remain true today. The fabric of the physical world hasn't changed. Gravity still pulls down, and does so with the same force (9.8 m/s^2) as it always has—Newton's laws haven't been repealed. Leverage still works. While it's true that few of us in the developed world have to worry about being eaten by a big cat or trampled by an elephant, we still get the flu, sneeze bacteria out of our body, and have to watch our step lest we break a leg. Most importantly, although there are many more people around now than ever before, each of us is the product of one mother and one father; we have relatives, friends, and enemies; and we belong to groups of various sizes. The difference between the modern social world and the ancestral social world is large, without a doubt, but it would be a mistake to think that there aren't many similarities as well. Don Brown's *Human Universals*[16] is a nice place to look for things that are true cross-culturally, and might well have been true of our human ancestors as well.

We're going to be talking a great deal about adaptations designed to navigate the social world in much of what follows. Similarities between the past and the present are important because our minds work pretty well—and relatively predictably—when they're faced with problems they were designed to solve. Differences between the past and the present often lead to cases in which our minds don't do quite so well, and occasionally lead us into trouble.

A toast[er] to specialization

Organisms, including humans, are, essentially, machines. But while machines that people make are usually designed to do something that is helpful to us, organisms are machines that are designed to reproduce.*[17] (Before continuing, it's worth a brief aside to mention that these ideas are so familiar to people that it's easy to forget that before Darwin, this wasn't obvious at all. It was once possible to think that organisms and their parts functioned

---

*Technically, what I've written here isn't precisely right. Nonetheless, from here on out, with some loss of precision, I'm going to talk about selection without retaining the emphasis on genes rather than individuals.

not in the service of their own reproduction, but rather for things like keeping an ecosystem in balance, providing diversity of nature, or even for exploitation by humans.)

So, organisms, designed to survive and reproduce, have various parts that work in the service of this goal.[18] The organisms that successfully reproduce, of course, will be the ones, in general, that, compared to others in a population, are best able to execute the functions necessary for survival and reproduction. Because selection has had a long time to act, even very small advantages matter, which is why when you go to the zoo or stand in a field, it is easy to be awed by just how well organisms' parts serve their functions.

On my desk I have a mounted specimen of *Phyllium celebicum*, a gift from a former graduate student on the occasion of his receiving his PhD.* More commonly known as a "leaf insect," this creature has a body that is outrageous in the degree to which it resembles a leaf. My favorite part of the animal's disguise is that it has slight indentations in its form and slight browning of parts of its otherwise green coloration, making it look like a leaf *that is partially eaten and slightly decayed.*

The function of the coloration of my leaf insect is to blend in with the surrounding environment to avoid detection and predation. Of this there can be no doubt. Clearly, in the same way one can know that the eye is for seeing, because of all the properties we observe—green coloration, vein-like structures on the body, leaf-shaped contours, etc.—*it's possible to know the function of the coloration of this creature even though I don't have fossil specimens and I haven't done any genetic sequencing.* I mention this because it's easy to forget that when we talk about evidence in favor of an adaptationist hypothesis, we're looking for this: design features that contribute to some particular function.†[19]

In the case of the leaf insect, observing color and form allows the inference about function. The only way that such improbably useful arrangements of matter could have come to exist is the process of evolution, and

---

*Yes, it's embarrassing that the gift went in the wrong direction. Or perhaps it is testimony that I instilled in him the most important aspect of graduate training: the betterment of one's mentor.

†The failure to understand how shape informs hypotheses about function is probably why evolutionary explanations are (incorrectly) seen as unfalsifiable. Many critics seem to think that hypotheses are about history rather than function. Hypotheses about history require different sorts of evidence than hypotheses about function.

color and form are the evidence that allows us to infer what the structure is for. In the same way that the physical properties of an object provide data that inform hypotheses about function, *human behavioral data inform hypotheses about function of the computational mechanisms that comprise the human mind.* This is because the equivalent of color and form in the human mind is computations. That is, minds do useful things because of the computations they perform in the same way that objects do useful things because of the details of their form. The nature of the mind's computations is, of course, informed by behavioral data; these behavioral data, which tell us something about the computations, inform function. Data from psychology experiments—including the ones discussed here—contribute to our understanding of the functions of the mind's modules, or subroutines.

So, organisms are machines with parts that have functions, such as helping to avoid detection and predation. This brings us to engineering. Engineering is relevant because an organism's features have functions and, because natural selection is an inherently competitive process, even slight advantages in the efficiency with which the organism's parts execute their functions can matter a great deal.

One basic, even fundamental principle of engineering—which is so basic that it extends to other fields like economics and computer science—is that *specialization yields efficiency.* As a very general rule, *machines with narrow functions are more efficient at executing their tasks than machines with broader functions.* A very specialized machine necessarily can't be used to accomplish an indefinitely wide range of tasks because different tasks are solved most efficiently by different shapes. There are always engineering trade-offs, and each form trades off one set of functions for another.

The logic follows from the fact that specialized machines have parts that work very well for solving the narrow function they serve. To function well, objects need to have very particular forms or shapes, which is why a ripsaw looks so different from a ladle. As an object's shape conforms to the requirements of a particular task, the shape simultaneously—and necessarily—becomes worse at others.

This applies to computational "shapes" as much as physical ones—as a computational mechanism becomes better at solving an information-processing problem, it becomes worse at solving any number of other ones, which is why the guts of a chess-playing program look really different from the guts of a word processor (and why you could beat Word at chess but wouldn't want to write a book using Deep Blue).

For some reason, I've always liked to use toasters to illustrate. Toasters have all sorts of design features that make them really good at toasting. A toaster has two slots, open on top, large enough for one slice of bread each, but small enough to deliver the heat efficiently to the sides of the bread.* It has a clever little plastic handle on the side that allows me to lower the bread into the toaster body, but the plastic handle itself stays pretty cool. It has a little timer that automatically ejects the toast (or Pop-Tart or whatever) when a certain amount of time has gone by. It also has a power cord and heating elements, which allow it to perform its function.

Note that the various parts contribute to the overall function of the toaster. They make it *good* at toasting bread. Not only that, but the features of the toaster provide evidence regarding its function. It's not hard to persuade someone what the function of a toaster is. Even if no one told you what the toaster was for, you could probably make a pretty good guess that it was designed to turn bread into toast. Its construction is too well suited for precisely this for it to be for anything else.

Contrast a toaster with, say, a butane torch. You could, I suppose, use a butane torch to toast bread. It wouldn't be as efficient, though. A lot of the heat would be wasted, and the bread would be unlikely to be toasted evenly—or it might just be immolated; I've never tried it. The toaster, designed to toast bread, in an important sense "assumes" many facts about the problem it has to solve—that bread will be of a certain shape, that toast needs to be heated for a certain period of time, that a certain kind of socket consistently delivers electric power, and so on. The torch's design embodies no such assumptions. The toaster has a narrow function, and would be terrible at doing a multitude of other kitchen-oriented tasks, such as opening cans, brewing coffee, or dispensing paper towels.

---

*My toaster can't accommodate bagels very well. I now know that there are toasters with larger slots that are designed for bagels. I don't know if these toasters are worse at toasting bread. I would think they might be, since a wide slot means the heating elements are further from the surface of the bread. Readers who know the answer to this are welcome to contact me.

Note, of course, that toasters *could* be used to perform other functions. You could use one as a paperweight, I suppose. You could use one as a weapon, as Bill Murray's character found out in *Scrooged*. You could, if your toaster was shiny, use it as a mirror to adjust your hair before going out on a date. You could use it to make crumbs, which collect in a little tray in my toaster.

Note, however, that a toaster is not really a good paperweight. It's too big and bulky. It's not a good weapon either, and would be hard to wield effectively. It's a poor mirror—it's curvy, so it distorts your image. And it's not really a good crumb-maker: It makes only a little bit of crumbs for each slice of bread it toasts—horribly inefficient.

Why am I telling you all this about toasters? It's because brains are machines with functions, just as toasters are. So, whether you're talking about human tools or biological machines, *to the extent there is a problem whose solution has regularities, an efficient solution to that problem will embody those regularities, making the mechanism specialized for the task and efficient in solving the problem.* In the context of organisms, to the extent that there are regularities in the environment, natural selection will favor designs that reap the advantages of specialization because efficiency of design is crucial in the context of evolution.

Returning to our leaf insect, its leafy contours and coloring are specialized for the ecology it lives in. If slightly eaten and decaying green leaves were not part of its environment, its coloration, specialized for this environment, would not be an effective solution. Wouldn't the leaf insect be "better off" with a body whose shape and color could change depending on the background it finds itself in? Well, maybe. But in evolution, there are always trade-offs. A dynamic color scheme comes with costs, and the costs of an organism's features, as well as their benefits, determine their evolutionary success. Even if a shape-changing, color-changing leaf insect were possible,* the specific color and shape that are nearly always hard to see in the environment in which it finds itself are the ones that did best in the evolutionary sweepstakes.

---

*Something like this is in fact found in nature. The mimic octopus (*Thaumoctopus mimicus*) has many disguises, and its pattern of colors can change surprisingly rapidly.

There are any number of other reasons that selection might not yield a design that is "optimal." Because natural selection operates on a random process, mutation, if a mutated gene happens not to appear, it cannot be selected. There could be engineering constraints that make some new structure problematic, in the same way that new buildings and new streets in cities are constrained by the layout of the buildings and streets that are already there. So, while it's perfectly reasonable to expect circuits in the brain to be well engineered to solve adaptive problems faced by our ancestors, it's also reasonable to expect any number of imperfections, suboptimalities, and so on, a matter to which we'll return.

Getting specific

The function of brains is to process information, so we should think about trade-offs and the advantages to specialization in information-processing systems. Computer scientists, who have spent a lot of time thinking about how to build mechanisms to accomplish information-processing goals, have generally found that it is useful to break down larger programming tasks into a number of smaller, more narrowly defined problems. Anyone who has tried to write a subroutine or a macro will find this intuitive. Along with the other advantages of modularity, the more you can assume about the problem you need to solve—including the format the information is going to be in (integer, real, string, etc.)—the easier it is to write code to perform the function in question.

Indeed, in computer science, as I understand the field, the question of whether or not modularity is a good idea in the context of complex information-processing systems is not really a question. As it was recently put, modularity, or "separation of concerns," is "a key guiding principle of software engineering."[20] Computer scientists have understood for some time that good system design requires breaking down computations into subsections, which allows the system to be flexible, easily changeable, and fault-tolerant. Even the notion of "hiding" information "inside" modules—which has a close analogy with many of the ideas we'll explore in later chapters—is far from new. It is unclear why, given this recognition in computer science, modularity has been so controversial in psychology.[21] I leave that puzzling question for another time.

Consider the distinction between what are being called "domain-specific languages" and general-purpose languages. According to Wikipedia, which I am usually hesitant to use, but will for this purpose:

> Creating a domain-specific language (with software to support it) can be worthwhile if the language allows a particular type of problems or solutions to them to be expressed more clearly than pre-existing languages would allow, and the type of problem in question reappears sufficiently often.[22]

The contrast is as follows: "The opposite is a *general-purpose programming* language, such as C or Java. . . ." Basically, domain-specific languages are very good at accomplishing narrowly defined tasks, and can do so efficiently and effectively. General-purpose languages fall on the other side of the trade-off, and can be used to do many things, but doing any one thing in them is less efficient because the language isn't specifically structured to serve the goal.

The Wikipedia entry notes that the "problem in question" has to be one that "reappears sufficiently often." It doesn't make sense to build a mechanism to process information unless you're going to need to perform the same operations over and over. The same idea applies in the context of evolution, but in the case of natural selection, it is not just a good idea, it's a rule. Because selection acts over the course of many generations, in order for a gene to be selected, it must confer an advantage on its own rate of reproduction sufficiently frequently that it can increase in the population. A gene that causes an advantage in one generation, and then a disadvantage in the next, would not be expected to survive the process of selection.

A computer science text talks about how different kinds of systems are better for different types of problems because of inherent trade-offs. I quote it at length here in part because the authors use the same analogy evolutionary psychologists have used[23] in order to drive home the point of the advantages of a having a bundle of specialized tools:

> At some times in the past it was thought that a single language could be best for all programming tasks. . . . As time has passed,

however, more languages, not fewer, have come into use, and new ones still appear. . . . Just as any able mechanic will carry several different tools for working with a 10 mm nut (open-end wrench, box wrench, crows-foot wrench, shallow socket, deep socket, etc.), any able programmer will carry knowledge of several different languages so that they can select the best one for a particular circumstance.[24]

The mind, too, is a bundle of software with programs and subroutines. The claim here is not, of course, that humans don't acquire information, learn from others, transmit information, and so on. Nothing about specialization says anything about where the information necessary to build the mechanism so that it operates correctly comes from. Many modules are designed to acquire information about the world—language learning systems being the most famous example[25]—but nothing in this argument says that modular systems don't learn, are inflexible, or only come in the color green. Lots of people make inferences like these (not the part about being green), but specialization is emphatically not the same as being fixed, genetically determined, or any other silliness.

Indeed, as we saw with Vehicles, *adding modular systems enables complexity and flexibility*, a lesson computer scientists have learned very well.

Not just computer scientists. The success of Apple's iPhone stems in large part, I think, from the fact that it runs a very large number of small, specialized programs. The iPhone is so (broadly) useful—and now has competitors with similar properties—because it can run so many (narrowly) useful applications, which are analogous to modules. Human engineers hit on the same solution that evolution did, bundling lots of specialized applications together, leading to a flexible and useful information-processing device.

Generally speaking

In sum, because specialization generates efficiency, and efficiency confers evolutionary advantage, we should expect organisms' bodies and brains to show specialization of function in the form of bundled interacting modules.

This general idea seems to be relatively uncontroversial in physiology. Signs in zoos often discuss organisms' adaptations for their particular ecological niche. One of the best-known examples of specialization, because of the role it played in Darwin's thinking, is the differentiation in the shapes of finch beaks on the Galápagos Islands. Jonathan Weiner's excellent book *The Beak of the Finch*[26] details how the particular ecological circumstances on the different islands led to the evolution of beaks specialized to exploit the local ecology.

The idea also seems to be uncontroversial in the arena of animal behavior. Spiders all by themselves are poster children for functional specificity. Their teeny-weeny brains have circuits for spinning different kinds of webs: orb webs, funnel webs, sheet webs. . . . Each web requires a particular set of movements at particular times, specific to the shape of the web being built. Each normally developing web-building spider has programs in its brain selected for their effectiveness in web-construction.

There are countless such examples. Bowerbirds decorate small territories to attract mates, honeybees dance to communicate the location of food items to each other, bats use sonar to locate and eat insects, and Virginia opossums engage in the apparently effective ploy of playing possum, appearing dead with the hope that a would-be predator will lose interest.

This idea is relatively uncontroversial in human physiology as well. People acknowledge that specialization of function is visible in gross morphology. Hearts are well designed to pump blood, but are not well designed to filter blood. Livers are well designed to filter blood, but not to pump it. The same is true at the cellular level. Neurons are very good at transmitting information, not so good at storing energy. Fat cells are the reverse.

Interestingly, the idea that specialization is the key to competition is enshrined in the bedrock of economic theory. According to the economic principle of "comparative advantage," a centerpiece of theories of trade and exchange, countries ought to specialize in certain products, namely the ones that they are, roughly, better at producing. Importantly, this means "better" in the sense of "better than they are at producing other products," not "better than other countries are at producing them." In David Ricardo's original discussion of this principle, he showed it was better for England to specialize in cloth rather than producing (any) wine, even though Portugal,

England's trading partner, could produce cloth more cheaply than England could. The advantage of specialization is central to realizing the benefits of division of labor.

I mention all of the domains in which the advantages of specialization are acknowledged and relatively uncontroversial—cell physiology, animal physiology, animal behavior, human physiology, economics, not to mention computer science—because it seems to me that the claim ought to be uncontroversial in human psychology as well. Indeed, in some cases, it is.

The study of vision—which is part of human psychology—embodies the two basic principles of the approach described here, even though by and large vision scientists don't consider themselves to be evolutionary psychologists. Vision scientists are inherently oriented toward function— they assume that what they're studying is designed to do something.[27] This something is, roughly, taking information contained in energy from one part of the electromagnetic spectrum (visible light) and generating a representation of the physical world.

More importantly for the present discussion, vision scientists, in no small part driven by the many discoveries over the last several decades, have looked for and found many mechanisms with exquisitely specialized and narrow functions. For example, the visual system includes specialized components whose function is to detect edges in the visual field at particular orientations. Similar kinds of specialization occur at various levels of vision, as well as in other sensory systems. How specialized these systems are, to be sure, remains the subject of debate.

My point is that there is no reason to expect that specialization applies to everything we have ever discovered or created that has some function *except* the parts of the human brain designed for social behavior. For some reason, many people are uncomfortable with the fact that the logic applies just as much to selecting a mate, choosing friends, joining groups, and so on, as it does to detecting if there are any edges in the visual field. Yes, these might be very *complicated* functions, but the logic of solving these social problems is exactly the same: efficiency from specialization.[28] Am I saying that natural selection has led to systems in people's minds that are specifically designed for such things as selecting a mate, choosing friends, and morally condemning others? You betcha.

Before moving on, I'd like to make one final plea for the argument that systems are likely to be functionally specialized. I'd like to do it by coming at it from the opposite direction, the notion of a general function. I've been collecting instances of "general-function" objects in real life. My current favorite is the bubble sheet we give students to take exams. You've probably seen it—it consists of many rows of five circles that the student fills in with a number 2 pencil to indicate the answer to each question. At the top of the form we use is written "General Purpose." I love this because it's "general purpose" as long as your "general" purpose is to record the answers of students on a multiple choice exam to be read by a special machine that generates a computer file of their answers and the number they answered correctly. . . .

I've come across "general-purpose" cleansers, scanners, screwdrivers, calculators, filters, flour, prepaid credit cards, lenses, fertilizers, light bulbs, and even "general-purpose vehicles," whose purpose, oddly, seems to be attacking people in their homes. Each of these seems to have an awfully specific function. Indeed, it's hard—for me, anyway—to imagine anything that is useful at all that *doesn't* have a reasonably narrow function.

Things with very narrow functions can, of course, still do a great deal. Google is a good example. Google's search engine has a specific function—searching for text (and now other things, such as still images and videos)—but it can do so on (roughly) the whole Internet.[29] That doesn't seem to mean that its function is not well captured by the notion of "searching for information."

People who want to claim that the mind has general rather than specialized devices tend to focus on learning, and they tend to make arguments like this one: "The immune system, for example, contains a broad learning system. . . . An alternative would be to have specialized immune modules for different diseases. . . ."[30] This argument confuses specialization for particular *things* for specialization of *function*. The immune system, independent of the fact that it can do its job for many, many pathogens, can still be nicely and accurately described as specialized: defending the body against harmful pathogens. Surely the ability to fight many different pathogens is a nice feature to have in an immune system, but that doesn't seem to make me want to change what I take its *function* to be. To return to toasters, consider toasters built before the invention of Pop-Tarts. Such toasters can still toast them. This also doesn't make me want to change what I think toasters are designed to do.

Whenever something useful is made, whether through human artifice or the process of natural selection, it must assume some form that enables it to carry out its task. There are no general-function artifacts, organs, or circuits in the brain because the concept itself makes no sense. In the same way that if someone told you to manufacture a tool to "do useful things," or write a subroutine to "do something useful with information," you would have to narrow down the problem considerably before you could get started. In the same way, natural selection can't build brains that "learn stuff and compute useful information." It is necessary to get considerably more specific.

A leg to stand on

Am I saying that *everything* with a function is *necessarily* specialized? Well, yes, it seems to me that everything designed is designed to do something in particular, but that doesn't mean there's nothing more than semantics at stake. Functions can be more or less specialized, and the trade-offs are important.

Oscar Pistorius came to the attention of the international media in the run up to the 2008 Olympic Games in part because of some specialized tools. He styles himself "the fastest man on no legs" because he is a double amputee with prosthetic attachments at the knee. His case generated controversy because the International Olympic Committee had to decide if the prosthetics conferred an unfair advantage. He was initially banned from competing, then the ban was overturned, and he was allowed to try to qualify.*

Pistorius's prosthetics illustrate the value of specialization and the engineering issues associated with running and walking. Humans do both, but the design requirements for running are different from those for walking, and so human physiology makes various trade-offs.[31] Pistorius has different kinds of legs for running and for walking. Each one makes it more difficult to

---

*He didn't make it. Sad.

do the other. According to Chris Maume, a journalist for *The Independent*: "The blades are designed for running, so when he walks away he looks like a crane or flamingo strutting away from the water hole."[32]

That's nothing compared to Paul Martin's collection. He's got nine different sets of legs, specialized for various tasks, including sprinting, skiing, walking, and biking.[33] The legs have appropriate design features for improving performance in each area.

So, specializing in legs that run means trading off the other function, walking. Again, if you want something that's multipurpose, you either have to compromise function or bundle systems with different functions. Given all the things that brains do, you'd expect a lot of bundling.

Me, myself, I, and . . .

That last piece of evolutionary psychology, which is important for what follows—and it's a really important piece—combines the idea that the mind consists of lots of specialized devices with the discussion of Vehicles that opened this chapter. If it's true that the human mind consists of a large number of modules—and we'll assume it does for the purposes of the rest of this book—then how these different modules are connected to one another becomes an important question.

A key point is that *any given specialized computational mechanism— any module—might or might not be connected up to any other module*.

This is why we discussed patients and various illusions in chapter 1. Those are cases in which the nature of the connectivity—or the lack of it— is evident. In the case of the split-brain patient, the lack of connectivity is obvious because the physical connection between the hemispheres was severed. My claim is that this unnatural separation, which leads to phenomena like the confabulation of the relationship between the shovel and the chicken claw, *is exactly analogous to natural separations in normal brains*.

Richard Nisbett and Timothy Wilson[34] conducted a study that has become one of psychology's all-time classics. In this study, people were shown four identical pairs of panty hose, laid out in a line, and asked which they liked best. The subjects didn't know they were all identical, and duly chose, and it turns out that when faced with an array of identical panty hose, people choose the one all the way on the right. That is, the *position* of the object is what seems to be driving the choice. However, just like split-brain patients, the people making the choice weren't able to say what really caused them to make the choice that they did; instead, they referred to some feature of the panty hose, such as color or texture, even though these were the same for all four.

Why are normal people, like split-brain patients, sometimes unable to identify the real reason for their choices? As Nisbett and Wilson put it, "there may be little or no direct introspective access to higher order cognitive processes."[35] In other words, the cause of the decision in this case—whatever it was, and whether you want to call it "higher order" or anything else—is not available to the modules that are explaining the decision. The part of the mind that talks just doesn't get the information from the decision-making modules.

Most fundamentally, if the brain consists of a large number of specialized modules, then information in any one of them might or might not be transmitted to any other module. This crucial insight is the origin of the claim that your brain can represent mutually inconsistent things at the same time. As long as information is "walled off," many, many contradictions can be maintained within one head.

This idea, which is called "informational encapsulation," is central to the logic of my later arguments. Because the brain has lots of different modules with very specific functions, and because evolution edits these systems in the way evolution does—that is, haphazardly, dictated by the path of history and the whims of the chance process of mutation—because of all of these things, it is by no means certain that the brain is going to be wired up such that any given piece of information will be consumed, shared, or transmitted to any other module.

My claim is going to be even stronger than that. The weak version of the claim is that modules in your head might or might not be connected to one another. So, to return to the visual illusions, when some part of your brain acquires the information that the two checkerboard squares are the same shade, this does not affect the "percept"—the way the image is perceived. On the other hand, telling people that they are about to hear about "a girl with a weasel in her mouth" does change the experience. For whatever reason, in the former case the information changes the percept but in the latter it does not. I note hastily it need not be this simple, and, just to add one complication, perhaps in the shading case the information gets "in" to the visual system, and it is simply not used, but this need not concern us for the moment.

The strong version of this argument is that some systems might be engineered specifically *not* to get information from (or send information to) other modules.[36] Your brain might be designed to keep certain kinds of information away from other parts of it. Suppose it actually *hurts* the function of some module to have access to information. This idea isn't really that crazy—and others have advanced similar ideas before[37]—and in later chapters we'll visit many cases in which receiving more information undermines function.

If it can actually be useful *not* to have certain kinds of information in some module in your brain, then selection might have acted to keep some kinds of information out of those modules. Artificial computational systems—human-made computer programs—have this property. Many subroutines are constructed in such a way that the details of their operation are made unavailable to other parts of the program through the use of locally defined variables, private subroutines, and so on. Other parts of a large program have access to only the output, not the underlying operations. This is not an accident. Encapsulating a subroutine's procedures—putting them behind what is called an "abstraction barrier"—carries important advantages, including the ability to modify the code without having to worry what other parts of the program will be affected.

In any case, an even more extreme version of this claim is that not only do some modules work better when they have *less* information, some might work better when they have *wrong* information. This is, obviously, a very strong claim, but I think that there is powerful evidence in favor of it, as we'll see.

chapter 3

Who Is "I"?

■ *Using Walt Disney World's attraction Cranium Command to illustrate, I explore the idea that the mind consists of a large number of modules, only some of which seem to have consciousness associated with them. The modular view of the mind makes one wonder if there's such a thing as "me" or "the self." In the end, the mind is just a bunch of modules doing their jobs.* ■

When I worked at Walt Disney World,[*] one of the attractions I worked on was *Cranium Command*. Getting to work on it was a stroke of wildly good fortune: This was perhaps my favorite attraction in any of the parks, and it's good to work on an attraction you like because you have the opportunity to see it over and over and over and over. And over.

Cranium Command is based on the whimsical idea that inside each person's head is a little person called a Cranium Commando, a specially trained brain pilot who sits at a control center and directs the action of the person whose brain it is. In the preshow, the (literally) animated General Knowledge tells us that someone at HQ has assigned our hero, Buzzy, a small—even by Cranium Commando standards—pilot, the job of operating "the most unstable craft in the fleet": a twelve-year-old boy. This particular craft is named Bobby.

After the preshow, which provides a lively introduction to the brain in general and the attraction in particular, we move into another room, the

[*] Disney World is the one in Florida, for those of you who confuse World and Land.

Cranium Command theater, which shows Buzzy—an animatronic version of the animated character we just met—sitting in a chair with knobs and buttons. When we came into the theater, we moved inside Bobby's head. Large screens and readout displays surround him. Buzzy gets information from the hypothalamus, the hemispheres of the brain, the heart, the stomach, and so on, represented by various thematically appropriate characters. (Bobcat Golthwaite is the adrenal gland, "ready to freak out at any second.") Buzzy sees and hears what his craft, Bobby, sees and hears, and the members of the team report to him. Buzzy issues commands to the various parts of the body, getting information as he needs it, directing action and, of course, scripting the words spoken by his adolescent craft.[*]

Buzzy runs the show, as it were.

The attraction itself is wonderful, and I won't give away any more details than I need to here, just in case you haven't seen it yet but might have the opportunity to enjoy it later.[†]

I mention *Cranium Command* because, although it's a thoroughly enjoyable attraction, *it has to be wrong about the way your mind works*.

OK, that's not too surprising. It's not all that reasonable to expect that a Disney attraction is going to be scientifically accurate, since its purpose is to entertain as much as or more than to inform.

But it's important to pause to consider precisely *how* it's wrong. It won't take long to realize that the problem (well, *a* problem) with positing that Buzzy is piloting our young hero's brain is that it raises[‡] a crucial question: *Who is piloting Buzzy's brain?* Where is Buzzy's Cranium Commando? Is he or she an even smaller Commando, running Buzzy's behavior? And if so, who's running the even smaller Commando? There's no way around this problem. The right answer to how the mind works is never going to be to

---

[*] If you haven't seen *Cranium Command*, it's not unlike the bit in the movie *Men in Black* in which Rosenberg (played by Mike Nussbaum), it turns out, is actually a very small creature called a Baltian and had a similar setup to Buzzy's. The Baltian sits inside Rosenberg's head, controlling Rosenberg with various buttons and levers and such. He's intensely cute, with a large head and big, soulful eyes.

[†] *Cranium Command* lost its sponsor and is, sadly, as far as I know, closed indefinitely.

[‡] People these days are using the expression "begs the question" as a synonym for "raises the question," but that's not, historically, what it has meant, and I find it really irritating. To "beg the question," at least up until recently, referred to a circular argument, such as explaining that opium causes sleep because of its soporific qualities, a question-begging "explanation."

posit a Commando.[1] You can't explain how a big brain manages to be so smart by positing a smaller brain within it that is just as smart. Big brains get smart by having a lot of pieces.

Having said that, *Cranium Command* does get some things right. First, it divides the brain up into different parts, which is already pretty great, but, more importantly, it divides it up into different *functional* parts, just as we discussed in the first two chapters. There are eyes for seeing, a hypothalamus for monitoring things like heart rate, and so on. This might not seem like a big deal, but I think it is. The idea is that the right way to break down the brain is in terms of what the different bits of it *do*, thinking of it in terms of a bundle of pieces, each with a function.

This allows me to say another word or two about the term *modularity*. Recall that by a "module," I just mean something that has a function; I *don't* mean that every module is cleanly and tightly localized in space in the brain somewhere. Because neurons are long and twisty, connecting up to one another in complicated ways, something that is *functionally modular*—having a well-defined function—is not necessarily *spatially localized*—well defined and nicely bounded in space.

Modern electronic gadgets also have functional modularity without necessarily having spatial modularity. A selling point of the iPhone is that you can stick lots of specialized applications on it to make it more useful. These very much resemble modules, but if you bore a hole in your iPhone, it's not like you can aim for the "Your Age in Dog Years" application* and disable it while leaving everything else intact. This idea is why I'm not going to talk at any length about where putative modules are, physically, in the mind—*modules don't need to be localized to be specialized*. Note, by the way, that functional modules *can* be localized, and some modules, such as elements of the visual system, do seem to have relatively nicely constrained locations.

So, *Cranium Command* gets modularity, in a kind of rough way, right.† But what's wrong about *Cranium Command* is, first, that it cuts the brain into far too few functional parts. It's just not correct to talk about "the right

---

*Nope, I'm not making that up.

† In this way, I think *Cranium Command* can safely be called the first theme park attraction to take cognitive modularity seriously.

hemisphere" of the brain—played by the effervescent and delightful Jon Lo-vitz—as though it has *a*, singular, function. There are many, many different systems in the right hemisphere of the brain, with a very large number of different things going on. This, in some sense, might not have been the best cut of the brain; the right hemisphere isn't a "module" in the sense that it has a distinguishable function. (Those of you who learned something like "the right half of your brain is for creativity and the left half is for logic" have to be ready to let that go.)

Second, and more fundamentally, no *part* of the brain can, at one and the same time, also be a *whole brain*, like Buzzy. That is, each functional unit, each module, is just that, a module. It can't be that any module or set of modules is itself a whole brain.

Which is not to shortchange modules. I have no doubt they can be very complicated, consisting of many, many sub-modules, working together to do their jobs. But *positing that there's a Buzzy can't be right*. Any theory that requires a little-brain-in-a-big-brain is wrong. The explanation for all the things that the big brain does is going to be an explanation of how lots of little modules—none of which has all the capabilities of the brain as a whole—work together. As Marvin Minsky put it, the question is, "How can intelligence emerge from nonintelligence?"[2]

On the other hand, one thing I like about *Cranium Command* is the way it wrestles with the issue of consciousness. Generally I try to avoid discussing consciousness, since it's, like, hard, but I can't avoid it here.

Cranium Command invites us to reflect on "Bobby": He runs to school, daydreams about his lab partner, and ducks out of the way of a flying lasagna, but all the while he—the aware, experiencing "Bobby"—doesn't seem to know that Buzzy is running the show. At the end, Bobby finds himself in the principal's office coming clean about his role in starting the food fight, but the audience is given the very strong sense that it was Buzzy—after consulting with both the left and right hemispheres—who made the decision to tell the truth. In this way, *Cranium Command* gets at the idea that there must be lots of modular systems—functional parts of the mind—that are not accessible to consciousness. So, if we understand Buzzy to be a modular system—rather than a whole brain—he's not unlike the systems that we visited earlier, making decisions that are not available to consciousness. "Bobby"—whatever you take that to mean—can't talk about how Buzzy made his decision because of the way Buzzy works.*

This illustrates an important point about the relationship between modularity and consciousness. Let me put it like this: The way that "Bobby"—whatever that might mean—doesn't seem to know exactly how he decided to confess to the principal is basically the same way that split-brain patients can't say why they pointed to a shovel—*the part of the brain that's doing the talking just doesn't have access to the relevant information.*

So, the modular view allows us to talk sensibly about the way information moves—and doesn't move—in the brain. If we assume that some modules send information to the parts of the brain that are "conscious"—holding aside exactly what that means for the moment†—and some modules have functions that don't require that they send information about what they've done to the conscious modules, then there are going to be many, many cases in which the modules that run the speech system don't have access to the relevant information, as in the experiment looking at how people choose panty hose. When the subjects were asked why they made the choice they did, some part of the brain generated a plausible reason, even though it wasn't the right one.[3]

This idea illustrates the way in which normal brains are like split-brain patients' brains. In a split-brain patient, modules are artificially separated by the surgical procedure, and this prevents certain information from moving from one module to another. In normal brains, different modules might or might not be hooked up to one another, and when they're not, information doesn't move from one module to another.

Cranium Command gets things importantly right in another subtle way. When things are going poorly for our hero, General Knowledge chimes in to remind Buzzy that *his crew* can't tell the difference between real stress and imagined stress, *but Buzzy can*, basically making the claim that some modules get certain types of information while others don't. And not to ruin it, but the take-home message is really about getting all one's different modules all working together, a notion that fits very well with the modular view I'm endorsing here. And not only *that*, but Buzzy even uses the plural to refer to himself/Bobby: "She likes us," correctly implying that "Bobby" is a collection of modular entities. *Cranium Command* was really ahead of its time.

†For most of this discussion, I'll use the term loosely, and just ask you to consult your intuitions. Basically, you can think of "consciousness" the same way Supreme Court Justice Potter Stewart felt about pornography: you know it when you experience it.

Actually, it's even worse. Because all the different modular systems in the brain are the product of evolution, there is no sense in which connections among modules is the necessary or default state of affairs. Selection must act to link up systems in a way that enhances overall function. If one imagines a new module coming along—though of course they don't simply appear like that—there's no reason to think that it will automatically be hooked up to any given existing system, any more than new modules of Vehicles are automatically connected to old modules.

So, informational encapsulation—the *lack* of information flow across modules—is, oddly, the default. Evolution must act to connect modules, and it will only act to do so if the connection leads to better functioning.

Which information gets shared will, of course, depend on the details of the functions of the modules in question.

Self/conscious

Cranium Command is wrong about how the mind works in a way that mirrors a discussion of dualism by the philosopher Daniel Dennett. Dennett introduced the term "Cartesian Theater" in his book *Consciousness Explained*,[4] published in 1991, just a couple of years after *Cranium Command* opened at Walt Disney World. The idea is that we have this (incorrect) intuition that there's someone—a "me"—inside the brain, watching what the eyes see and the ears hear, much as Buzzy does.

There is a striking, even eerie similarity between what Dennett described and what Disney's Imagineers created. In his book, Dennett made the persuasive case that whereas there is some sense in which people "understand" that the little-brain-in-a-big-brain must be wrong, there is still some sort of strangely powerful intuition that there's some special something in our brains, a sort of observer, or Wizard-of-Oz-like person behind the curtain. Dennett writes:

> The idea of a special center in the brain is the most tenacious bad idea bedeviling our attempts to think about consciousness . . . it

keeps reasserting itself, in new guises, and for a variety of ostensibly compelling reasons. To begin with, there is our personal, introspective appreciation of the "unity of consciousness". . .[5]

There really is something strangely compelling about the notion of someone *in charge* in the brain, someone watching the action, someone in control. Indeed, the philosopher Jerry Fodor is insistent on this point: "If . . . there is a community of computers living in my head, there had also better be somebody who is in charge; and, by God, it had better be me."[6] I don't really know what Fodor means by "somebody," "in charge," or "me" in that sentence, so I'll just pass discreetly on.

The modular view means that we ought to be really careful about how we think about consciousness. Because we don't really know the *function* of the modules that happen to be conscious, we should be very wary of the notion that conscious modules are necessarily going to turn out to have really big roles to play in what the brain, as a whole, is up to. It might seem as though they should, but it could be that we only feel this way because consciousness is the only thing the brain does that feels like something. My guess—and I think the evidence in psychology is with me on this—is that whatever the conscious modules actually do constitutes relatively little of what the mind, in total, does.[7]

So, there are many, many things going on in your brain, and "you" have consciousness—experience—of only some of them. Your visual system is doing all kinds of complex computations—it takes an insanely complicated set of operations to turn the light on your retina into something other bits of the brain can use, and you don't experience any of those. You just experience the visual world.

Further, there's no particular reason that we ought to expect that consciousness is or must be associated with any particular process. We know more today than we used to about consciousness, but I think I'm on firm ground when I say that there's still a lot we don't know. In particular, I don't think we know what the function of consciousness is, or even if it's reasonable to talk about consciousness *having* a function.[8] I won't get into the philosophy of this, but it's worth keeping in mind that if we don't really understand it, we probably shouldn't make any sweeping claims about it.

There's a strong intuition that the conscious modules are "us," and that "we" need to know, basically, everything. But while Bobby does just fine asking Annie out at the end of Cranium Command, the modules that implement this excellent idea probably don't have information about how that decision was made. Many, many modules are busily doing their jobs, giving conscious modules the information necessary to do theirs, but quite possibly not much beyond that.

It's easy to forget this. It's easy to think that the conscious *I* is "in charge," originates decisions, and, basically, is every single module. But it's not. I think Dennett got it right when he said that while there is *some sense* in which we all reject dualism, nonetheless, as he put is, "the persuasive imagery of the Cartesian Theater keeps coming back to haunt us— laypeople and scientists alike—even after its ghostly dualism has been denounced and exorcized."[9]

I think what Dennett pointed out in 1991 is probably just as true today, and the intuition that there's some person-within-a-person in control makes it hard to think clearly about what it means to be "us." One of my favorite examples of this comes from a famous experiment in psychology by Benjamin Libet. In his research, subjects were hooked up to EEG machines to measure certain kinds of brain activity and told to perform a simple movement— a flick of the wrist—at a moment of their choosing. Libet and his colleagues looked at the relationship between activity in the brain and the subjects' report of their awareness of the decision to move the wrist.

Before I tell you the results, consider how this process might work. As you're reading these words, there are many parts of your visual system performing their functions that you don't have any experience of. For example, you don't know how you identify the letters on the page; this job is done by "low-level" modules, and you don't have any experience of how they work. You can think of vision as a modular cascade, with many different systems interacting with one another, building up the percept that is experienced. We have awareness of only the last step in this complex process. Most of the modules in vision are nonconscious, giving rise, eventually, to the conscious experience of seeing.[10]

So, when you're going to move your hand, there are a number of modules involved, and some module has to make the initial decision in this cascade. It seems to me that there are really only two possibilities. One possibility is that the *very first computation* in the *very first module* that starts the string is one of the operations that's conscious. In this case, the conscious experience of the decision and the brain activity will be at the same time. The only other possibility is that in the long string of operations that occur, from the initiation of the decision to move the wrist to the eventual movement of the wrist, some operation *other than the very first one* is associated with consciousness.[11] Some module tells Bobby's arm to reach for some ammunition for the food fight; shortly thereafter Bobby experiences the feeling of choosing to reach for chocolate pudding.

First of all, let's be clear. One way it *can't possibly turn out* is that brain activity occurs only *after* the decision to move the wrist. Whatever is making a decision to move the wrist, it's a module of some sort, and for certain *it's part of the brain*. You can't have a module in the brain that isn't, well, part of the brain. A module has to have *some* physical existence. If it didn't, it would be, in the philosopher Gilbert Ryle's famous term, a "ghost in the machine."

As you can probably guess, Libet and his colleagues found that brain activity *preceded* subjects' reports of their wish to move their wrist. In 1999, Libet talked about these findings, saying "In the traditional view of conscious will and free will, one would expect conscious will to appear before, or at the onset of, RP."*[12] But how could "conscious will" appear *before* anything happened in the brain? Whatever "conscious will" is—and I agree that this is a difficult issue—we all agree that it must be physical, something that happens in your brain. The decision to move the wrist can't be made, initially, by a nonphysical Buzzy-like entity.

Similar studies, using more advanced technology—fMRI rather than EEG—have shown similar effects. A recent headline in *Wired* magazine, discussing a study similar to Libet's, read: "Brain Scanners Can See Your Decisions Before You Make Them."[13] Why is this news? The only way brain scanners would *not* be able to see the initiation of a decision before the subject can report the awareness of "making" it would be, again, if it just happened

---

*RP, or "Readiness Potential," is the electrical activity in the brain that indicates the initiation of the activity.

to be true that the very first little module that initiates the long string of processes necessary for decision making just happened to be one of the very
small number that was associated with conscious awareness. In this case, the
brain activity and the sense of deciding would be simultaneous. But there's
just no scenario in which the sense of deciding comes before brain activity. It
just can't happen that way because all deciding just *is* brain activity.

Once you start thinking of the brain as made up of all these different
modules, and consciousness as nothing special, then headlines like this are
surprising only insofar as it's surprising that people aren't thinking about the
brain correctly yet.[14] One might be similarly surprised to find that today, not
just in the press, but also in top-tier psychology journals, the homuncular
Buzzy is still constantly around, usually hidden under innocent-looking but
deeply problematic terms such as "one," "the person," "the self," or similar
phrases. We visit such a case in the next chapter.

Speaking of being surprised by obvious things, let's pause to consider
a wonderful example of a similar phenomenon. Deena Weisberg, a psychologist, did some clever research while a graduate student at Yale. She
presented different groups of subjects two different explanations for psychological phenomena. Some subjects got the "regular" explanation, while
other subjects saw the same explanation with additional material saying
that "brain scans indicate" that some particular part of the brain already
known to be involved in the process in question caused the process to occur. In other words, the additional neuroscience didn't add anything explanatory. As the authors of the paper reporting these findings put it: "The
neuroscience information in the With Neuroscience condition thus did not
affect the logic or content of the psychological explanations, allowing us to
see whether the mere mention of a neural process can affect subjects' judgments of explanations."[15] Despite the lack of additional information, even
students enrolled in an introductory cognitive neuroscience course at Yale
rated the "With Neuroscience" explanation to be more satisfying.

The only way you can find the additional neuroscience information more
satisfying is if you somehow have the intuition that finding that *it's the brain
that does something* is surprising. In short, Dennett seems to be right, and
the Cartesian Theater creeps back in.

So who are "I"?

If everything I've said to this point is right, your brain, which consists of a large number of modules, has some modules that are conscious, and many, many more that are not. Many of the ones that are nonconscious are potentially very important, processing information about the sensory world, making decisions about action, and so on.

If that's right, it seems funny to refer to any particular module or set of modules as more "you" than any other set. Modules have functions, and they do their jobs, and they interact with other modules in your head. There's no Buzzy in there, no little brain running the show, just different bits with different roles to play.

What I take from this—and I know that not everyone will agree—is that talking about the "self" is problematic. Which bits, which modules, get to be called "me?" Why some but not others? Should we take the conscious ones to be special in some way? If so, why?

If you do think there's a sense in which there's a "self" in your head somewhere, that's OK, but it seems to me that at minimum it's clear it can't be Buzzy, or anything like him. It can't be a little person in your head seeing what "you" see, hearing what "you" hear, and making the decisions "for" you. If there's a "self," it has to be some part or parts of your brain, because that's all that we have to work with.

OK, you say, I understand there can't be a Buzzy in my head. But—and this is still you talking—I *feel* like there's a "me." As Fodor says, "I" seem to be in control. When *I* want to say something, words come out and all that. *I*'m in here somewhere. Right?

There's no doubt that parts of your brain cause your muscles to move, including the very important muscles that push air out of you lungs past your vocal cords, lips, and tongue to make the noises that we call language. Some part of the brain does that. Sure.

But let's be clear. Whatever is doing that is some *part* of your brain, and it seems reasonable to ask if there's anything special about it. Those modules, the ones that make noises with your lungs, might be "in charge" in some sense, but, then again, maybe they're not. It's easy to get stuck on the notion that we should think about these conscious systems as being special in some way. In the end, if it's true that your brain consists of many, many little modules with various functions, and if only a small number of them are conscious, then there might not be any particular reason to consider some of them to be "you" or "*really* you" or your "self" or maybe anything else particularly special.

Understanding the *function* of these modules helps in figuring out what they're up to, and that's the issue to which we next turn.

chapter 4

Modular Me

■ *One modular system in the mind is the press secretary, designed to communicate with other people . . . in Machiavellian fashion.* ■

In the television series *The West Wing*, a key plot arc in the second and third seasons was that the President, played by Martin Sheen, had hidden the fact that he had multiple sclerosis from the electorate. Inevitably, he was found out, generating all sorts of interesting twists that keep shows like *The West Wing* humming along.

When the White House Counsel spoke to the Press Secretary, C.J. Cregg (played by Allison Janney), he asked her a series of questions about how she had asked about the President's health. Had she asked if there was anything else she *needed* to know about his health, or anything else she *should* know about it? C.J. had, we discover, asked the President the former question—*needed*—and for good reason. C.J. had been careful to ask only if there was anything else she *needed* to know because if she'd asked if there was anything else she *should* know, then—his MS being something she *should* know but did not necessarily *need* to know—the President would have been put into a tricky position. If she uses the word *should*, and he doesn't tell her, then he's lying to his Press Secretary and, by extension, the press and the American people. If he does tell her, the game is up, and she would then have to reveal that he has MS.

What's the point? By asking if there's anything she *needs* to know, she can remain ignorant of the President's condition. If anyone asks about the President's health, she can honestly and convincingly say that she has no knowledge of any potentially serious medical condition that might undermine his ability to lead the country, command the most awesome military force the planet has ever known, and perform ribbon-cutting ceremonies.

This illustrates how it is sometimes a good idea for the Press Secretary to remain ignorant. If she doesn't know a particular fact, she can honestly deny knowledge of it rather than having to lie, which can be found out; and she can avoid accidentally revealing it, which can be damaging.

The Press Secretary has a function. Her job is to communicate various things about what's going on in and around the executive branch of the government to the outside world. Because of this particular function, she has to be very careful about what information she receives. Later in the series, C.J.'s successor in the job, William Bailey (Joshua Malina), succinctly states how important ignorance is in the job of the Press Secretary: "I do my best work when I'm the least informed person in the room."[1]

Of course, to say that the Press Secretary's job is to "communicate" with the press understates her responsibilities. Press secretaries do not simply transmit information from the White House to the Fourth Estate; they spin it, framing issues in ways favorable to the administration. For example, they make liberal use of euphemisms, making unpleasant elements of policy sound positive, turning a new tax into "revenue enhancement," a retreat into a "strategic redeployment," and torture into "enhanced interrogation techniques."

Suppose that some of the modules of the mind have the job of communicating—and framing—various things to the outside world, in particular, to other people. How would these modules be designed? Well, if there are reasons that these systems might, like the Press Secretary, execute their function *better* if they have incorrect information or no information, then we might expect that the part of the brain that talks might be designed in a way that allows them to be good at their function in the same way Will Bailey was.

The crossing-the-street-in-Philadelphia example is one case in which ignorance helps. I'm going to present a few more examples because it's a little counterintuitive that knowing less can be a good thing. Nobel laureate Thomas Schelling, drawing on principles from game theory, pointed out a number of such cases in his book *The Strategy of Conflict*, arguing that "genuine ignorance can be an advantage to a player if it is recognized and taken into account by an opponent."[2] Being ignorant can prevent other people from using a threat against you,* for example if you work in a store that advertises that employees do not know the combination to the safe.[3]

Consider the game of chicken. You and I are traveling in cars at high rates of speed toward each other, and the object of the game is for each of us to get the other to swerve. One strategy you can use is to rip off your steering wheel and throw it out the window of the car, ensuring that I see you do it. This last part is important—if I don't see you throw your steering wheel out, then I don't know that you've prevented yourself from swerving, and the gambit won't work. But I have a counter-strategy. I can put on a blindfold. If I prevent myself from seeing you commit to going straight, then your strategy has no effect on me, and you're back where you started.

That's obviously an unusual example, but there are similar kinds of things happening in everyday life.

And, more importantly, the process of natural selection seems to have hit on the same strategy, and designed the modular mind to keep certain kinds of information out of the press secretary system because of the strategic value that (correctly perceived) ignorance confers.

Moral modules

Jon Haidt, a psychologist at the University of Virginia, presented subjects with the following story:

Julie and Mark are brother and sister. They are traveling together in France on summer vacation from college. One night they are staying

---

* Consider how useful it would have been for Dustin Hoffman's character in *Marathon Man* to have been able to establish his ignorance of the answer to the question, "Is it safe?"

alone in a cabin near the beach. They decide that it would be interesting and fun if they tried making love. At very least it would be a
new experience for each of them. Julie was already taking birth control pills, but Mark uses a condom too, just to be safe. They both enjoy
making love, but they decide not to do it again. They keep that night
as a special secret, which makes them feel even closer to each other.
What do you think about that, was it OK for them to make love?[4]

As you can imagine, people answered that no, it was not OK. Haidt fol-
lowed up this question to try to get at *why* people thought it was not OK.
Some subjects gave answers having to do with inbreeding—which is irrelevant given the double-contraception. The experimenter explained why
each reason subjects gave was either contradicted by the story or irrelevant.
Finally, subjects gave up justifying their view that it was not OK, but sticking
to the view.

Haidt dubs this "moral dumbfounding," and I think it's one of the most
interesting findings in this area of moral psychology. At least for some kinds
of moral judgments, people can't give good reasons for their views, though
they often try quite hard.[5]

Just as people can't articulate the real reason they chose a particular
pair of panty hose, when making potentially important moral judgments,
people can't articulate the real reason behind them. While we might not
be all that worried that people don't know how they choose panty hose, we
might want to start to get a little more worried if people go around morally
condemning other people's behavior without being able to give a principled,
coherent justification. If people don't know why they think others should be
punished for having sex with their sibling, selling their kidneys, or cloning a
chicken, then that's potentially scary. We revisit issues of morality in more
detail in the final chapters of the book. The present point is that the range of
decisions we can't account for is large.

The lessons that Haidt takes from the incest case and ones like it are not
all that different from my view. In his book *The Happiness Hypothesis*, he
says that "To understand most important ideas in psychology, you need to
understand how the mind is divided into parts that sometimes conflict. We
assume that there is one person in each body, but in some ways we are each

more like a committee whose members have been thrown together working at cross purposes."[6]

I couldn't agree with this more (except I would have gone stronger than "in some ways"). But he goes on to say that "Our minds are divided in four ways,"[7] and this is the point at which he and I part conceptual company. Haidt divides up the brain in terms of left and right, old and new, emotional and rational, and "controlled" and "automatic." I think the granularity of these divisions is far too coarse.

If the modularity view is right, then we should be thinking in terms of dividing up the mind with respect to the *functions* of the modules that are doing the work rather than location or age.

There is, however, one binary division I favor. If the press secretary view is right, then it's reasonable to think that some bits of the mind are going to have design features that are useful in the context of *communicating* with others. These modules transmit information about lots of more or less mundane things we say or hear on a day-to-day basis, like "your keys are on the table," "grades are due on the fifth," or "get that thing out of your nose."

But communication is obviously useful for manipulating what others think in a way that works to one's advantage, and many modular systems in the mind seem to be designed for this purpose. Indeed, I think there is some sense in which *the part of you that feels like "you" is, more or less, designed to serve this public relations function*.[8] It's useful to think of these modules, the ones that we experience, at least in part, as having functions rather like the Press Secretary. These modules, the public relations system of the mind, seem to get certain kinds of information from other bits of your brain and communicate with other people.

If this is correct, then the modules that you experience as "you" can be thought of, at least in part, as more or less a mouthpiece for the organization. "You" are the Machiavellian spin doctor and, as such, only a small part of the sum total of what's going on in your head. "You" aren't the President, the central executive, the Prime Minister, or Buzzy.

"You" don't even know why you believe that incest is wrong; "you" just try to justify your belief.

Dan Dennett, discussing consciousness, advanced a similar view, referring to "PR," the Public Relations component of the mind: "PR takes as input *orders to perform speech acts*, or *semantic intentions*, and executes these orders" (his emphasis) and that "[t]he picture of a human being as analogous to a large organization, with intercommunicating departments, and a public relations unit to 'speak for the organization' is very attractive and useful."[9]

Later, in another book, this time in a chapter co-written with Nicholas Humphrey, Dennett advanced another version of the argument that closely resonates with the one I am advancing:

> On this view, selves are not things at all, but instead are explanatory fictions. Nobody really has a soul-like agency inside them: we just find it useful to imagine the existence of this conscious inner "I" when we try to account for their behaviour (and, in our own case, our private stream of consciousness). We might say indeed that the self is rather like the "centre of narrative gravity" of a set of biographical events and tendencies; but, as with a centre of physical gravity, there's really no such thing (with mass or shape or colour).[10]

Further on they say: "The analogy with a spokesman may not be far off the literal truth. The language-producing systems of the brain have to get their instructions from somewhere."[11]

So, to the extent there's a "you," it turns out that "your" job is public relations.[12]

No computation without representation[13]

Quick review: I've argued to this point that the brain consists of a large number of specialized systems, or modules, with various functions associated with solving our ancestors' adaptive problems. I've argued that some of these systems feed information to one another and some don't. Some instances in which information doesn't flow are evident in the patient cases we discussed in chapter 1, as well as in moral dumbfounding. In moral dumbfounding (and purchasing panty hose), some part of your brain is making a judgment, but the part that talks doesn't seem to have access to the information or the procedures that are driving it.

This notion of restricted information flow among the brain's many modules—informational encapsulation—explains why brains can contain inconsistencies. If two different systems are designed to get input from different sources, and there's no overarching purging of inconsistencies, then contradictions can easily remain. In the case of blind sight, the visual system has information about what's in the world, but the system that causes speech has no access to the information. One part of the brain can "see," but another part of the brain doesn't know this fact.

It's useful, in talking about these ideas, to introduce a term from cognitive science, *representation*. The word "representation" simply means information stored in your brain. In the Müller-Lyer illusion discussed in chapter 1, it must be that somewhere and somehow, the visual system has a representation of the two lines as unequal in length—in order to have the perceptual experience, the information "about" that experience has to be in your brain somewhere. Similarly, when I tell you the lines are of equal length, there is a representation of that fact in your head somewhere as well. That representation could be in something that might be called *propositional form*—something like the form of a sentence in natural language.

The two representations here are in what's called different representational *formats*. For example, two watches can both *represent* that it's 2:30 P.M., but one can be in digital format—numerals from 0 to 9—and the other can be analog—hands pointing to different positions on a disc. Representational formats are important and interesting, and I'm going to ignore them for the most part, except to mention that some great ideas in this area come from Zenon Pylyshyn, who, in my view, has, by a wide margin, the coolest name in all of cognitive science.

Most people are already very familiar with representational formats. If you've ever tried to open a computer file with the wrong application, then you're aware of the problem. Programs that "consume" files need to have them formatted in just the right way, or they can't understand them. The large number of picture types—.gif, .tif, .bmp—illustrates how the same information can be put into different information formats.

There is plenty of disagreement about the particulars surrounding formats in the brain, and, again, I don't want to engage in any of these debates because the argument I want to make doesn't require it. The language of "representation," however, is very useful, and I'll lean on it, but I also want to admit now that for purposes of getting ideas across, sometimes I'm going to cheat. So, for example, instead of saying "it must be the case that somewhere and somehow, the visual system has a representation of the two lines as unequal in length," I'm just going to say things like "your visual system thinks (or believes) the lines are unequal." You should take this as shorthand for saying that I think there's some subroutine in your head with a certain function that has to have appropriate representations in appropriate formats to get its job done, and it's easier to use words like "think" and "believe" instead of "representation."

Different representations, then, are found in different modules. Complicated evolved creatures like us, with many different modules with many different functions, are, for this reason, likely to have a substantial number of inconsistencies. Note that some have argued that these inconsistencies represent a problem, and the very large literature on "cognitive dissonance"—which has made its way out of psychology classes and into the mainstream media—suggests that there is an important "motive for consistency" that works to homogenize things. The view I'm endorsing here is very different, and I would argue that there are many, many cases in which any number of discrepancies coexist quite comfortably. I am deeply skeptical of the cognitive dissonance literature, a very brief discussion of which I relegate to an endnote.[14]

From here to hypocrisy

So the brain contains various inconsistencies in various systems. Are there a lot? Should we worry about them? Is it a big deal if we can't say why we think incest is immoral?

Maybe. For one thing, the modular view changes the way we think of what the mind does and how it does it. It suggests that instead of thinking of something like a Buzzy in charge, we should think of different modular systems being more or less in charge at different times. What's "driving our motors" depends on the situation we're in. In a Vehicle, when there's a lot of light, the light-fearing module takes over and drives the Vehicle away. It's not exactly the same—but also not altogether different—but when there's a bear, the predator-evasion modules in human minds take over, and drive us away. Different modules come online and go offline at different times, having more or less influence depending on the situation.

This is important because adaptive responding requires different kinds of strategies. As we'll see, for example, sometimes seeking out information is a good idea, and sometimes it isn't. Modules, shaped by evolution, are designed to implement strategies that are appropriate for the relevant problem. Because the details of the strategies that modules are using depend on what the module is for, modules have to be designed to become active when the problem they were designed for is being faced, and otherwise lie more or less inactive until their turn comes.

Sometimes modules are activated by what's going on around you. In the case of the bear, this is obvious. When there's a predator nearby, it's best to pretty much shut off other modules and prepare appropriately. The well-known "fight or flight" response is really just a bunch of modules, and physiological systems, getting turned on.

The effects of what's going on around you can be subtle; and, as always, these effects are not always, maybe not even often, subject to conscious awareness. One of the first studies I ran in graduate school involved having people play a very simple economic game. Subjects were given a certain amount of money and had to decide between keeping it or investing it in a "group account," in which case the money increased in value, but was shared with other people in the study. This method, called a "public goods game," essentially asks people to choose between acting selfishly and cooperatively. In one condition of this study, I had subjects share a brief mutual glance with one another. They just had to peek at their neighbors out of the corners of their eyes. I didn't change the economic incentives, just had them share a fleeting oblique glance. People were more cooperative under these conditions than when they didn't do any such peeking.[15] Looking at one another seems to have activated the more pro-social modules—or perhaps suppressed the selfish ones.

People are frequently unaware of how what's going on around them affects their decisions. For example, how do men decide whether or not to call a woman they recently met to ask her out? One possibility is that some modules are designed to assess how attractive others are as mates, and these modules generate "arousal" as an output. Suppose the modules that make the decision about whether or not to pursue someone operated based on how much arousal was being experienced when the woman in question was encountered. If so, it might be possible to "trick" these modules by putting men in arousing circumstances, and seeing if the arousal influences this decision. In one classic study,[16] psychologists had an attractive female confederate approach unsuspecting male subjects on one of two bridges, one that was high and wobbly, the other one on safer ground. About half the participants in the "wobbly bridge" condition later called the woman, compared to a much smaller fraction in the "safe bridge" condition.

Marketing professionals have various ways to manipulate your modules. They probably wouldn't put it that way, but certainly the people who decided to fill breezeways with aromas from the kitchens in Walt Disney World when I worked there seemed to have a pretty good idea about what would activate my meatball-seeking modules.*

Which brings up the next point, which is that which modules are on or off depends not just on what's going on around you, but also on what's going on inside. When you get more and more hungry, the food-seeking modules tend to wield greater and greater influence. This is why you shouldn't go grocery shopping when you're hungry—those modules make you buy things your other modules will later wish you hadn't, an issue to which we return in chapter 8.

By the same token, the relative influence of different modules changes over the course of the lifespan, which is why it seems as though eighteen-year-old boys have only one module, designed around various sorts of transactions with eighteen-year-old girls. By the same token, new parents find that some very profound modules, ones that must have been lying more or less dormant, now pretty much take over. The point, of course, is that which

---

*Of course I don't think evolution sculpted meatball-seeking modules per se. But I do think there are systems designed to cause us to seek food and eat it when we haven't eaten recently and there is food about. The technical term for this is "hunger."

particular adaptive tasks—which functions—are most important depends on how old you are, which is why the influence of different modules changes systematically.

Speaking of which, it might seem that the dynamic activation and de-activation of modules is complicated, influenced by one's age, current state, current context, and so on. How is this symphony of modules coordinated? The short answer is that I don't know, and I don't think that anyone really knows, and that the answer is that there's no one answer, but that, yes, it's all very interesting. To a first approximation, the answer might be that this is one convenient way to think about what emotions are. You see a bear, and your modules designed for foraging, mating, and pretty much everything else get shut off, and your modules for evasion turn on. "Fear," then, is this process, the suite of reactions that lead to some modules gaining priority over others given the current context.[17]

The modular view is really, really different from the view of the mind that many really, really smart people seem to have of it. Many people, in particular philosophers, think of the mind as unitary. For this reason, they worry a lot about contradictions within the mind. And, really, they can get themselves into a complete tizzy about this. In *Self and Deception: A Cross-Cultural Philosophical Enquiry*,[18] a whole bunch of philosophers worry a lot about this problem, so much so that you can almost sense them collectively wringing their hands. In one chapter dramatically called "On the Very Possibility of Self-Deception," the author discusses two subsystems, which he denotes S1 and S2, in the brain of a person. What if S1 believes one thing, but S2 believes another? This can't possibly be. Why? Because "the person cannot, of course, be both S1 and S2."[19]

I love this, especially the "of course." It's not obvious—at all—that "the person" can't be S1 and S2. If people's brains consist of lots of modules, and talking about "John, the person" in the way that Ramachandran did is problematic, then "the person" *can be*—and, in fact, *is*—S1 and S2 . . . and S8,571, and each of those systems can have its own beliefs, and they can contradict one another. The lines can be equal in one part of the brain, and unequal in another.

Finally, the modular view sheds light on why people are wrong and in-consistent. If some modules function better by being wrong, then we start to have a way to understand why people seem to be wrong about so many things, particularly about themselves. To return to the idea at the beginning of this chapter, if there is something like a press secretary module, and the mind's press secretary, just like the U.S. Press Secretary, can benefit from being ignorant or wrong, then other modules might be designed to keep information away from it, or even to give it bad information because the job of the press secretary—persuasion—is not always served by knowing what's true. So, while some modules are guiding what we say, other modules might be guiding action, leading to potential inconsistencies.

Disbelieving belief

So, there's lots of stuff going on in your head that the press secretary module does not know, and so is unable to talk about. Most of the rest of this book is a discussion of the implications of this view. But before moving on, I'd like to clean up just a little bit of remaining brush.

While the modular view shows how some seemingly mysterious things are not mysterious at all, it also does the reverse, making some very intuitive ideas problematic, sufficiently so that if we're trying to understand human psychology, we need to look carefully at some deep but potentially misleading intuitions, and be willing to abandon intuitions that get in the way of doing good, clear psychology.[20]

The first thing to worry about is the use of sentences that are deceptively simple, like "John believes X." The seemingly straightforward notion of someone believing something might not be straightforward at all.[21] Recall again the Müller-Lyer illusion. Given that there are contradictory beliefs in the observer's head, it seems funny to say that the observer "believes" something about the lines just because there are two different and conflicting representations in different modules. Yes, we can decide for some purposes that we only care about one module or another, but that doesn't mean it's going to be sensible to talk about what John, *as a whole*, believes. This is why I use quotes in many places here. While it seems sensible to talk about what a module represents, it is problematic to talk about what a "person" believes.

The second thing you want to worry about is that you can't assume that it's the one that talks—such as the one saying the lines are equal—that constitutes what "John believes." Consider two ways you might evaluate my math skills.[22] You could ask me if I, say, can do calculus. Or you can give me a calculus test. The first kind of measurement is susceptible to both lying and the possibility that the bit of me that answers the question doesn't know that I've forgotten everything I learned in calculus class by now. It seems pretty safe to say that to the extent there "really" is a set of math skills in my head, the bit that talks isn't as good a source as the bit doing the exam. Young children are especially bad—in some cases, outrageously bad—at telling you how good their performance is going to be on a memory task, claiming that they will be able to remember vast strings of digits.[23]

There's a huge body of literature in social psychology using what is called the "Implicit Association Test." As the name implies, this test is designed to measure the association between two concepts. It is "implicit" in the sense that the test does not consist of asking people how much they associate X with Y—that is, it doesn't ask people to make an explicit judgment; instead, it uses their reaction time to measure the strength of the association. The general idea is that if there is a close association between two concepts, then those two concepts will "activate" each other more strongly than if they were more distantly associated.[24]

This research tool has been used in particular in the domain of racial stereotyping. In one version of the task, subjects see African American and European American names as well as certain words with either good (e.g., "rainbow") or bad (e.g., "kill") connotations. The task is straightforward. If the word is *either* an African American name *or* something negative, there is one button to be pressed. If the word is *either* a European American name *or* something positive, a different button is pressed. Then the pairing is reversed: One button signifies African American or positive, the other, European American or negative. Reaction times are measured for each of the two pairings. As you might guess, people's reactions are slower when the categories are [African American names, good] and [European American names, bad]. The idea is to measure the implicit association between the names (and presumably the people in the category) and positivity or nega-

tivity: The difference in speed between the two tasks is taken to be a measure of the (implicit) association. One can be forgiven for the intuition that
this association, measured in this way, is somehow a more "true" measure of
the subject's attitudes than simply asking the subject how much she associates African Americans and negativity, but researchers in this area treat this
quite sensibly, and explicitly deny this construal of an IAT score.[25]

The IAT illustrates that there's no reason to say that the information in
the modules that talk represents "real" or "genuine" belief; but there's also
no reason to say that information to which this part of your brain *doesn't*
have access should be considered to be "real" or "genuine." Note that I'm
not saying anything about lying here. People who have (modules that contain) a strong implicit association between African Americans and negativity are not necessarily lying when they report that they don't. It's just that
this association isn't available to the modules that talk.

Nonetheless, there is a deep intuition that it's reasonable to talk about
what someone *really* believes. People routinely talk about what they believe
in their "heart of hearts," what they believe "in their gut," or what they "truly,
truly" believe. But there are very good reasons to worry that this isn't right.
First, the intuition behind the notion of what one "really" believes seems to
be along the lines of Dennett's Cartesian Theater and Buzzy. The "real" belief
seems to have something to do with what you think Buzzy believes. If Buzzy
were in there, that's what he'd think. That's what the *guy in charge* thinks.

That's one good reason to worry right there. Again, in the case of optical
illusions, blind sight, and so on, there does seem to be *some* sense in which
"you" "really" believe that the lines are the same length. But I think this
intuition comes from the fact that we tend to give priority to the bit of the
brain that talks, and, in this case, this module thinks it knows something that
is actually true. That makes the belief seem more genuine.

But what about cases like split-brain patients, blind sight, and choosing
panty hose? Did the patient *really* choose the shovel because it's used to
clean up after the chicken? It seems not, yet that's what you hear them say.
Did subjects choose the panty hose because they liked the fabric, or whatever they reported to you? It seems almost certainly not.

From this, we can conclude that *to the extent that the mind does consist
of separate modules, there's just no reason to talk about what one module*

believes as being more "genuine" or "real" than another one. The next time you hear a psychologist try to talk about what someone "really" believes, you should really not believe the psychologist. You should also worry about the expression that people believe something "at some level."

In the same way, it's important to be careful not to be drawn into saying things like "you tell your brain to do this" or "one can tell one's brain to do that." It's fine for Homer Simpson to say, as he did, "All right, Brain, you don't like me, and I don't like you. But let's just do this, and I can get back to killing you with beer." But this can't be right. Whatever is doing the saying is—for real people, anyway—part of the brain. So, Homer's quote here runs into the little-brain-in-a-big-brain (i.e., the Buzzy) problem. If there's one *part* of the brain communicating with another part of the brain, that's fine, but it's not OK to say that "you tell your brain" something, because whatever "you" might be, it's some part—and *only* some part—of the brain. It's not all of it; it can't be. And, whatever sets of modules you think are "you," they're just that, modules.

I mention this to highlight that while thinking about modules is very, very helpful, *not* thinking about modules has tripped up many people, including the professionals who get paid to do this stuff for a living, psychologists. Recall Dennett's warning, that the homunculus creeps into thinking about psychology, often without people realizing it. In psychology, people often refer to "one," "the person," and "the self" with no clear idea about what, specifically, those innocent-looking words refer to.

I myself came across an example recently in the context of a debate surrounding the issue of sexual jealousy. In what sounds like the beginning of a joke but isn't, in a paper about the psychology of sexual jealousy, David DeSteno and coauthors described a hypothetical case of a potentially jealous woman, a husband who got home late, and a transit strike. My colleagues and I suggested that in thinking about such a case, it was useful to consider how information in one module about transit strikes—and how they might delay people, including one's spouse—might influence the module or modules that generate feelings of jealousy. Modules that *generate* jealousy, it seems, might well be influenced by jealousy-relevant information, such as whether there is a good reason for one's spouse getting home late. We thought that this was a pretty reasonable idea.

DeSteno and colleagues begged to differ. They suggested *instead* that "awareness of a transit strike might allow one to tamp down rising jealousy stemming from" a module.[26]

See that "one" after "allow"? It's a small word, but it speaks volumes. That "one" is just like Homer talking to his own brain. They're saying that our view that one *part* of the brain is inhibiting the module that generates jealousy isn't right. Instead, they think that *one*—the "person," the "self," a little-brain-in-a-big-brain, Homer, Buzzy, whatever you want to call it—is.

Once you translate what they're saying into the language of modularity, it's easy to see that they're just very deeply confused about the mind in the same way that someone who still believes in the Cartesian Theater is—someone's still in there—"one"—watching the screens, eating popcorn, drinking Duff . . . and "tamping down" jealously. It's not a module. It's "one," a little Buzzy. Oops.[27]

Without modularity, dualism creeps in.

Conscious modules?

It is appealing to talk about what "I" "believe," or what "you" "believe"— and, in real life, it's often good enough. But, when you're trying to figure out how the mind works, it's important to think about modules, even when making seemingly simple claims that Person X believes p. To do good psychology it's best to be as specific as possible about what you mean when you talk about belief.

It's useful to think of beliefs, or other representations, as being "in"—or, at least, associated with—some module or set of modules. It's easy to say that the representation of unequal lines is somewhere in the visual system, or that the visual system represents the lines as unequal, and that there is another module that contains the proposition that the lines are equal. As psychology progresses, we'll be able to talk more and more sensibly about which modules have which representations. And, in fact, there's quite a lot of that already. Researchers in cognitive science, linguistics, and neuroscience know a great deal about various modules in your brain—though they use a range of terms to talk about it—and the field is doing better every day.

In the same way that I think it's a mistake to be content to say "John believes X"—because different modules of John might believe not-X—there's a problem with "is aware of," "is conscious of," and "is in control of." To the extent that only some modules have consciousness associated with them, *it's also a problem to say that "John is conscious of Y."* Really, it's going to turn out that more precision is required, and that *some of* John's modules are conscious of Y.

It's pretty much uncontroversial by this point that some things in your head have consciousness associated with them and some don't. Simply saying "I" am conscious of "X" loses all the work we've done to this point worrying exactly what that innocuous one-letter but philosophically loaded capital "I" might be.

While this is sort of an odd way of looking at things, any modular system is going to have this basic problem. But I think it gets even odder. Suppose some modules in your head have consciousness associated with them, and some don't, and some systems in your head pass information to one another, and some don't. Fine. It follows that not only is there a lot going on in your brain that your press secretary—the "you" that "talks"—doesn't know about, but there's a lot going on in your brain that your press secretary *can't* know about. In the same way that you can't know what it's like to be a bat—an idea discussed in a wonderful essay by the philosopher Thomas Nagel[28]—you, that is, again, the "you" that has experience, can't know what's going on in those other bits of your brain that don't send you information in a format that your press secretary can process.

Now suppose that some other parts of your brain *did* have experience or consciousness. Suppose that it was actually *like something* to be an edge detector in the visual system or it was *like something* to be the part of the brain that regulates breathing and heart rate or some such. If so, *how would "you" know?* Just as it is impossible for you to know what it's like to be a bat, or, for that matter, for you to know what it is like to be me, how do you know that it's not *like something* for the other bits of your brain? Yes, I'm suggesting that it's not, in principle, impossible, that all of us are carrying around parts of our brains that have experience but can't communicate anything about those experiences.

That might sound pretty strange—carrying around silent, conscious modules in your head. But maybe it's not *that* strange. One of my former graduate students, Marc Egeth, is working on communicating with people who might be able to process information but not respond to it. Imagine you're in a kind of a coma in which you're paralyzed, but the systems needed to keep you alive are still functioning. Say further that you can hear and you have experience, but that's it. How would you let someone know? If there are modules in your head that have some sort of experience, but don't control speech or muscles, how would anyone know about their experience?

It's a tricky problem, and Dr. Egeth is working on solutions, but his work illustrates that communicating with modules that don't link up to parts of the system that communicate is a tricky business.

This issue was raised poignantly in the film *Awakenings,* with Robert De Niro and Robin Williams. Williams, playing Dr. Sayer, is talking to another doctor about patients infected with a virus (*encephalitis lethargica*) who have been in comas—speechless, motionless, unresponsive—for many years.[29]

SAYER: What must it be like to be them. . . . What are they thinking?

OLD DOCTOR: They're not. The virus didn't spare the higher faculties.

SAYER (*hopefully*): We know that for a fact.

OLD DOCTOR: Yes.

SAYER: Because . . .

OLD DOCTOR: Because the alternative is unthinkable.

Reinventing one's "self"

This concludes my discussion of the theoretical foundations of modularity. These ideas are helpful in understanding a large number of issues in psychology, including self-deception, strategic ignorance, and hypocrisy, all of which we explore in subsequent chapters. The key idea is that the human mind is like an iMind, with lots of killer apps all bundled together. Did our ancestors face a particular adaptive problem? Yeah, there's an adaptation for that.[30]

The best summary of this view comes from absurdly intelligent Marvin Minsky, best known for his work in artificial intelligence, in his book *Society of Mind*. In an unpublished draft of the book from 1976,[31] Minsky wrote:

The mind is a community of "agents." Each has limited powers and can communicate only with certain others. The powers of mind emerge from their interactions for none of the Agents, by itself, has significant intelligence. . . . In our picture of the mind we will imagine many "sub-persons," or "internal agents," interacting with one another. Solving the simplest problem—seeing a picture—or remembering the experience of seeing it—might involve a dozen or more—perhaps very many more—of these agents playing different roles. Some of them bear useful knowledge, some of them bear strategies for dealing with other agents, some of them carry warnings or encouragements about how the work of others is proceeding. And some of them are concerned with discipline, prohibiting or "censoring" others from thinking forbidden thoughts.

I don't think I could put it better than that. *Society of Mind* is still an excellent read two decades on. The book is both wonderfully well written and more generally just wonderful, and I like it because Minsky has a nice, terse way of putting the Buzzy problem: "The idea of a single, central Self doesn't explain anything. This is because a thing with no parts provides nothing that we can use as pieces of explanation" (p. 50). He saw clearly how a large number of simple machines can make a big, smart machine. He is, I think, one of the smartest machines, ever. Minsky had the notion that thinking about agents—or modules—requires thinking about their function, but, as far as I can tell, he didn't *quite* get the next step, which is that it requires thinking about their *evolved* function, which will play a key role in answering questions such as the following: Why are some modules designed to avoid getting potentially useful information? Why are some modules designed to make systematic errors of inference? And, of course, why are (other) people such gosh-darned hypocrites?

chapter 5

The Truth Hurts

■ *For biological organisms, knowing what is true is, everything else equal, an obviously good idea. However, there are many cases in which the function of some evolved system will be harmed by gathering true information.* ■

Prominent philosopher Jerry Fodor, in *The Mind Doesn't Work That Way*, asserts that "there is nothing in the 'evolutionary,' or the 'biological' or the 'scientific' worldview that shows, *or even suggests*, that the proper function of cognition is other than the fixation of true beliefs."[1] Philosophers in general and Fodor in particular talk that way, but all he means is that *all* your brain is good for is figuring out what's true. So, he's saying that pretty much all of the stuff I've been trying to argue for—that your brain has modules for solving adaptive problems—is bunk. Fodor's main arguments for his view are, first, that evolved mechanisms interact with one another—which seems true but unpersuasive in itself—and second, that belief is for doing, and doing is facilitated by knowing true things: "It's generally not much use knowing how the world is unless you are able to act on what you know."[2] I'm going to argue in this chapter that Fodor is right in that it's often good to know what's true. But I'm also going to argue that he is also deeply wrong.

Don't misunderstand me; to be sure, there are lots of good reasons to know what's true. Knowing what's true is *useful*, and in biology, function is everything.

Not only is truth useful for guiding behavior, but it's also good for generating more true beliefs. If you know *All men are mortal*, and you know that *Socrates is a man*—and you can apply some formal logic—you can infer something that bodes ill for Socrates.

Truth can be useful when compared to untruth. "Knowing"—i.e., having a representation in your head—things that are untrue can be damaging. A certain Zulnun Arghun had the belief that he was destined to defeat the Uzbeks, as a result of which, he "did not put the fort in a defensible state; did not prepare ammunition and warlike arms; did not appoint either an advance or pickets to get notice of the enemy's approach, nor even exercise his army, or accustom it to discipline, or battle-array. . . ." He held his ground with his 150 against 50,000 Uzbeks, with the predictable results.[3]

But it's a mistake to think that having only true beliefs, and as many of them as possible, is always going to be a good thing. And, consequently, it would be a mistake to think that the mind's modules are designed only to perceive, discern, store, and infer truth. Philosopher Patricia Churchland put it this way: "The principal function of nervous systems is . . . to get the body parts where they should be in order that the organism may survive. . . . Truth, whatever that is, definitely takes the hindmost."[4]

I couldn't agree more, except it's not survival but reproduction that is the heart of the matter. Close enough.

TMI

Let's begin with some easy cases. First, it should be obvious that people shouldn't be motivated—that is, your brain shouldn't have modules designed—to try to find out all true information it is possible to find.

Some information that is, in principle, obtainable simply isn't useful, and the time spent getting information could be used for doing useful things. Barry Schwartz has done some very interesting work in this area, showing that some of us often don't stop gathering information even when it's not worth our time.[5] If you have ever been in a supermarket stuck like a deer in headlights staring at rows upon rows of shampoos that are roughly equally priced and, from my perspective at least, equally good, then you know his point. People often try to optimize their purchases even when the absolute best deal is only a tiny amount better than the next best deal.

This idea has been formalized by Peter Todd and colleagues in the context of looking for a mate. If you don't stop looking for a mate until you're certain that you've found the absolute perfect match for you, then the most likely outcome is that you never stop searching. Sad. But how do you know when to stop? Some very nice mathematical models address exactly this question.[6] These models make the reasonable assumption that the extra information you get about mates keeps getting smaller and smaller as you search longer and longer, and so at some point searching is more costly than the benefit of getting more information. It remains to be seen how well people do at stopping their search in various domains. Cases like the ones that Schwartz focuses on show that while some of us, obsessed with getting the best possible option, spend too much time searching, others of us, satisfied with getting something "good enough," do just fine. A good thing to remember next time you have found a pretty good parking spot but can't help wondering if there might be one just a little closer.

Other kinds of information aren't worth searching for because they won't change your behavior in any way. A vast amount of information is in this category, and we restrict our information-gathering to a narrow band of domains, including what's going on with our friends and relatives—often 140 characters at a time these days—information relevant to our work, and, for reasons that seem obvious but I don't think are, sources like *People* magazine, which has information on how much fat tissue has accumulated in the body of a young woman living in southern California who has a pretty good acting career going and who essentially no one reading *People* will ever meet.

There is, of course, a great deal of true information out in the world that we don't seem to seek out. Do you care about the price of apples is in New Zealand? Probably not. But what about information about your health? Surely our information-seeking modules should be designed to find out information about our health.

Right?

And the truth shall hold ye hostage

There are several ways in which not having true beliefs can make you better off. One of my colleagues at Penn, Jason Dana, has investigated this phenomenon in a clever set of experiments.[7] He used an economic game in which subjects are brought into a lab and faced with a choice between two options. The first option is $5 for themselves and $5 for someone else. The second option is $6 for themselves and $1 for the other person. So, their choices are between $5/$5 and $6/$1. Roughly two thirds of the people who participated in this experiment chose $5, foregoing $1, making their counterpart $4 better off than they otherwise would have been. So, people are, on average, generous. Right?

But a different group of subjects played a different game. In this one, the players making the decision can, as before, choose $5 or $6 for themselves, and some other person then receives either $1 or $5. In this game, however, while players choose their own payoff, they don't know whether the other person will receive $1 or $5 as a result of the choice. In effect, then, the person is facing a choice between $5/$X and $6/$Y, but without knowing what X and Y are, $5 or $1. In this situation, a generous player has no way of knowing which option will give the other person $5 rather than $1, and hence, won't know which option to choose.

Here's the twist: People making the choice can, if they want, find out the other player's payoffs. They simply have to click a button. If they do, they will be told whether they are choosing just as in the first game—a choice between $5/$5 and $6/$1—or the reverse—a choice between $5/$1 and $6/$5. From the standpoint of the subject, clicking on the button might reveal that by choosing the $6 option—the one she would rather choose—she is costing the other person $4. By *not* clicking on the button, the subject can choose the $6 option and say, honestly, that she didn't know what effect that choice would have on the other person.

Indeed, roughly half the people in Dana's study refused to look at the payoffs of the other player. And, not surprisingly, many more subjects chose $6/? rather than $5/?. Having chosen not to click the "reveal" button, these subjects could honestly say, if asked afterwards, that they *didn't know* what effect choosing the $6 option had on the other player. If you were in the study, and you wanted to be able to look someone in the eye after it was over, and say that you didn't know that choosing the $6 option left him with only $1, then you would have to refuse to look at the information you were offered.

Dana likens his study to the following moral dilemma. Suppose you knew that a sinister person was going to call one number at random in your city at noon on Saturday and give the following ultimatum: "Unless you cut off your left pinky, I will kill an entire family." If you knew that such a call could be made, would you somehow be away from your phone around noon?

Dana's studies should remind you of the Frogger/crossing-the-street distinction because the multiple effects of one's choices mirror considerations in the real world, where people face choices that have costs and benefits that can be conveniently divided into *instrumental*—the tangible stakes in terms of money, health, and so on—and *social*—what other people will think and do given that you have selected—or not selected—various options. Finding out information can affect social payoffs.

Sometimes obtaining information changes social payoffs because of the consequences of lying. The moment that you find out that a close friend has committed a serious crime, your social payoffs change. Before you know, if you are interrogated, you can truthfully say that you know nothing, thus allowing you to protect your friend without running the risk of perjury. Once you find out your friend is guilty, you are faced with a difficult decision if forced to testify under oath. With the extra information in your head, a previously costless decision (to say nothing) turns into one that is costly no matter what you do. Under oath, either you have to perjure yourself, or you have to give up your friend.

People who have been kidnapped are in the same situation. Once kidnap victims see their kidnapper's face, a bad situation becomes even worse. As long as the victims can't identify their captor, he can free them without worry that doing so will lead to his arrest. However, once they see his face, the victims become a liability if they're freed, making release problematic. The same thing applies whether the kidnapper gets the ransom or simply changes his mind. Absent some kind of insurance that the victims won't turn him in, the kidnapper can't free them.[8]

A little knowledge is a dangerous thing

Having information can cause social problems with subtle and wide-ranging effects. I'm going to discuss issues related to one's reputation in the context of perceived *duties*. Many philosophers have written extensively on this—most notably Kant—so I'll just make a few general remarks.

People's reputations suffer to the extent that they are perceived not to discharge a duty. If you can save a drowning child at little risk to yourself, people perceive you as having an obligation to do so. So, getting access to new information can give you a new duty that you didn't have before.

Suppose you're standing outside a house that's burning to the ground, and you're feeling bad for the people who are losing their belongings, because you're empathic. Good for you. A small boy comes along and points out to you that there is, just visible in the smoke, a cat in the window, and its exit is blocked by the flames. Now, holding aside the benefits you might get by being a cat-saving hero, consider that prior to finding out about the cat you could stand by and not suffer any adverse reputational damage. Now that the boy knows you know about the cat, you have two options: You can try to save the cat, at a risk to yourself, or not try to save the cat, and endure the reputational damage of allowing the cat to die.*

The boy pointing out the cat did you no favors. Having information—especially information others know you have—changes how your choices—and, consequently, actions—are evaluated by others because there is the reasonable sense that you now have a duty to act on that information.

In my lab, we have been looking at a classic moral dilemma, the so-called "trolley problem."[9] The story goes like this. You're standing on a footbridge and you see a runaway trolley that is about to hit and kill five people standing on the tracks. There's not enough time for them to get away, and they're too far away for you to be able to yell and warn them. A man with a large backpack is standing next to you, and if you push him off the footbridge, the backpack is heavy enough that it will stop the trolley, saving the five people on the track. Do you push the man off the footbridge, killing him in order to save the five people?

---

*You could kill the boy, but then you've got other problems.

In many variations of this problem, people say it's not OK to push the man with the backpack.[10] In our own studies, when we ask people if it is morally wrong to push the man, nearly everyone (87%) says that it is. For the present purpose, what is interesting is that when we ask people if *not* pushing the man is wrong, a majority of people, 62%, say that's wrong too. If you're on the footbridge, people think that whether you push or not, you've done something morally wrong. Knowing you can kill one person to save five in this way puts you in a no-win situation.

This problem is accentuated for people who are perceived as having a duty to enforce rules or laws.[11] People generally think that those who break laws ought to be punished. That's clear enough. But it's not at all clear that people want to enforce the rules if they can avoid it. The problem facing rule-enforcers was illustrated in HBO's exceptional drama, *The Wire*. If you're a cop, a problem with drug laws—a topic to which we'll return in chapter 9—is that if you see drug use, and people see you see drug use, then if you don't enforce the law, the people who have seen you know you're not enforcing the law. This means that, in principle, it's easy to wind up spending all your time on petty busts rather than focusing on more important matters. One of the characters, Bunny Colvin, talks about this problem eloquently in the context of alcohol. I'll quote him at length here because it captures the basic idea so nicely. Colvin is addressing a room of Baltimore police officers, explaining the value of ignorance:

> Somewhere back in the dawn of time, this district had itself a civic dilemma of epic proportions. The city council had just passed a law that forbid alcoholic consumption in public places. On the streets and on the corners . . . but the law's the law. The Western cops rolling by, what were they going to do? If they arrested every dude out there for tipping back a High Life there'd be no time for any other kind of police work . . . and if they looked the other way, they'd open themselves to all kinds of flaunting and all kinds of disrespect. Now this is before my time when it happened, but somewhere back in the '50s or '60s, there was a small moment of goddamn genius by some nameless smoke-hound who comes out of the Cut-rate one day and on his way to the corner he slips that just-bought pint of elderberry

into a paper bag. A great moment of civic compromise. That small, wrinkled-ass paper bag allowed the corner boys to have their drink in peace, and gave us permission to go and do police work.[12]

Colvin applies this basic idea to the enforcement of drugs in his area and designates an area where the police don't arrest drug vendors and users. Setting aside this area where people can safely sell and use drugs, without worry of enforcement, improves crime rates elsewhere in the district and helps get treatment and clean needles to addicts. In a nod to realism, when the scheme is discovered by his superiors, they put an end to it and Colvin is punished for improving the lives of addicts and citizens.

Police are, then, sometimes better off not knowing when crimes are being committed. Ignorance relieves them of their duty with respect to particular infractions, and allows them to make better decisions about law enforcement.* Parents know this as well. Not being one, I can't say if it's true that parents will frequently take pains to avoid seeing a minor infraction they don't wish to police, but, having had parents, it sort of felt that way to me.† What I can say is that as an instructor, I think I would much prefer someone do the crossword puzzle in my class discreetly, rather than out in the open. Every time I let an obvious puzzle-doer go, my authority erodes just that little bit. And there's no way that I've found to call out a student for doing a crossword puzzle without seeming draconian. So, I try to look like I don't notice puzzle-doers.

In effect, the value of ignorance comes from the costs of others seeing you know something that puts you in a position in which you are perceived to have a duty and must choose to do one of two costly acts—punish, or ignore. In my own lab, we have found that people know this. When our subjects are given the opportunity to punish someone who has been unkind in an economic game, they do so much less when their punishment won't be known by anyone. That is, they decline to punish when the cloak of anonymity protects them.[13]

---

*Remember, it's really *other people's* beliefs that they are ignorant which is doing the work here; it's not the ignorance per se but *the perception of ignorance* that matters. By the same token, it's worth remembering that if one were sure no one would find out, then, as a purely strategic matter, we're back in a Frogger situation, in which information can only help for purposes of decision making.

†I was usually the villain who got away with something, so this isn't a complaint so much as an apology.

Ignorance is institutionalized in the United States military. The so-called "don't ask, don't tell" policy prevents soldiers from disclosing information about their sexuality that would disqualify them from further service in the military. Importantly, the "don't ask" part keeps commanders from asking about soldiers' sexual orientation, the knowledge of which would lead to discharge.

Returning to television, this was illustrated by the famous final episode of *Seinfeld*, in which the four main characters not only observed a car-jacking, but filmed it, even commenting on it as it occurred. They are arrested and tried for violating a "duty to rescue" law, which compels observers to help others under certain conditions. (I hold aside the legal details here. I simply note that this is often referred to as a "Good Samaritan" law, but "Good Samaritan" laws actually protect people who try to help others.)

To the extent that our modules are designed to confer advantages, these arguments suggests that some, maybe many, modules in our minds are designed to avoid getting information because of the strategic consequences. It's at least plausible that in the world in which humans evolved, being observed by others while finding out certain things was to our detriment, and so it's not unreasonable to suppose that some modules are designed to guide us away from certain kinds of discoveries.

So ignorance, or simply having the wrong facts (there was a *cat* in that building? If only I had known . . .), is best when having correct information makes your available options less desirable than when you didn't have the correct information. That is, in such cases, accurate knowledge—with others knowing you know—is a negative. What I'm saying is that, yes, *we're designed for ignorance*. Mostly, this design will be visible in strategic settings—when my ignorance helps because of others' perceptions. A little knowledge really is, and often has been, a dangerous thing.

Is Ignorance Bliss?

Related to strategic ignorance is plausible deniability. Consider the issue of testing for sexually transmitted infections. Knowing that one has a particular infection can be valuable for getting treatment. Because getting treatment is important for one's continued health, one might imagine that people would get themselves tested if they thought there was a chance of having been infected. However, seeking to maximize health is not the only goal in a brain that has many modules in it, some of which are, I argue, designed for strategic ignorance.

Consider a person with the following reasonably plausible preferences:[*] (1) He wants to have multiple sexual partners; (2) he does not want to be able to be (correctly) accused of knowingly risking a sexual partner's life;[14] (3) he doesn't mind being (correctly) accused of not finding out information that would have led him to conclude that sexual contact would risk his partner's health. Such an individual might resist testing, knowing that a positive test puts him in the position of having to forgo sexual partners to avoid an accusation of knowingly risking someone else's health.

Preference (3) might seem odd. Finding out such information is trivial in terms of time and money compared to the costs of putting someone's life in danger. Why don't people mind being accused of *not* taking relatively easy and cheap steps that could have prevented them from endangering someone else's life? That's an interesting question, and, like so many interesting questions, I'm going to ignore it here.[15]

How should we think, in general, about which modules might be designed for ignorance? In Douglas Adams's *The Restaurant at the End of the Universe*, a principle character sports a pair of "Joo Janta 200 Super-Chromatic Peril Sensitive Sunglasses," which turn black when danger looms, allowing the user to remain blissfully ignorant of whatever might otherwise be alarming. This is funny exactly because this is a case in which ignorance isn't a good solution to immediate danger.[†] When, just as in Frogger, you're playing a game with Nature, and there are no people involved, ignorance is typically not going to be useful. The arguments that turn on duty and the condemnation of those who don't fulfill their duties get their traction

---

[*] Later I'll suggest that we shouldn't think of people as having preferences so, yes, this is inconsistent with that. Here, the notion of preferences is useful to make the point.

[†] The thing about ostriches burying their heads in the sand is a myth. It had to be. Imagine two ostriches, one that sticks its head in the sand when a lion is approaching, and one that *runs away*. The ostrich that runs is going to be scared as hell for a while, but it has a chance of escaping. Yes, the head-in-the-sand ostrich might have some nice moments of peace, but ostriches that ignore impending predation don't leave many offspring to do the same.

because of *people*, in particular the way that people evaluate others based on their choices. Ignorance when the payoffs are not social is generally a bad thing.

Having Joo Janta 200 sunglasses when you're playing Frogger won't help. You'll lose every time. Suppose you had them in Jason Dana's experiment. If they go dark before you can see the other person's payoffs, you're free to choose $6 for yourself, and no one can fault you for it . . . as long as they can see that your lenses have gone dark.

Ignorance is at its most useful when it is most public.

The value of being valuable

The preceding arguments are supposed to suggest that humans might have some modules designed to keep them away from certain kinds of information because it's too expensive to be worth the cost of gathering it, because some information makes choosing certain options very costly, and because some types of information lead to the perception of duties that carry social costs if left unfulfilled.

In some ways, these arguments are relatively straightforward. The next part of my argument is going to lean heavily on the ideas about modularity and the press secretary model, and I'm going to need a bunch of assumptions to get me where I want to go. My destination is going to be that the press secretary module might be designed to contain certain kinds of information that are useful for certain purposes *even if other modules have information that not only conflicts with this information, but is also more likely to be accurate.* That is, my claim is that some modules are designed to acquire systematically biased—i.e., false—information, *including information that other modules "know" is wrong.* To return to *The West Wing* analogy, it's like C. J. Cregg *wants* the President to lie to her.

OK. If I'm going to claim that some modules are actually designed to be wrong, I'd better have a good argument. Here we go.

The first assumption I need is relatively uncontroversial. If you compare humans to nearly any other species on the planet, we're incredibly social. If you're, say, a stick insect, then your fitness depends largely on nonsocial stuff, like how much you look like a stick, which helps you to avoid predation and that sort of thing. Some of the things you do are social—you have to mate successfully—but largely your design as a stick insect is to solve nonsocial adaptive problems such as looking sticklike.

Humans are very different. Humans' success no doubt has to do and had to do with avoiding predation, finding food, and so on. But human success is deeply tied to our ability to navigate the social world. Indeed, in the ongoing debate about why human brains are so big—and relative to body size they're really large—a major contender for what drove this process is competition in social domains.[16] Individuals' abilities to form friendships and alliances must have played large roles in reproductive success over human evolutionary history.

Intriguing evidence of the importance of social life is found in our sensations of pain and pleasure. A very simple way to think about these feelings is that pain is evolution's way of telling you something bad is happening, and pleasure is evolution's way of telling you that you're doing what you ought to be doing.*

And evolution is telling you to be social. Findings over the last several decades have shown that people who live alone are more prone to physical and mental illness,[17] that one's health is negatively affected by having fewer stable social relationships,[18] and, on the flip side, that having positive social relationships correlates strongly with emotions like happiness.[19]

Creative experiments have illustrated the same idea. Kip Williams devised a clever study in which, in the fine tradition of social psychology, he led subjects to believe they were waiting for an experiment when they were already actually in it. In the room with the subject were two confederates—research assistants who were in on the whole thing—one of whom picked up a ball that had been placed in the room and started tossing it around. In the key condition, the hapless subject was thrown the ball a few times, and then ignored. (Subsequent versions of this study have moved it from the real world into the virtual world, and subjects play over a computer network, where they are virtually ignored, as it were.) Subjects excluded in even this seemingly minimal way reported very high levels of distress, anger, and sad-

---

*It's obviously more complicated than that.

ness. In describing some of the research in this area, Williams writes that the pain levels reported by people reliving socially painful events, especially ostracism, "were comparable to pain levels observed . . . for chronic back pain and even childbirth."[20] So that's pretty bad I guess.

Anyway, humans are extremely social, and our survival and reproduction are determined in large part by how well we navigate the social world. Given this, it's reasonable to expect that our minds are designed to compete fiercely—if often subtly—for the benefits in the social world: the best mates, the best friends, membership in the best groups, and so on. The outcomes of these competitions would have had massive effects on reproductive success over the course of human evolution.

In some areas, competition is relatively easy to understand. For example, the benefits of having a higher quality rather than a lower quality mate are obvious. Indeed, the centrality of having a good mate is so important, psychologist Geoffrey Miller has suggested that it is the competition for mates that drove the evolution of our absurdly large brains. For Miller, brains are like peacock tails, flashy advertisements that allow us to do various feats—athletics, poetry, writing books about human brains, and so on—aiding us in our quest for attracting the best possible mate.[21]

Other aspects of the social world over which people compete might be less obvious, such as the competition for friends. As usual, I think the best illustration of this comes not from the scientists who are supposed to be carefully examining and explaining human social behavior, but rather from television. Consider the first line of this dialogue, and see if you can tell what's going on.

What I give to you, what—what I share, I do with no one else. I like to think what you give to me, you do with nobody else.

This is a line from the television dramedy *Boston Legal*, shortly after Denny Crane, played by William Shatner, "catches" his best friend Alan Shore (James Spader) having an intimate (but certainly Platonic) conversation with another man. Denny continues:

Now that - that may sound silly to you. But here's what I think is silly—the idea that jealousy or fidelity is reserved for romance. I always suspected that there was a connection between you and *that* man. That you got something you didn't get from me.

Alan Shore reassures Denny: "I love you, Denny. *You* are my best friend. I can't imagine going through life without you as my best friend." To which Denny adds, "I don't want you on my balcony . . . on *any* balcony, alone—with *that* man." (The balcony is a special place where Denny and Alan bond at the conclusion of each night's episode.)

The importance of friendship jealously is, in my view, underappreciated. There is some work in developmental psychology—research with young children, who, unlike adults, often are quite happy to tell others where they rank in their list of top friends. Adults, however, are cagey, and don't part all that willingly with this kind of information.[22]

The general idea, however, is straightforward. Each of us can have only one best friend. Best friendship is, then, a scarce resource. Being someone else's best friend is valuable. A best friend is likely to help you in times of need. More importantly, if you're someone's *best* friend, then that person is also likely to take your side in essentially all of the inevitable conflicts that arise in social life.[23]

Having many people consider you to be among their best friends is one of the most valuable commodities social creatures such as ourselves can have, and it would be surprising if people didn't have various modules designed to cause them to try to be especially valuable to others. People report getting satisfaction from helping their friends, and of course from making new ones.

Finally, people like to be part of groups. Some groups are explicitly exclusive, carefully picking their members—sororities and fraternities on college campuses are examples of these. Other groups have a less formal structure, but are no less important. Any number of movies about adolescents trying to get into the group of the "in" crowd illustrate that being part of the best group can loom very large in one's social world.

More generally, much of what we do might well be geared toward making us more valuable to have around. Our efforts to acquire knowledge, skills, and resources might well be driven at least in part by adaptations designed to make one valuable in the social world. And at every turn we're competing against people equally cultivating themselves to be liked, loved, adored, and needed by others.

Persuading others that you are valuable is an important, even crucial adaptive problem for humans,[*] and it would be reasonable to expect that our brains would be designed both to make ourselves valuable and to demonstrate our value.[24] Our value to others is made up of many things about us— our wealth, skills and abilities, existing social connections, intelligence— and probably many others. One factor is particularly important: health.

Humans live a long time. Indeed, for our body size, we live a somewhat surprisingly long time. What's important for the present point is that one's value as a mate, friend, ally, and so on depends in no small part on the most basic precondition for providing benefits to others: not being dead.

Most human relationships involve, at least to some extent, the exchange of various goods and services over time. You water my garden while I'm on vacation, I'll babysit your children after I've come back. This kind of exchange, in which people can reap benefits of gains in trade, is at the center of what some people think has led humans to where we are today.

And central to gains in trade is being around. If you water my garden while I'm away and then I die shortly after I get back from vacation, your investment is wasted. For this reason, everything else equal, it's good for others to believe that your prospects are good. As you can imagine from what I've said to this point—and this will anticipate the basic argument I want to make here—it's good for others to believe your prospects are good *even if they aren't.*

Finally, the last piece of the argument: To this point, I've argued that for humans, sociality is crucial, that there's a lot of competition in the social world, that one's value in the social world is determined by many factors, and that one central factor is how long one is likely to be around.

The last bit is a monkey wrench: At its most basic, the world is complicated. How do you know if someone is a good mate? How can you judge who

---

[*]Also for anthropomorphized reindeer. Nobody liked poor Rudolph until it happened to turn out that he and his shiny red nose were actually *good* for something. He couldn't even join in any of the reindeer games, which doesn't seem like it would have been that big a deal. Anyway, it was only *after* Santa came knocking to guide the sleigh that all of the reindeer loved him.

is likely to be loyal, caring, and giving? How can you tell who is intelligent? What is intelligent? Is it having a PhD, or knowing how to retune a carburetor? (I'm not sure a carburetor is something that gets tuned. I'm just saying.)

So, while there might be fierce competition for becoming a mate, friend, or group member, making judgments about who would make a good mate, friend, or group member is difficult. People vary in any number of different ways, and figuring out which traits are important is difficult enough; evaluating people on relevant traits is difficult as well. It's not as though SAT scores or a "loyalty quotient" is tattooed on people's faces.

Which is not to say that there's nothing at all to go on. Obviously, we learn a great deal about others from what they say and what they do. Yes, there is often objective information to be had—particularly now in the era of Google—and there is third-party information. But it is reasonable to think that in human evolutionary history, *what people say and do provided a large part of the information content for evaluating others.*[25]

Indeed, we learn a lot about others in a surprisingly small period of time. A large body of research in psychology known as "thin slicing" refers to people's ability to make judgments about others from small amounts of information, usually from observing someone for short periods, usually 30 seconds to 5 minutes. Judgments about any number of traits have been investigated—extroversion, personality, intelligence, etc.—and the basic results are that people are pretty good at it and that 30 seconds is as good as five minutes. Basically, small amounts of information might be better. In a review article on the subject, two prominent researchers in this area said their result "contradicts the commonsense notion that more information leads to greater accuracy; the additional information might be redundant, or even counterproductive,"[26] a conclusion that anticipates some of what Gladwell would go on to say in *Blink*.

I confess I have a special place in my heart for the possibility that people can learn a great deal about others in a short period of time. Having studied speed dating, I can say that people seem to agree on who the most desirable partners are at speed dating events. Having said that, it appears this is driven, not too surprisingly, by looks,[27] so it might not be worth getting too excited about.

Leaking the story

The key point here is that people judge others by word and deed, and word and deed are caused by various modules. Our actions, caused by various modules, influences others' judgments of us. These ideas suggest that *the modules that cause the speech and behavior that lead to others' impressions should be designed to generate as positive a view as possible of our traits and abilities.* You can think of the way we talk and behave as "leaky"—some set of representations give rise to behavior, and behavior gives rise to judgments about the representations that caused the behavior. In this sense, speech and act are ways to give others evidence about what's in our brains.

As always, there's a good movie example to illustrate the point. In *Catch Me If You Can*, the con artist Frank Abagnale Jr. executes various scams, his success turning on the confidence with which he behaves in the role he's playing. To impersonate a doctor, he acts as though he's a doctor. Very generally, and even more in the past than today, the best source of information about a person was, generally . . . that person. If you show doctor-like qualities, whatever those might be, I'm inclined to perceive you as doctor-like, and maybe even think you're a doctor. (In the case of *real* doctors,* who require actual credentials, this is potentially tricky, which I suppose is why Abagnale is such an interesting case.)

But what about other traits? Take something abstract, like being a good potential friend or romantic partner. There is no "true" valuation of someone's worth as a friend or mate. For doctors, there are medical degrees, but no such credential exists for other roles that people play in social life. So given the competitive nature of the social world, *press secretary modules should be designed to cause people to behave in a way that sends out the most positive defensible message about the person's worth, history, and future.*

The most positive *defensible* message. It does no good to act as though you're a great lion tamer if you're going to be thrown into the ring with a lion. As Roy Baumeister put it, "Self-presentation is . . . the result of a trade-off between favorability and plausibility."[28]

---

* I'm excluding "doctors," like me, who have PhD's, but can't be leaned on to give you a prescription for Demerol or anything like that.

So, to persuade others that you have various positive qualities, it's good to have representations of those positive qualities, because by acting *as though*, yes, you really are *that* good, you can persuade others that you are. For this reason, you want your behavior to reflect as much about you that is good as possible.

Some things, of course, aren't caused by what's in your head. Thinking that you're six feet tall isn't going to make someone less likely to notice that you're five six. But there are many other qualities that are debatable, or, at least, harder to measure. Having certain representations in your head, even if those representations aren't "accurate," can alter others' behavior. If you act as though X is true, others, everything else equal, might come to believe X is true as well.

So, what is the point of all of this? Let's return to the idea that there are modules that work like a press secretary, and these are the modules that, more or less, talk to other people. Let's suppose that there are modules that have particularly central roles to play in social interactions. If others judge you by how you behave, and your behavior is caused, in part, by various beliefs in these modules, then there are going to be certain kinds of beliefs that would be good to have in these systems. In particular, you're better off being wrong—or, perhaps, not knowing—about things that will cause you to miss benefits from the social world you might otherwise obtain.

For example, as I suggested above, it's useful for other people to think that you're not going to die anytime soon. People who are about to die are bad investments of time and energy because they won't be able to repay the favors. One might expect the mind's modules to reflect this, and, in fact, they do. We tend to avoid learning about our own medical conditions if the condition in question is both (1) serious and (2) untreatable.[29] Why learn about facts which, if leaked, can only hurt you, with no offsetting benefits?[30]

Further, it's better to have beliefs that make you a valuable social partner—mate, friend, group member—even if they're not true.[31] Recall that natural selection designs systems to have features that lead to benefits (in reproductive terms). True representations will often fit the bill, but not always. If being wrong can be systematically beneficial, you might find that some modules are, in fact, systematically biased.[32]

This idea is not unlike Robert K. Merton's notion of a self-fulfilling prophesy, discussed in *Social Theory and Social Structure*.[33] First let's take the example he used to illustrate his point. Imagine a bank that, for whatever reason, is rumored to be in danger of failing. People hearing this rumor will—quite sensibly—want to withdraw their money, causing a run on the bank. Others, seeing the run, will do likewise, potentially leading to its failure; all this on the weight of only the incorrect rumors about its being in trouble.

As with so many ideas in psychology, William James seems to have thought of it first.[34] In *The Will to Believe*, he writes:

> How many women's hearts are vanquished by the mere sanguine insistence of some man that they *must* love him; he will not consent to the hypothesis that they cannot. The desire for a certain kind of truth here brings about that special truth's existence; and so it is in innumerable cases of other sorts. Who gains promotions, boons, appointments, but the man in whose life they are seen to play the part of live hypotheses, who discounts them, sacrifices other things for their sake before they have come, and takes risks for them in advance? His faith acts on the powers above him as a claim, and creates its own verification.[35]

In other words, love, like bank runs, can be self-fulfilling.[36]

Of course, for many kinds of problems, it's just best to know the truth. If you are hungry, it won't help to think, erroneously, that there are ripe berries several miles away, there for the picking. For other kinds of problems, there might not be objective truth, and, even if there is, because of social influences, it might not help to know it.

Most interesting of all are cases in which it's best to have *both* the "truth" and something less than the truth. Suppose that it's good to be seen as a good lion tamer. Even if you're not, it might be a good idea to have a representation that you are, potentially earning all the associated benefits. Note that I'm not suggesting you lie; lying is a separate issue.[37] But suppose you could have a representation in one module that you were a good lion tamer in every single context in which there were no lions to be tamed. Then, when there were such an opportunity, you'd want the "true" representation, living in some other module, to "take over."

Christopher Columbus might have taken advantage of this idea. Though there is some scholarly dispute, it seems that during the first voyage to the New World, he had two estimates of how far the ship had traveled. One estimate was for propaganda purposes: a deliberate underestimate to reduce the crew's worries; the other estimate was his best guess, to be used for practical purposes.

The point is that if it were possible to maintain one set of representations that were designed for "public consumption," to maintain the most positive possible information about one's traits and abilities, and keep unfavorable representations "walled off," to be used only when necessary, that would be the best of all possible worlds.[38]

And that's the world I think our brains are in, and the focus of the next chapter.

Getting along by being wrong

But first, a quick detour. I can't quite move on without discussing perhaps the most spectacular way in which people are wrong: supernatural beliefs. Much ink has been spilled on this, pretty much since there has been ink to be spilled, so let me make some disclaimers right up front.

First, I take religion and supernatural beliefs to be objects of scientific study. I'll treat them that way, and so, if you get easily offended by reading about beliefs that are very important to you by someone who thinks you're wrong about them, you might want to skip this section.

Next, I want to be clear that here I'm just going to talk about supernatural beliefs, not organized religion or, at least, not any organized religions in particular. By "supernatural" I just mean anything that cannot be explained by natural laws.

And I'm going to assume here that all supernatural beliefs are wrong. Before you get too upset, consider that, as Richard Dawkins pointed out,[39] to a first approximation, independent of your particular religious beliefs, so do you. Most people have only a very small, indeed minuscule, subset of all possible supernatural beliefs. Indeed, they have only a small subset of the supernatural beliefs anyone has ever had. Consider all the supernatural beliefs ever held by anyone, including beliefs about the Greek gods, spirits inhabiting various animals and plants, the effectiveness of rain dances, and so on.

Whatever your particular supernatural beliefs, you must believe that nearly all of these are wrong, not least because many supernatural beliefs are mutually inconsistent.[40] One can't be both a monotheist and a polytheist, for example. More broadly, it's a pretty good bet that if you were introduced to virtually any of the world's supernatural beliefs, you would reject them as false.

So, in many respects, the approach I'm taking here makes me pretty much just like you and just like everybody else. We all reject almost every single supernatural belief, holding only to our own, thinking everyone else is wrong. The only way I depart is that I take the view that supernatural beliefs are guaranteed to be wrong because I think everything has a natural explanation.

If one combines the view that supernatural beliefs are wrong with the idea that our minds have evolved to acquire beliefs that are useful, one arrives at the question of why humans' brains seem to have systems that cause them to acquire beliefs that are guaranteed to be false. In this sense, supernatural beliefs are weird. Not only are they all wrong, but historically they've caused people to do all sorts of seemingly odd things, from spending precious time in rituals to destroying property to wearing silly hats.

Many people have tried to answer this puzzling question, and I refer interested readers to some excellent books, including my favorite, *Religion Explained,* by Pascal Boyer.[41] I'm not going to try to answer this question myself.[42] Instead, I just want to point out that having true beliefs rather than false beliefs can be especially costly when it comes to the supernatural. In particular, having supernatural beliefs that are not the same as others around you, especially those in power, can be very dangerous. Having unpopular supernatural beliefs can have many unpleasant consequences. As Steve Pinker put it, "People are embraced or condemned according to their beliefs, so one function of the mind may be to hold beliefs that bring the belief-holder the greatest number of allies, protectors, or disciples, rather than beliefs that are most likely to be true."[43]

At its most extreme of course, such as during the Inquisitions, having the wrong (i.e., locally unpopular) supernatural beliefs could lead to death. Among the most famous victims of this era was Giordano Bruno, who, according to some sources at least, was burned at the stake for, among other things, his views on transubstantiation, which were at odds with the powers in Rome at the time,[44] illustrating that the correct belief that bread does not turn into human flesh on Sundays in certain special places can be a dangerous one in just the right, or maybe just the wrong, circumstances.

History is replete with similar examples, and the details of which supernatural beliefs were espoused by whom played a central role in warfare in Europe for hundreds of years. Conflicts that derive, at least in part, from differing supernatural beliefs are not actually all that difficult to find in modern times either.

With respect to individuals, it seems to me that there are high costs associated with having the wrong—or no—supernatural beliefs. For example, it looks like I'm going to be unable to run for President, since recent surveys indicate that some 60% of Americans would refuse to vote for an atheist.[45]

Picking the right supernatural beliefs has important consequences even for people with no political ambitions. Because communities are frequently—though of course not always—built around collections of supernatural beliefs, it is easy to imagine that those disposed to rejecting any and all of them risk at least some forms of social exclusion or ostracism. The details seem to vary a great deal from time period to time period and from place to place, but it is not hard to imagine that, on balance, the social benefits of conformity in supernatural beliefs have been profound.

So, that's one way in which being wrong is an awfully good idea from a functional standpoint. Now we move on to some others.

chapter 6

Psychological Propaganda

■ *The first of two kinds of "self-deception" is addressed. Sometimes it is benefi-cial to be "strategically wrong," being wrong in such a way that, if everyone else believed the incorrect thing one believes, one would be strategically better off. Being strategically wrong is a pervasive part of human affairs, from beliefs about the extent to which one has control over events, to corners of science, in which being strategically wrong about what others believe allows one to persuasively argue that one's own ideas are more novel than they actually are.* ■

Modularity implies that there isn't one, unified "self" in your head, that there isn't a "real" "you" in there somewhere. The intuition that there is might be useful for various purposes, but if modularity is right,[1] then this intuition is wrong.

So what?

Well, modularity makes certain phenomena that are otherwise very puzzling easy to understand. We'll look at several examples, but this chapter begins with a perennial favorite in psychology and philosophy, "self-deception," which, as Shelley Taylor puts it, "has always presented philosophers with a logical paradox: How can a person know and not know information at the same time?"[2]

How *can* "a person" simultaneously know and not know something?[3]

Without modularity, this question does seem to be quite a pickle. We all have the sense that people are sometimes "deceiving themselves," but what can this mean? The notion of deception seems to require something—usually, some*one* —doing some deceiving, and something being deceived. "Deceive," a proud member of the class of transitive verbs, needs both subject and object. The problem in *self*-deception is to identify what is doing the deceiving and what is being deceived. Is the mind deceiving the mind? How can that be? A paradox.

It's going to turn out that "self-deception" is actually two different phenomena that get lumped together. We'll look at them one at a time. The first one is slightly harder to describe, easier to explain, and the subject of this chapter. Let's start with an example about me. Examples of this kind of self-deception tend to make people—individually or as a group—look foolish, so it seems only right to go first. Further, this work is about how each of us overestimates our traits and attributes, so it's satisfying to start with how this effect is all about me.

I generally believe I'm a pretty good instructor, certainly no worse than average. Apparently, many of my colleagues have similar beliefs about their own skills in the classroom. In a widely quoted passage, K. Patricia Cross wrote that "faculty members reveal what may as well be starkly labeled smug self-satisfaction. An amazing 94% rate themselves as above-average teachers, and 68% rank themselves in the top quarter on teaching performance."[4]

Because it is obviously impossible that 94% of college instructors are above average, many of us—including, quite possibly, me—must be wrong.

This finding is one of a larger class of findings often referred to as the "Lake Wobegon Effect," named after Garrison Keillor's fictional town in which "all the women are strong, all the men are good-looking, and all the children are above average." Similar effects have been found in other areas, such as traits, like fairness, and abilities, such as driving.[5]

These effects aren't all that mysterious if different people just happen to have different criteria for what it means to be a "good" driver or a "good" teacher.[6] Is a good driver a very safe driver, or one who can execute difficult maneuvers, even if they are unsafe? Is a good teacher someone who successfully conveys information, or one who gets high teaching evaluations?[7] Very generally, to the extent that the issue at hand is ambiguous, people tend to be more self-serving. For example, in laboratory studies, the Lake Wobegon Effect is bigger for wiggly traits like "impractical" than for more objective traits like "mathematical."[8] Similarly, when you compare people's actual performance with their self-ratings of their abilities in domains like sports—where winning and losing are there for all to see—there is a much closer relationship than when you compare self-ratings to measures of performance in social domains, such as interpersonal skills.[9]

What about cases in which there's a genuinely correct answer? Consider a recent study in which participants were shown pictures of a number of faces, including one picture of themselves, along with a set of pictures of themselves morphed with highly attractive (and unattractive) features that made them look more (or less) attractive. Participants frequently identified one of the faces morphed with the highly attractive features—the better-looking face—as their own.[10]

Cases like this are often called "self-deception" because the subjects seem to believe something they somehow shouldn't, and the thing they shouldn't is, in some way, "good" for them. Here, we expect that people see their own faces, not digitally enhanced, every day in the mirror. Surely we *know* what we look like. This intuition—*c'mon, you know what you look like*—makes it seem like "we're deceiving ourselves." We *really* know what we look like, but we're *telling ourselves* that we're more attractive than we really are.

I want to be clear that *I don't know what the italicized words in that last sentence might mean*. I don't know what it means to "really" believe something, or who or what is doing the telling or the listening. Indeed, without invoking Buzzy or something like him, expressions like "we're telling ourselves" make no sense. Using phrases like this is just bad psychology because it implies a little Buzzy, with "real" beliefs, who is communicating with some unspecified something.

Modularity clarifies things. There's no deception here. What's happening is that a particular representation in a particular module is what I call *strategically wrong*.[11]

In what sense is it *strategically* wrong to have a representation of your face that is more attractive than it is in reality? A representation is strategically wrong when it is inaccurate in a way that confers an advantage in the social world. Being strategically wrong can be an advantage, for example, because of the possibility of persuasion: *If everyone else had the same (overly positive) representation of you, your traits, abilities, and likely future*—all things we visit in this chapter—*then you would be better off*.[12] And by "better off" here I mean that the design of the system can be explained by virtue of the effects over evolutionary time.

The idea here turns on the one I sketched in the last chapter regarding the function of the press secretary module, and it gets its traction from the assumption that having a positive representation in your head, because of the way that representation affects your own behavior, might persuade others that the strategically false thing in your head is actually true, making you better off. If you behave in ways that lead others to believe whatever it is, then, within the limits of whatever people will believe, you're better off. In short, the systems that lead you to be strategically wrong are part of the evolved propaganda machine.[13]

As an example, let's move away from humans for a moment. Consider a hungry baby bird in a nest of other hungry baby birds. Suppose that chicks of certain species compete with their brothers and sisters in the same clutch to get food that mom regurgitates. For reasons that are not important, mom's fitness interest is (roughly) in giving food to the hungriest of her offspring. (This has to do with the fact that a bit of food is of the most value to a hungry organism.) The individual birds' interests, however, are different from mom's, and—again, roughly—each baby bird wants to get the lion's share of the food even if it isn't in desperate need.

Mom's problem is that she has little to go on in allocating food. One piece of information that she has is the "food calls" the chicks make—loud cries with open beaks. Birds that act as though they're really hungry are at an advantage, leading to an evolutionary arms race—birds are continuously being selected to appear more hungry than their siblings.[14]

Of course we don't know the details of how "hunger" is represented in the chick's head. One possibility is that the chick has one module with "true" information, representing its best estimate of how hungry it is, getting information from the digestive system, and then the chick, through its behavior, "lies" to mom, acting as though it were more hungry than that. The alternative is to have a representation of being "over-hungry," in one module—something like the press secretary module—and acting in proportion to that representation. I'm not sure how one would go about distinguishing between these two possibilities. My point here is simply to illustrate how being *strategically* wrong can, in principle, straightforwardly confer an advantage. Here the driving force is, as usual, social—convincing mom of something that's intrinsically hard to know. I hastily add that a bird foraging for itself—where spending time searching for food must be balanced against the costs of foraging, including risks of predation—probably is best off by simply getting its level of hunger right or, at least, as right as possible. Briefly—and maybe a little vacuously—when there's no one to deceive, honesty is the best policy.

So, being strategically wrong in a way that is somehow communicated to others can be beneficial because of its potential for *persuasion*.[15] In the case of these chicks, it's about calories. For humans, because we get so much of our information from others, evolution could have built systems that are designed to be wrong in ways that are beneficial in the service of convincing others in any number of areas.

By the way, many of us come across machines that are strategically wrong all the time. The grocery store closest to where I live has cash registers with the peculiar property that they are frequently wrong, but always in the same direction: higher than the price indicated on the shelf. I don't know if there is intention behind this or not, but in these cases, being wrong is strategically advantageous indeed, leading to a literally better payoff.*

Positive delusions

Probably no one has done more to advance our understanding of the various ways in which people are strategically wrong than Shelley Taylor and her colleagues in a body of research looking at "positive illusions." In a seminal paper in the late eighties, Taylor and Jonathan Brown argued that, in contrast to conventional wisdom, accuracy wasn't always such a good thing. They presented evidence suggesting that people (1) think they have more favorable traits than would be realistic, (2) think they have more control over what will occur than they do, and (3) are more optimistic about the future than facts justify. Their focus was on the value of incorrect, but favor-

---

*For the owner of the store, not the register itself, obviously.

able, beliefs for one's mental health. My concern is not with mental health; it is with the adaptive value of the systems that give rise to these systematic errors. That is, my argument will be that the ultimate explanation for these phenomena lies not in any mental health benefits of positive thinking, but rather in the strategic benefits of being wrong.

Firstly, broadly, people think they're better than they are. Roughly one million takers of the SAT answered questions about various traits such as leadership ability, athletic ability, and getting along with others. These are, obviously, subjective, perhaps maximizing the amount of wiggling. And wiggle these students did: A quarter of the respondents indicated that they were in the top 1% in their ability to get along with others.[16]

One of my favorite studies in this area was conducted in 1965 in which two groups of 50 people were asked to rate their own driving skills and, not surprisingly, people—in both groups—gave themselves generous ratings, and the mean ratings of the two groups were "almost identical."[17] This might not seem too surprising, given that driving skill is subjective. Except that one group of 50 drivers consisted of *people who had been in traffic accidents sufficiently severe to put them in the hospital*; 34 of these were judged by police to have been responsible for the accidents. Twenty-two of the accidents were classified as "hit fixed objects" or "overturned on roadway." Apparently crashing into reality is insufficient to make people more realistic about their driving abilities. Indeed, a more recent study shows that people in accidents serious enough to send *someone else* to the hospital rate themselves nearly identically to control subjects on self-reported measures of driving skills and safety.[18]

The effect is broad. In one large study, Mark Alicke and colleagues asked students to rate themselves on a number of traits, 20 positive and 20 negative. One group of subjects was asked how they rated compared to an average college student, in the abstract. Another group was asked to compare themselves to a particular person whom they did not know, but was in the same room with them as they filled out the scales. In 38 out of 40 cases in the former group and 31 out of 40 cases in the latter group, subjects rated themselves above average on the positive traits and below average on the negative traits. One trait that people rated themselves as much *lower*, compared to an average college student, was "liar."[19]

Recently Elanor Williams and Thom Gilovich (the latter of whom, I ought to disclose in the spirit of openness, was my statistics instructor at Cornell, and I now consider a friend) have done some work extending this research, asking if people *really* believe they're better than they are. They used a clever method. Cornell students in the experiments guessed where they ranked relative to other Cornell students on a number of traits, one of which was intelligence. They were then given the opportunity to choose between two wagers. One wager was a simple random draw—picking a token from an urn—in which they had X% chance of winning $1, where X is the subject's estimate of his ranking relative to other Cornellians. If the subject said that he thought that he was smarter than 60% of Cornellians, he was offered a simple 60% chance to win $1. In the other wager subjects could choose, if the subject guessed he was smarter than 60% of Cornellians, he was told that one Cornellian would be selected at random, and if that particular Cornellian was, in fact, less intelligent than he was (as measured by a test), he would receive $1. In effect, he could have his fate determined by the random pick of a token from an urn, or by the random pick of a Cornellian.

Suppose everyone guesses his rank exactly correctly. In this case, the two wagers are identical, and subjects might be expected to be indifferent between the two types of wager. But, suppose that subjects overestimate their rank. Someone who guessed she was smarter than 60% of Cornellians but was in fact only smarter than 10% of them—*and knew this*—would, to have the best chance of winning, choose to pick from the urn rather than having her score compared with that of a randomly chosen Cornellian.

The results were that Cornellians, on average, thought themselves to be above average, guessing that they were at roughly in the 61st percentile for four desirable traits (intelligence, creativity, maturity, positivity). More importantly, Cornellians stood by their guesses—they didn't take the draw from the urn particularly often, suggesting they *really* believed their guess about where they ranked.[20]

"Really?" We revisit issues of using economic choices to evaluate what people *really* want or prefer later on, but for the moment, two points. First, suppose that each Cornellian overestimated where she stood on the distribution by 10 percentage points—which is roughly correct, given the data.

By choosing the "wrong" lottery—that is, avoiding the random draw—she's costing herself roughly a nickel per wager—the expected value of the difference of the bets. For 20 cents, she can appear consistent to the experimenter, that she "*really*" believes she is as smart as she initially said she was.[21] (In fact, the stakes were even smaller: Subjects were deceived about what was going on and did not in fact get the payoffs from their choices of wagers. Instead, at the end of the study, everyone drew randomly from a jar, being paid between $0 and $4. In effect, no money was at stake.)

Second, to return to the issue of what it means to say that someone "*really*" believes something or other, maybe the modules guiding betting behavior have the incorrect, inflated sense of one's traits, but there are other representations elsewhere that have the correct ones. Finding that people are willing to pay to back up an inflated view of themselves doesn't seem to speak to the issue of whether there might be a more accurate representation lurking about in the modular brain somewhere. That is, if it's true that our Cornellians have two beliefs in different modules, one correct and one inflated, and the inflated one is in charge in this case, then it seems to me that it's hard to say that the module with the incorrect belief is the one that counts more.

Errors like these are made possible by mechanisms such as selective memory: We are more likely to remember events that suggest that we have positive traits; events that cast shadows over us are apparently more likely to be ejected from memory or at least more difficult to recall.[22] While some errors might be due to the inherent ambiguities and uncertainties in making judgments and predictions about oneself and others, [23] the fact that we remember events that are positive rather than negative is a phenomenon that needs to be explained, and my guess is that the answer is that our propaganda modules are designed to be strategically wrong.

Finally, the icing on the cake in this literature is delightfully recursive: We think we're better than average *at not being biased in thinking that we're better than average*. A sample of undergraduates were told about biases like the ones discussed here, and asked how susceptible to them they were. They uniformly judged themselves less susceptible than the average American.[24] These students are saying: Everyone *else* is biased; *I* am dispassionately realistic. And, yes, I really am *that* good.

Lies, damned lies, and self-perception

We tend to be strategically wrong about the very effects that we have on the world. People are more likely to think that they caused an outcome if it was positive rather than negative.[25] Because in the real world it's often difficult to pin down exactly who or what caused what, much of this research has been conducted in the laboratory. In a typical study, subjects (usually college students) come into the lab and perform some task that supposedly measures an attribute, such as intelligence. Students are then given false feedback, and then asked why they got the result they did. The essence of these findings is that if the result is good, subjects think they were responsible.[26] Bad outcomes are attributed to factors outside the control of the subject. The experimenter, of course, knows the real source of the outcome: chance. The feedback subjects get is usually determined by some randomizing device.

The view suggested by the perspective I'm taking here is that drawing inferences about success or failure is part of the design of the system. In this sense, the bias observed in these studies isn't—or at least, isn't necessarily—a result of subjects' *lying* about credit and blame for outcomes. My claim is that these modules are designed for a world where, unlike the lab—in which assignment to condition can be genuinely random—figuring out what caused what is hard. It's not a bad design that takes advantage of this ambiguity to advertise—to the extent it is plausible—that one is the bringer of good things.

One study looking at the possibility that people engage in what the authors refer to as "descriptive distortion" (and what the rest of us refer to as "lying") used a cute method called "the bogus pipeline." Subjects were wired with electrodes and hooked up to a machine experimenters referred to as an "electromyograph." By sneakily recording the answers given to a questionnaire earlier in the study, experimenters could persuade subjects that the machine—which in reality did nothing— could detect when they were lying. They simply asked questions the experimenters already knew the subjects' answers to, and told the subjects to give some true and some false answers. Because the experimenters were controlling the machine, they could make the machine "detect" a lie any time the subject gave a false answer. In this way, (sly) psychologists can make a machine appear to be able to detect subjects' lies.[*]

Subjects in this experiment took a test of "social intelligence" and were then given a (false) score that was either very low or very high, and then asked while connected to the electromyograph why they got the score they did: luck or skill? The question is, when people get high scores, do they indicate that they think their score is due to their skill *even when they're hooked up to a machine that they believe will detect when they're "descriptively distorting"*?

Yes, they do. Subjects reported that the result of the test was due to skill when their score was high, but due to other factors—luck, something about the tests—when their score was low, whether they were hooked up to a well-functioning electromyograph or not. The researchers conclude that "self-serving attributions are not merely misrepresentations in their public descriptions of causality used by subjects in the service of self-presentation. Instead, this attributional asymmetry seems to reflect actual bias in private perceptions of objective causality."[27] (Note that the words "actual bias" suggest the authors believe that there's a "real, true" belief in there, rather than some representation in a propaganda module.[†])

Before moving on, it's worth noting that the studies reported here have met with the usual academic caveats and limitations.[28] There is lively discussion about whether people everywhere indulge in self-enhancement, or if there are important cross-cultural differences.[29] In addition, there are cases in which people underestimate their abilities.[30]

In any case, finding examples outside the lab and in the real world in which people divert blame for bad outcomes that were in fact their fault and take credit for good outcomes even when they haven't done anything to bring them about isn't very difficult.[31] Like many people these days, I play in a "fantasy football" league. I and nine friends choose professional football

---

[*] A parallel to this can also be found in HBO's *The Wire*, in which police persuade suspects using a similar method that a photocopier can detect lies.

[†] Subjects in this experiment were debriefed after they were done, told about how they were lied to about the electomyograph, and so on. Then, interestingly, they came back to the lab about one week later and were *lied to again*, told that some scales they were asked to fill out were unrelated to the previous study, while, in fact, they were related. Instead of psychologists worrying about how much subjects lie to psychologists, it seems to me that subjects ought to worry about how much psychologists lie to subjects.

players to be on our team, and each week of football season our teams score points depending on how well those players do according to the official statistics: yards gained, touchdowns scored, and so forth. While there might be some skill in choosing players, which team one plays against on any given week is pure chance. So, even if your team doesn't do well one week, if you happen to play one of the teams that does even worse, then you get a win. One year, one player in my league was paired over the course of several games with teams that had particularly bad weeks, and so even though his team wasn't scoring many points, he was ahead in the standings. In the league's discussion board, when this was brought up, the player pretended (I hope) shock at the suggestion that he was only winning because of this run of luck. "Luck? No way. Just good fantasy football defense."

Members of Congress are by no means exempt. In August of 2008, world oil prices were falling after meteoric rises over the preceding few years. Changes in these prices depend on any number of factors, mostly having to do with current and expected future supply and demand. Many believed that the dip had something to do with the fact that the economic slowing in the United States might reduce demand for oil in the future. Representative John Shadegg from Arizona's 3rd district had a different view: "The market is responding to the fact that we are here talking. . . ."[32]

Comparatively friendly

If it's true that being strategically wrong is akin to a propaganda ploy designed to persuade others that you're a valuable social being, then we might expect that being strategically wrong is not just about being good, but specifically, being better than others. As we've seen, people tend to overestimate where they fall relative to others on traits like intelligence and getting along with others and skills like driving. If people must make decisions about whom to have as friends, mates, allies, and so on, then the most important thing is to be *better* than others. Being "very good" at driving isn't helpful if everyone else is "excellent."

This idea is related to one introduced by John Tooby and Leda Cosmides which they dub the "banker's paradox." The name comes from a problem with lending money: The people who want to borrow money tend not to have a lot (or they wouldn't need to borrow it), and people who don't have a lot of money are less likely to be able to pay back loans than people who do. The point for social life is that it's possible (if not particularly sentimental) to think of friends as people one invests in now so that when one is in need later, they'll be able to help.[33] So, the argument goes, people who need help now are likely to want to be your friend, but they are also potentially poor investments.

Tooby and Cosmides argue that one solution to this problem is to cultivate skills that make you uniquely valuable—irreplaceable as a friend. So, what kind of modules might your mind have to guide you toward being valuable in the social world? One thing you can do is be better at something than everyone else around. If you are the best at something, then you are irreplaceable insofar as there's no one else who can do whatever it is you do as well or better.

Taking the banker's paradox argument together with the general line of argument I've been advancing, one would expect people to advertise that they have unique skills. They should try to persuade others—perhaps by maintaining appropriate representations for the press secretary to work with—that they have skills that are valuable and, importantly, better than others'. That is, this view predicts that people specialize in areas that might be of value, and are particularly conscious of comparisons. We should observe that people accentuate domains in which they have a comparative advantage, particularly when it matters, as in their social networks, those with whom they spend time: their friends.

William James, again, seems to have thought of it first:[34]

> I, who for the time have staked my all on being a psychologist, am mortified if others know much more psychology than I. But I am contented to wallow in the grossest ignorance of Greek. My deficiencies there give me no sense of personal humiliation at all. Had I "pretensions" to be a linguist, it would have been just the reverse.[35]

Not only that, but James pointed out a singular oddity about our species. Being better than everyone except one person is vastly different from being better than everyone else:

So we have the paradox of a man shamed to death because he is only the second pugilist or the second oarsman in the world. That he is able to beat the whole population of the globe minus one is nothing; he has "pitted" himself to beat that one; and as long as he doesn't do that nothing else counts.

James noticed that people care a great deal about social comparison. The second best pugilist or oarsman is surely a very good pugilist or oarsman. But it's the relative skill that matters to people, perhaps because in a competitive social world, in which demand is what's really at stake, *relative* standing is absolutely important.

Extremely interesting research related to these areas has been around for decades. Leon Festinger's social comparison theory suggests that people evaluate their traits and opinions relative to those around them.[36] Festinger's ideas have been extremely influential, but I'll ignore them here in favor of some ideas from Abraham Tesser's work on what he referred to as "self-evaluation maintenance."

Tesser began with the idea that people are motivated to maintain a positive view of the "self." In one of Tesser's experiments, pairs of friends participated in a laboratory study in which they were asked how important it was to them to have good esthetic judgment and "social sensitivity." They were then given tests they were told would measure how they rated on these variables. Subjects were given false feedback about their performance on these tests and asked how well they thought their friend and a stranger did on them. The basic prediction was that for tasks that were important to subjects, they would evaluate their friend's performance negatively, but not the stranger's. This is essentially what happened: If doing well at something is important to me, I see my friend, but not a stranger, as bad at it.

I don't just *see* my friend as being bad at it: I *make* him bad at it. In another classic experiment (with Jonathan Smith), Tesser had participants play a game like the old television show *Password*. The goal was to figure out a mystery word given a set of words that clued the answer. The task was described to (different subjects) in one of two ways: either as "a measure of an important verbal skill" or as a task "having no relationship to important skills," being simply a "game."[37]

People came into the lab with a friend, and were asked to play the game with that person and with a stranger. They were then given a set of words that could be used as clues to get their partner to guess the mystery word. Some clues were good ones (e.g., "wheat" or "corn" to clue the word "grain"), making solving the problem easy, while some clues were obscure (e.g., "brookcorn" for "grain'"). Subjects gave either a friend or a stranger clues to help them solve a problem. When the task was described as important, they gave the *stranger* better clues than they gave their own friend. When the task was described as merely a game, they gave their *friend* better clues. Interestingly, when asked how helpful they had been to friends and strangers, people indicated they had given equally difficult clues to both. The press secretary tries to appear to be fair while some module causes one to hamstring friends when the issue at stake is perceived as important.

The results of Tesser and colleagues don't, in my view, lock down the case. But the line of work, and the line of reasoning, illustrates that while social relationships can be helpful, friendship is a competitive business.[38] For a social species, who gets the best friends and allies is important, and it's not unrealistic to expect the propaganda machine to work hard to make one valuable to friends. If that means making them worse off from time to time, well, that helps one's own skills (relatively) more valuable.

Control freaks

The second of the three areas Taylor and Brown discuss is the illusion that one has greater control than one really does. People appear to believe that they have control over outcomes in cases in which it ought to be obvious—and it is objectively true—that they do not.

Most events that occur in the real world are sufficiently complex that it's almost impossible to isolate how much any given cause brought about any given effect. For this reason, it's challenging to study people's perceptions of causality: It's hard to measure when they are right or wrong. That is, if we

---

*The experiment was conducted at the University of Georgia. It's possible subjects there knew what brookcorn was, though I certainly don't. It's also possible that there's a typo in this paper, and the clue was actually "broom corn," which is still pretty obscure.

don't know the precise cause of a given effect, we can't measure how accurate someone is at determining what the cause was. So, it's useful to look at one area in which we know the correct answer: gambling. Here, substantial efforts have gone into creating dice, wheels, cards, and other devices that generate random outcomes. When a seven comes up on the dice—assuming they are fair—we know that the only "cause" was chance.

Even in these cases people think they have control. A number of classic findings illustrate the point. James Henslin did a compelling ethnography of cab drivers who also played craps. He reported that people throw the dice harder if they want high numbers and "easier" (softer) if they want low numbers.[39] These same players advised the researcher, who was playing with them as a "participant observer," to take his time and to "work on it," and—inevitably —to talk to the dice when shooting. (Apparently none of this had the desired effect.) It's not just gamblers who think they have control; dealers working in casinos can lose their jobs for having "runs of ill luck" (for the house, that is).[40]

Ellen Langer's early work in this area remains among the classics in psychology. In one study, people in one group were allowed to choose their own lottery ticket, while people in another group had their lottery ticket selected randomly for them. Everyone, in both groups, paid $1 for the ticket. (It might be worth noting that the "lottery tickets" were football cards with the names and pictures of the players on them. I doubt that made a big difference, but one never knows.) Experimenters approached ticket holders on the morning the winning ticket was to be drawn and asked how much they would sell their ticket for. The prediction was that people who had chosen their ticket, thinking they had a better chance of winning,* would ask a higher price than those who had been given a random ticket. They did. The average selling price of people who had picked their own ticket was $8.67, compared to $1.96 for those who hadn't.[41]

In another study, Langer had subjects come into a room with a confederate who was either confident and well dressed, or shy and dressed in a sports coat that was too small. (Illustrating that experimental psychologists also have senses of humor, Langer referred to these as the "dapper" and

---

*They didn't.

"schnook" conditions, respectively.) Subjects, after talking with the confederate for ten minutes and having useless electrodes attached to their hands (to mask the real purpose of the study), played a simple card game like War in which each player randomly selects a card from a deck and whoever has the higher card wins. Subjects could bet up to 25 cents on each round. (These experiments were conducted in the early seventies.) People bet nearly 50% more when they were playing against the schnook than when playing against the dapper confederate.

There are any number of explanations for this phenomenon. One common explanation goes something like this. If you overestimate the control that you have over something good happening, then you'll be more motivated to try than you would be if you felt you had less control; and trying to get something good to happen is, well, good. This position was endorsed by the famous psychologist Albert Bandura, who is not infrequently quoted for having written that "optimistic self-appraisals of capability, that are not unduly disparate from what is possible, can be advantageous, whereas veridical judgements can be self-limiting."[42]

Except—and I mean this with all due respect to the venerable psychologist—that makes no sense. Overestimating how much control you have and therefore overestimating the chance of managing to do something good doesn't change the probability something good will happen—it just changes the chance that you'll do it. Imagine two different people, one who tends to overestimate and one who estimates correctly. The person who's right will allocate her effort better—the overestimator will waste time working on the wrong things. Imagine two people making bets. One is appropriately optimistic, and pays $1 for a 50% chance to win $2. The other—a devotee of Bandura, perhaps—pays $1.50 for the same 50% chance, not wanting to "limit himself." The second person is, for sure, worse off, whereas the person with "veridical judgment" is not.

So, choosing what to do is—holding aside the social effects surrounding the fact that what you choose to do carries information to other people— like playing Frogger. In Frogger, you don't gain any advantage by thinking, *I can make it across the road before that large truck splatters me*, unless you really can make it across before the large truck splatters you. "Veridical judgments"—making the best guess you can given the information, and choosing the option with the highest expected value—is the best thing you can possibly do—again holding aside influencing others—in games against The World. So, in the context of nonsocial decision making, for humans or other creatures, we should begin with the expectation that *mechanisms should be designed to maximize expected value.*[43]

Roy Baumeister and colleagues conducted experiments investigating this issue with, oddly enough, video games.[44] They had subjects come into the lab and play a game involving flying a biplane around some obstacles. This is really not so different from Frogger,* only by air rather than by sea. After playing the game for twenty minutes or so, subjects were told that they were going to play again, only this time they would get some money if they finished the game under a certain time. But they had a choice to make. They could either (a) choose to try beating the time limit set by the experimenter, in which case they would get $2, or (b) choose a shorter—and so more difficult—time to beat, in which case they would earn more than $2 if they did, in fact, beat that time. Some subjects were taunted with this instruction: "Now, if you are worried that you might choke under pressure or if you don't think you have what it takes to beat the target, then you might want to play it safe and just go for the two dollars." Subjects with high self-esteem were more likely to choose the more difficult option, choice (b),[45] and averaged lower earnings—25 cents—than the low self-esteem subjects, who averaged $2.80. In a second, similar experiment, experimenters found that those with high self-esteem "showed the greatest tendency to make high bets on themselves and then lose."[46]

The moral of this story is that, again holding aside the social effects of decision making, if you have an overly high opinion of your skills, then as long as the judge is cold, hard reality, you're worse off than if you simply had the correct opinion of your skills, even if they are modest. Because of the advantages of being right, *any explanation about why it's good to be over-motivated to do something needs to begin with an explanation why people are under-motivated to begin with.* Without that, the motivational story isn't logical, and it's a bad idea to be overly optimistic.[47]

More than that, it's wrong. One study looked at 107 traders from investment banks in London.[48] Researchers measured differences among the trad-

---

*I didn't know about this paper until after I'd chosen to go with the Frogger riff. Just a strange coincidence.

ers by using a little game in which a graph displayed a line going up and down on a dimension simply labeled "index." The traders' task was to get the index to go as high as possible during the course of the game. They had three different keys to press, which they were told "may" affect the index, but which, in point of fact, had no effect whatsoever on the path of the "index," which was programmed to be a random walk.* Subjects were asked to rate their success on the task, which was taken to be a measure of how much they imagined, incorrectly, that they had control over the task.

This measure was then compared to an independently generated index of how good a trader each of them was. Traders who showed a higher illusion of control earned less money and were rated as less effective at their jobs. The higher the illusion of control, the worse they were at their job, just like the gamblers in the thought experiment above.

So what's my explanation for illusion of control? I have two notions. I favor the second one because the first one is (a) not directly relevant to my main point, and (b) not my idea.[49]

The first possibility goes as follows. Consider how difficult it is to make things that are truly random. This has been a consistent problem for people who want to generate random numbers, and of course something with which casinos wrestle all the time. It's relatively unlikely that over the course of human evolution there would have been *any* artifact that was truly random; they're too hard to make. So, humans might not be designed for a world of perfectly random decks, dice, and dominoes. If it's true that our minds are designed for a world in which things like tools aren't simply random number generators, the default could be to assume that we can indeed control small tools, like dice, cards, and joysticks, because usually, this will be true. Illusions of control, on this view, are a manifestation of this default.[50]

But I favor a propaganda explanation. There is often a certain amount of ambiguity, both before and after the fact, about how much of an effect chance as opposed to skill played in any given outcome. In most cases— with exceptions such as casinos and certain experiments in psychology labs—it's difficult or impossible to make a clear call on exactly what role

---

*In a somewhat bashful section of the manuscript about the ethics of (possibly) deceiving their subjects, the authors emphasize that they used the word "may," never saying whether the keys would or would not have an effect.

chance played. Was that field goal kicked just right, or did the wind kick up and carry it inside the post? In ambiguity lies opportunity.

Within the limits of credulity, it's advantageous to persuade others that you have more control over events than you really do. To take a literary example, recall Mark Twain's Hank Morgan in *A Connecticut Yankee in King Arthur's Court,* who persuades King Arthur that he caused an eclipse, leading the king to elevate him to great power and influence.

By maintaining a representation that one has control, others are, possibly, going to be persuaded. As long as the benefits of the useful things that you can persuade others about outweigh the costs of being wrong—a condition not met for our hapless traders—thinking one is in control is a pretty good thing.

Optimally optimistic

The third and final category of positive illusions is unjustifiable optimism. People think that good things (like success in their career) will happen to them, and bad things (like car accidents) will not, in comparison to the average. Statistically, this can't be right.

Optimism pervades domains from the trivial to the life-threatening. On the (somewhat) trivial side, one researcher asked 1,000 Israeli soccer fans watching two different games to predict who would win the game they were watching, both before the game began and then again at halftime.[51] Half were given instructions "to answer objectively" holding aside their feelings, and half were not. Before the game, 1% of the people not given the instructions to be objective predicted that the team they were rooting for would lose. For those given the objectivity instructions, this figure climbed to a whopping 2%. Looking just at those fans instructed to be objective and whose team was behind by a score of 2–0 or 3–0 at halftime (big leads, in soccer),* 17% predicted (correctly) that the team they were rooting for would

---

* The paper that reports these results carries a slightly condescending remark for American readers who might "carry a baseball-oriented notion that a big lead may well be erased in one half-inning," and notes that "such an event is unlikely in soccer." This was, I might note, before the heartbreaking U.S. loss to Brazil in the 2009 Confederations Cup final, in which the Americans went into halftime with a 2–0 lead.

lose. The other 83% are people I would like to find to arrange friendly wagers with in the future.[52]

Predicting that your team will win is not restricted to sports. Granberg and Brent examined the relationship between one's preferred political candidate and predictions regarding who was going to win.[53] Using data from surveys in which people were asked who they predicted would win the presidential election and who they expected to vote for, they found that consistently between 1952 and 1980, roughly 80% of people predicted that their preferred candidate would win. (People who predicted Stevenson, Nixon [in 1960], Goldwater, Humphrey, McGovern, Ford, and Carter [in 1980] were wrong. The 87% of Democrats who said they were going to vote for Carter and predicted he would win in the race against Ronald Reagan were *way* wrong.)

On a more serious note, in an early and classic study of optimism, 258 college students were asked a range of questions about how likely various events were to happen to them compared to the same events happening to their classmates. A range of positive potential future events and negative future events were used. On average, students predicted they were 50% more likely to like their post-graduation job, 41% more likely to have a starting salary above $10,000 (this was meaningful back when the article was published, in 1980), and 35% more likely to travel to Europe. On the negative side, students thought they were 58% less likely to have a drinking problem, 56% less likely to attempt suicide, and 49% less likely to get a divorce.[54]

Moving along the scale of increasingly serious ways in which people are overly optimistic, a large study in the Netherlands showed a similar effect on estimates of the likelihood of becoming infected with the virus that causes AIDS.[55] Four groups of participants were recruited, and all judged that it was more likely that a person chosen at random would become infected over the next two years than that they themselves would be. This is relatively unsurprising given the evidence I've reviewed here to this point, but it's more surprising when one considers the details of one of the four sample groups. One group consisted of people recruited from an STD clinic who had engaged in "prostitution contacts" in the previous six months; on average, the males in this group had 21 sexual partners (7 "private" and 14 prostitution) in that period, and the females had over 500 partners. That is, people with very large numbers of sexual partners thought their risk was not very different from *a randomly selected person of their age and sex in the population.*

Optimism is, from the point of view of being an appealing social partner, a pretty good thing. If positive things are likely to happen to me—or, really, if I can *persuade* you I think that good things will happen to me—then I'm a good bet as a friend, ally, or mate. Not only that, but the nice thing about predictions about the future is that, being about the future, they aren't wrong, at least not yet. Being strategically optimistic seems like an eminently reasonable strategy. As Williams and Gilovich put it, "people feel free to give knowingly inflated estimates of their likely success far from the moment of truth and there is no possibility—or no imminent possibility—of their predictions being disconfirmed."[56]

Not only that, but there's a downside to pessimism. One set of researchers from Transylvania University (I'm not making that up) concluded that "pessimistically biased individuals were less socially accepted."[57] In addition, pessimistic people were found to be twice as likely to become werewolves and three times as likely to become vampires. (OK, that I'm making up.)

Again, however, I can't stress enough that, absent the *social* benefits of being *overly* optimistic, one should be exactly as optimistic as is warranted. To the extent that optimism guides effort and so on, creatures that are good at predicting what's going to happen and acting on those predictions appropriately are, everything else equal, going to do better than overly optimistic people, whether playing Frogger, an airplane game, or what have you. As we've seen, the claim that being overly optimistic is necessary to motivate doing risky, high-payoff things doesn't make any sense—being correctly optimistic will do this as well and, in fact, even better.[58]

It's worth appending a few notes. People are not always wrong in the direction of being overly optimistic: Areas in which people are pessimistic have been found as well.[59] Also, there's some debate about whether people's estimates that they're less likely to experiencing negative events is driven by low estimates of their own chances of having bad things happen or high estimates of others' chances.[60] I leave important questions like this one to others to explore.

It's also worth noting that, independent of the precise reason for the excessive optimism, these beliefs can have tangible consequences: Women who judge their chances of an unwanted pregnancy to be lower than others are less likely to use contraception.[61]

A leg to stand on

People vary in their susceptibility to these illusions, much the way some people find it maddeningly impossible to see the three-dimensional images in those stereograms that were popular for about twenty minutes in the early nineties.

In particular, there have been substantial discussions about the possibility that people who are depressed might be more accurate, giving rise to the notion of "depressive realism," about which I will say little, except that much of the work discussed in this chapter has its roots in Taylor and Brown's work in the eighties and nineties focused mostly on mental health. I mention this here because the approach I'm suggesting here changes the question from "How do positive illusions contribute to mental health?" to "How do (or, really, *did*) the modules that generate positive illusions contribute to achieving adaptive goals?"

It's also worth noting that Brown and Taylor worried that positive illusions might be simply "public posturing" rather than "privately held beliefs." The whole notion of "privately held beliefs" suggests they think it's meaningful to say that there's someone one can *really* believe, about which I'm skeptical. In any case, the idea that these positive illusions are really about public relations is bolstered by findings that people seem to be designed to portray the most positive *defensible* evaluation of their own abilities. Constantine Sedikides[*] showed that people who are given the task of grading their own essays assign lower marks when they know they'll have to justify their marks to others.[62] As Sedikides and Gregg recently put it, "self-enhancement occurs within the constraints imposed by rationality and reality."[63] Note that "reality" is really about what *other people* will believe. This fits very well with a propaganda explanation. If positive illusions were, say, all about feeling good about oneself, it's not clear why what others think would matter.

---

[*] Sedikides is far and away my favorite palindromic psychologist.

Having said *that*, the "constraints imposed by rationality and reality" are perhaps less binding than one might think. Paul Martin, the person with multiple function-specific legs whom we met in chapter 2, is a consummate optimist. Describing leaving the hospital after his leg was amputated, he says: "At that moment, I knew—*I knew*—that my future would be every bit as prosperous as I had ever imagined."[64] His optimism went further. He opens his book recounting his experiences by explaining that since he wanted to write his memoir, having a bunch of time "on his hands" was such a Good Thing that he "*couldn't wait to go to jail!*" (his italics and exclamation point).[65] He wonders, "What better opportunity could I have asked for to begin putting my experiences on paper?" It might be tempting to say something like, a better opportunity might have been, oh, an all-expenses-paid stay at a cottage on the shores of Maine overlooking the lobster boats and the changing tides, the craggy coastline and the wafting fog so conducive to literary inspiration . . . but a jail cell is also good, I guess.

Strategically wrong: interlude and case studies

Being strategically wrong is everywhere, and even scientists are not immune. In fact, there's some sense in which scientists have a particularly strong incentive to be strategically wrong, and their press secretary modules seem to be doing a singular job selectively seeking, forgetting, and interpreting information to reap all the multiple and myriad benefits of being wrong.

When I was a graduate student, I had, in retrospect, a Pollyanna-ish view of the way science worked. I thought that scientists read others' papers, evaluated the logic and evidence, and ran experiments to test their ideas against competing ideas. I thought publishing was the way in which arguments were made and settled.

And I actually still think that is how many scientists go about their business. But not all of them. The problem is that in science, there are big benefits to be had in being strategically wrong. It comes down to this: Scientists make a splash by making discoveries, figuring out or finding out something that no one else knew before. The more novel an idea, the more likely it is to get attention and sell books.

The trick is that novelty is in the mind of the beholder. One's old ideas can seem very new to anyone who isn't deeply enmeshed in the field. To make a splash, you have to persuade others that that the idea is new, even if it isn't.* To do this, the press secretary in one's head can be strategically wrong, "believing" the idea is new and portraying it in this light. Then, consumers of the idea—editors, other scientists, and the public—can thereby be made to think so as well. I'm not saying that these people are lying—I'm saying that, by design, the press secretary modules are getting it wrong.

Consider the following well-known joke:

> A shy guy goes into a bar. He sees a very attractive woman and, eventually, gathers his courage and goes over to her. He asks, tentatively, "Um, is it OK if I introduce myself?" In response, she yells at the top of her lungs, "No, I won't sleep with you tonight!" Everyone in the bar turns to look, and the guy, utterly embarrassed, slinks away. A few minutes later, the woman comes over to him and apologizes, saying, "Look, I'm sorry I embarrassed you. I'm a social psychology grad student and I'm studying how people respond to embarrassing situations." In reply, he yells at the top of his lungs, "What do you mean $200?!"

By careful theatrics like this, you can persuade observers that the person you're arguing with has said something that she didn't really say because in science, as in a loud bar, the people yelling the loudest can make themselves heard.

I suspect this happens in many fields, but I can speak only to the areas I have contact with. I offer a few examples here, which might seem like inside baseball, but I present them because it's the area I know best and because my field, evolutionary psychology, seems to be especially subject to this particular version of attack.[66]

Suppose someone—let's call him, for argument's sake, "David Buller"—says, in criticizing evolutionary psychologists, something that everyone who has spent a few moments in the natural world knows, that different

---

*Of course I recognize I might bear some guilt here. I have tried to credit people who have had ideas like the ones I present throughout, and I have tried to cite them appropriately. Minsky, Dennett, Trivers. . . . This footnote is my formal apology for my own errors of this type.

organisms have to contend with different issues to make a living, which is why the beaks of finches vary depending on which island they live on. When this person says that evolutionary psychologists need to understand that "the adaptive problems faced by a species are not independent of its characteristics and lifestyle,"[67] you might think that this very basic principle of biology had been lost on evolutionary psychologists. What? Evolutionary psychologists don't realize that birds *fly* and fish *swim*? They are *that* ignorant of biology!?

It's a little like the little boy who cried wolf. People who like to get attention, like the apocryphal boy, can yell and scream and generally throw a tantrum, and sometimes it's hard to tell if there was actually a wolf about when all the commotion began. I mean, who's going to check to see if the critic is right about all this? He seems to believe it—I mean, no competent scholar wishing to be taken even remotely seriously would publish books and articles that completely misrepresent the field he's critiquing, right? So there's no use even going back to check to see if the wolf he's screaming about is really there.

But the idea that "the adaptive problems faced by a species are not independent of its characteristics and lifestyle" has been a centerpiece of evolutionary psychology right from the start.[68] Tooby and Cosmides made this point vividly more than a decade before Buller's "corrective," in this passage:[69]

> "Appropriate" has different meanings for different organisms. . . . On smelling feces, appropriate behavior for a female dung fly is to move toward the feces, land on them, and lay her eggs. . . . But for you, feces are a source of contagious diseases. For you, they are not food, they are not a good place to raise your children . . . appropriate behavior for you is to move away from the source of the smell.

Evolutionary psychologists do not need to be told this—or essentially the rest of what our hypothetical critic is saying—because they have been making precisely this point since they began writing on the topic. If critics like Buller were right, it would be important to know. But there's no wolf here, and there never was.

As I say, evolutionary psychology is oddly subject to this type of scholarly malpractice. Martin Daly and Margo Wilson catalog various cases in which "scholars" have not only mis-cited them, but hung views on them that are the exact *opposite* of their position.[70]

Stephen Jay Gould was an absolute master of this sort of thing. Anyone who read him could not doubt his intelligence. With his pen he wove tapestries of linguistic elegance of such texture and subtlety that the rest of us could only admire from afar, awash in despair, frowning in contemplation of the distant inferiority of our own works.

Gould's mind was, no doubt, a sharp one and, whenever he comes to mind, I can't help but pack my sentences with metaphor.

But he was strategically wrong in truly spectacular fashion. Gould, with Richard Lewontin, wrote a heavily cited paper published in 1979 in which they argued that natural selection resulted in not just adaptations—the complex organized functional parts of organisms—but also by-products, the side effects of adaptations. So, for example, belly buttons aren't adaptations—they have no function—they're side effects of umbilical cords, which do have functions. Using an architectural metaphor, Gould and Lewontin referred to by-products as "spandrels," which are the triangle-shaped spaces where arches meet one another on the ceiling. To me they seem sort of like an arch's armpit. Gould and Lewontin's point was to illustrate that things with functions have nonfunctional parts.

Gould continued to pound the table about this for decades. He wrote piece after piece insisting that biologists recognize that evolution leads to not just adaptations, but also by-products. As Gould became aware of my field, he insisted that we, too, acknowledge by-products, writing that one of our problems was "a failure to recognize that even the strictest operation of pure natural selection builds organisms full of nonadaptive parts and behaviors."[71]

That's all well and good, except that evolutionary psychologists *already believed what Gould was trying to "persuade" them about*. My favorite piece of evidence on this—and there are so many to chose from—is from a chapter by John Tooby and Leda Cosmides, two of the main targets of Gould's pen, who wrote, eight years before Gould's chapter appeared, "In addition to adaptations, the evolutionary process commonly produces two other outcomes visible in the designs of organisms: (1) concomitants or by-products of adaptations (recently nicknamed "spandrels"; Gould & Lewontin 1979); and (2) random effects."[72] Not only is it clear that they think that there are by-products, but *they cite Gould and Lewontin's paper and even use their metaphorical term.*[73]

I think it's not that unlikely that Gould selectively read or skimmed the sources he was critiquing—I'm sure he was a busy guy—and the press secretary in his brain maintained a representation of the ignorance of his interlocutors that was "justified" by the limited information it received. He remained strategically wrong, and his reputation in the public never really seemed to suffer.

Why?

Gould was able to retain his status as a prince of biology because it didn't actually matter that he was wrong. A peculiar fact about becoming famous is that it becomes less relevant if you're right. When you write for a small community—say, of scientists—it's hard to be strategically wrong because most of your readers are in a position to correct you. And they often will.

But once you write for a larger audience, things change, and press secretary modules reflect this fact. Gould was writing for lay people, who probably quite reasonably assumed that the people in Gould's sights actually wrote what Gould said they wrote. As long as no one did any checking, he could spin whatever tales he wanted—another juicy irony given his penchant for accusing others of spinning "just so" stories—with no worry of being found out or called to account.

John Maynard Smith and Ernst Mayr—two hugely important figures in evolutionary biology who, outside of the scientific community, hardly anyone has heard of[*]—were heavily critical of Gould. Maynard Smith wrote in 1995 that Gould was giving the public a "largely false picture of the state of evolutionary theory,"[74] but such critiques didn't really matter. Gould's strategic errors, painting himself a defender of a completely sensible view in opposition to views *held by no one*, was thoroughly effective. He died famous, wealthy, and wrong.

[*] Gould beats Maynard Smith in a GoogleFight nearly 10 to 1. Mayr does better, but still loses by a wide margin.

If it seems odd for a scientist to give people "a largely false picture" of their field, consider first that in a world without written language and the Internet—the world in which our ancestors evolved—it would have been impossible to document the flagrant errors Gould made. When words are fleeting, as in spoken language, it's difficult or impossible to verify who said what. It's only in the modern world that the Machiavellian, strategically wrong press secretary system can be called to account.

Consider second that even now it doesn't seem to matter. Gould did just fine.

And others are pursuing similar strategies with equal success. Elsewhere I've written at some length about a book co-edited by Stephen and Hilary Rose, and I won't rehash that here.[75] Suffice it to say that contributors to this book are very angry about a mythical world in which people believe all sorts of silly things.

To take another example, consider Gary Marcus, whom, I ought to say, I quite like. We agree on lots of things, and I would even call myself a fan. He was a student of Steve Pinker's, whose work has heavily influenced me. Marcus, in his recent book *Kluge*, scolds evolutionary psychologists for thinking that all adaptations will function *optimally*, and he insists instead that evolution, because of path dependencies (i.e., history), trade-offs, and constraints, will yield "an outcome that is good enough."[76] The key here is the distinction between something designed well or well enough on the one hand, and something that is *optimally* designed on the other. Marcus's idea is that the mind might not be *optimally* designed.

To make his point, Marcus quotes John Tooby and Leda Cosmides as saying that "natural selection tends to cause the accumulation of *superlatively well engineered* functional designs."[*][77]

Here is how Marcus's strategic interpretation of this quotation would work at a dinner party.

MRS. SMITH: Why, Mister Jones, the soup is superlative this evening!
MR. JONES: Thank you, Mrs. Smith.

---

[*]The italics are in Marcus's version, not the Tooby and Cosmides version. Probably because the human memory system is not optimally designed, but is rather a kluge, Marcus forgot to indicate that he had modified the original.

> GARY: What!? This soup is truly excellent—I love the lentils!—but
> you cannot prove to me that it is the best soup of all possible
> soups which could ever be! Ha!
> MR. SMITH: Who let Gary Marcus in?

The Tooby-Cosmides quote is a linguistic gambit; Marcus is hoping by "superlatively well" you'll think they mean "perfect" or "optimal." They don't. In case it's ambiguous, is there any way to tell?

Well, two paragraphs after the material Marcus quotes in the very same paper, Tooby and Cosmides write that "adaptations are certainly suboptimal . . ."; and, *in the very same paragraph that Marcus draws the quotation from,* they refer the reader to Richard Dawkins's book *The Extended Phenotype* for "an extensive discussion of the many processes that prevent selection from reaching perfect optimality."[78]

But really Gould and Marcus haven't got a patch on the more recent critic of evolutionary psychology I mentioned above, David Buller. In late 2008 he wrote a brief article in *Scientific American* leveling the usual criticisms at the field. The article is filled with so many misrepresentations that it's hard to know where to start. I think my favorite part is when Buller writes: "Some human psychological mechanisms undoubtedly did emerge during the Pleistocene. But others are holdovers of a more ancient evolutionary past. . . ." He implies that evolutionary psychologists think that humans sprang out of nowhere during the Pleistocene, and that it never occurred to us that some modules predate recent evolution. While this is quite silly, it can be effective as a way to suggest that evolutionary psychologists are unsophisticated in the way they think about the history of the mind.

Being strategically wrong is a good—by which I mean "effective," certainly not "moral"—strategy when the costs of being wrong are low and the strategic advantages—when persuading others of whatever it is that you're wrong about—are high.

Because digging up the truth is often more trouble than it's worth, being strategically wrong is, sadly, often an excellent strategy.

Having said that, I want to be very clear that I'm not saying Gould, Buller, Rose, and their ilk are (necessarily) *lying.* It's possible they are, but I think it's more likely that at least in some cases they are reading (or remembering) selectively in order to build an argument—which they can use for persuading others—that the people they are critiquing hold the views they attribute to them. By keeping strategically ignorant of—or, again, strategically forgetting—where the authors they criticize make the relevant arguments, these authors can argue, without lying, that their criticisms are valid. If I've forgotten that you told me that you think the world is round, I can publicly correct you for thinking that it is flat.

Strategic error asks a lot of memory. To be strategically wrong requires mechanisms designed to recall facts that support the view one wants to endorse and forget facts that undermine it, and there is evidence for such mechanisms of memory, which is one important way that modules are designed to implement the strategy of being wrong.[79]

It's all in your modules

I close this chapter with a brief detour into one area that occurs to everyone when I talk about the benefits of being wrong: placebo effects. In a placebo effect, patients experience improvement after being given an inert substance, usually attributed to their belief that they are, or might be, getting a real drug. In this sense, they are "wrong" about the substance they receive. There is considerable debate surrounding the placebo effect, in no small part because it's difficult to study. For instance, in a typical study using a placebo control group, some set of patients get the treatment, some get the placebo, and recovery rates are compared to determine if the treatment is more effective than the placebo. If some fraction of the people in the placebo control group improve, we don't know, from this study alone, if the recovery would have occurred without the placebo.

I don't really want to get into this debate, which seems from my reading as acrimonious as any other academic debate (that is, very), but I do want to lay out the type of argument for placebo effects that the view I'm endorsing would lead you to.

First, let's dispose of the notion that it would be surprising to find that simply having someone tell you something (e.g., "Those pills you just took will dull your pain") can alter your physiology or your experience (of pain or whatever else).Of course it can. People have profound physiological reactions to what people tell them all the time. Surely if someone tells you about the death of a loved one, or that you won the lottery, we would be surprised if simply having the information *didn't* profoundly affect how you felt.

But it's actually a lot more basic than that. E*verything* that you hear affects your brain somehow. Again, if we're going to avoid dualism, all it *means* to process some information is that your brain changes in some way. Being surprised that the words a particular person—such as a doctor—utters when you take a sugar pill affects your *brain* is odd. How can the words a particular person—such as a doctor—utters, say informing you of the death of a loved one, affect your brain? Same way. Spoken words affect our brains and physiology all the time. In fact, that's *all* they do. That's all they *could* do.

So it seems to me that the question isn't really about how placebo effects could occur at all; it's in the details. And let's be clear about one answer that *can't* be right. It can't be right that, over evolutionary time, people susceptible to the placebo effect healed faster than others, so that susceptibility was selected for. On this account, you're getting something "for free." That is, if it's possible to heal better or faster—whether because someone gave you a sugar pill or you believe in a deity or what have you—then selection should simply favor whatever it is that allows one to heal faster or better, regardless of the placebo effect. The answer has to be more subtle than that. I have no idea if the answer that I'm sketching here is right, but this is one way to think about it, and it has to do with trade-offs.[80]

The pain system seems to me to be designed, at least in part, to cause you to change your behavior to prevent further damage. This is why it hurts to move when your ankle is broken—it's evolution's way of telling you to sit tight.[81] Yes, this might compromise your ability to do things like obtaining food, cultivating social relationships, or indulging your foot fetish, but these things must go to reduce the chance of further injury. And of course sometimes this system is suspended, which is, I take it, when you carry on past injury when it matters, as in key situations in sports or in combat. Consider the soldier on the battlefield who stops to nurse a stubbed toe. The pain is useful. Now consider the same soldier's experience of the pain just after his buddy yells, "*They're right behind us!*" The words we hear have profound effects on our experience; it's just good engineering.

Pain, then, is a mechanism involved in a trade-off. If I rest now, the body's resources can be used for healing rather than tending to other important tasks. Trade-offs are a big part of healing. Maintaining an immune system at full strength is enormously energetically costly; indeed, stress in lots of critters, including humans, suppresses the action of the immune system.[82] This reflects a trade-off—when the organism is stressed, resources must be diverted, and the immune system pays.

So, pain can be usefully thought of as a kind of information about how to trade off healing with other things that one might do. How to make this trade-off depends on many factors, but one factor, especially for humans, is the social world. If I'm in trouble, and the social world is supportive, it seems to me that I don't need to make healing my highest priority.[83] I can ratchet back the energy I spend on healing and use it for other useful activities. So, under certain circumstances, it makes sense to "turn down" the pain, confident that I don't need to devote all my body's resources to healing immediately. Placebo effects, on this view, are resetting the trade-off downward. Turn down the pain, get on with other tasks.

Many people have talked about the placebo effect as deriving from the relationship between the patient and the physician or healer.[84] Could be. If there's someone caring for me, and this person believes that whatever she's doing is useful, then it could be that I'm better off dialing down the expensive healing system. Why shouldn't the words of a trusted physician or friend affect our physiology in this way, in the same way that any number of words from physicians or friends do? As long as the claim isn't one in which the placebo effect gives the body "extra" healing powers—but rather just changes the physiological trade-offs—I can imagine any of a number of possible explanations for the phenomenon that might hold.

Recap

This chapter has covered a lot of ground so, before moving on, a brief recap. So far I've used the phrase "strategically wrong" to talk about a basket of phenomena that others would prefer to refer to using other kinds of words and ideas. While I think a term like "positive illusions" is felicitous to describe some of these effects, I prefer "strategically wrong" because it points to what I think is the function of these systems—persuading others of things that, if they believed them, makes you better off. Whereas I take an "illusion" to be something that happens in a funny environment as a by-product of the way that some mechanism is supposed to function, I think being "strategically wrong" is exactly the way various parts of your brain are supposed to function.

Some people have referred to effects like the ones we visited in this chapter as instances of "self-deception." The intuition is that these examples show that I might believe something that an unbiased person with the same information wouldn't believe—that my soccer team is going to win even though they're down two-nil at the half, that I'm an excellent driver even though I've just hit a stationary object, or that I can control the dice if I throw them *just so*. The whole brain *should* know what's right, and maybe even in some sense *does* know what's right—I "really know" "on some level"—but it is "deceiving itself" into believing something else.

This is all very mysterious without the modular view, but unsurprising with it. Some parts of the mind—some modules—are designed for functions other than being right because of certain strategic advantages. These modules produce propaganda, and, like the more traditional political propaganda, the information isn't always exactly right.

In all of this it doesn't seem to me that there's anything plausibly called "self-deception" going on. This labeling problem stems from the insistence in psychology on the word "self," and thinking of a unified "self" instead of a collection of modules. As we'll see in the next two chapters, almost any time you come across a theory with the word "self" in it, you should check your wallet. Here, I don't see why being *wrong* in some systematic way suggests that there's any deception of any "self." I think there's arguably a little deception in some sense of *others* going on, but it's not like one module is pulling something over on another module.

If some social strategic problems are best solved by having less than the best guess about what's right—because of the value of persuasion—we would expect many modules designed to be strategically wrong about one's traits, abilities, and future.

Sometimes, perhaps often, the truth is useful. So it wouldn't be surprising to find that the mind has some modules designed to discover truth.

So what if there are two different modules with different functions, one of which requires being strategically wrong—for persuasion purposes—and the other of which requires being as right as possible—for some other purpose? It might be fine to have a representation that one is an excellent driver right up to the moment when one has to decide whether or not to attempt a bootlegger at high speed. Ideally, what you would want is the public relations modules to have the strategically wrong representation, but the system that will drive decision making to have the right one. This leads to the peculiarity of needing to have two mutually contradictory representations in the same head.

This should sound familiar. We visited such cases at the start of the book. These ideas come in handy in the next chapter.

chapter 7

Self-Deception

■ *The second of two kinds of "self-deception" is addressed, which is the simultaneous representation of mutually contradictory beliefs in the same brain, one of which is "strategically wrong" in the sense discussed in chapter 6. Viewed this way, problems of self-deception are finessed.* ■

Fred has cancer, a kind that is, unfortunately, terminal. He has been told that he has roughly six months to live, nine at the outside. Not only that, but in order to have a chance of making it even to six months, he needs to undergo some painful procedures once a week.

Fred says that he thinks a positive attitude is important for cancer patients. When people ask him how he feels, he tells them that he is going to surprise the doctors and pull through, making a full recovery. In fact, he's so sure that he is going to be fine that he says he doesn't even *need* the painful treatments once a week. Oh, well, yes, he's going to have them done; after all, he promised his little sister that he would. It will make her feel better. *My sister and I are very close. I'd do anything for her, and if it helps her get through this. . . .*

As promised, Fred undergoes the treatments, maintains a healthy attitude, puts down a $50 deposit to reserve a spot on a cruise in a year's time, and dies seven months after his initial diagnosis.

Was Fred deceiving himself?

People take this to be a case of "self-deception" because Fred seems to have a belief—that he will recover—that is unjustified by the facts at his disposal. In addition, there seems to be some evidence that Fred didn't *really* believe what he said he did, since he went to the trouble of getting treated. It feels somehow right to say that Fred was deceiving himself, and cases like Fred's have frequently been used as examples of self-deception.

What distinguishes Fred from the cases we visited in the last chapter is that Fred seems to have two different, mutually contradictory beliefs in his head, whereas positive illusion cases are generally those in which there is—or might be—just one (unjustifiably positive) belief at issue.

As we've seen, depending on how one thinks the mind works, the idea that Fred has "two different, mutually contradictory beliefs in his head" is either a problem verging on the paradoxical or a straightforward consequence of the modular architecture of the mind.

With a unitary model of the mind, believing two contradictory things is troubling. If you have a bunch of information coming in, and you shake it up and mix it all together, then some conclusion is reached by the combination of everything that you've put in. A unitary mind should reach a compromise or simply get rid of one belief in favor of the other. This is why psychologists and others worry about "self-deception," when "a person appears both to know and not know one and the same thing."[1]

I'm not saying that anyone actually thinks this is the way the mind works. (By the way, I actually *do* think that, but I'm just not *saying* it because it's not really relevant to the present point.) I'm saying that *if* you think of the mind as rationally chewing up information and coming up with the best guess about what's true, *then*, roughly, contradictions will get resolved in the direction of whatever guess is most likely.

But I think this whole business is confused to begin with.

Am I lying to myself about self-deception?

I find the philosophical and psychological hand-wringing about self-deception a little hard to understand. If you are persuaded by the arguments here about modularity, then you might too, so it's useful to visit a little of the historical development in this area and notice how the intuition of the mind as unitary has driven thinking.[2]

One of the most important moments in this area was a paper by Ruben Gur and Harold Sackeim.[3] They had subjects make recordings of their own voices and then try to identify their recordings among recordings of others' voices. In addition to giving verbal responses, subjects were hooked up to electrodes that recorded their galvanic skin response (GSR). The idea was to use arousal measured by GSR to find when people were misidentifying the voice. Gur and Sackeim, based on previous work, assumed that when a subject identified a voice that was actually himself as someone else, his GSR would be high.[*][4] The key idea was that the only way that GSR could be high when subjects made a mistaken identification was if the subject (somehow) knew—that is, somewhere there was a representation in the brain that— the voice was his when he said it was not. These researchers took various steps to ensure that subjects weren't simply lying, and we'll assume they were successful.

Gur and Sackeim were concerned mostly with simply demonstrating that self-deception existed, and in this they declared themselves successful: "When subjects misidentified the voices of self and others, they showed that at some of level of processing correct identifications were made," and that while subjects "simultaneously held contradictory beliefs," they "were not aware of" the fact that they were misidentifying voices.[5] They concluded that they had indeed found evidence of self-deception. (We return to the issue of being "aware" later in this chapter.)

More recently, Anthony Greenwald looked at this question, also beginning with a story much like the one I open with, about "a cancer patient who maintains the expectation of recovery even while surrounded by the signs of an incurable malignancy. Presumably this patient knows unconsciously that the disease is incurable, but manages to prevent that knowledge from becoming conscious."[6]

Greenwald poses three questions:

How does the person both know and not know *p*?
What good does it do not to know *p* consciously?
Why is the faster, more accurate system unconscious?

---

[*] I like to think of this as "their lips said no but their skin said yes."

The questions illustrate how these issues have traditionally been viewed. Greenwald wonders about "the person" knowing things and, in what he calls a "drastic step,"[7] suggests the possibility of abandoning the "assumption that each person's knowledge is organized into a single, unified system."

The predominant explanation for what's going on with Greenwald's cancer patient is *motivation*.[8] The gist is that Fred doesn't *want* to believe that he's going to die, so he's *motivated* to believe that he's not. You'll often read things like "the patient is motivated to protect the self."

My basic problem with this is that, not to put too fine a point on it, I *have absolutely no idea what this means*. First, I don't think there's a "self" to be protected, and, as far as I know, there is no coherent account of what, exactly, is being protected and what, exactly, is doing the protecting. Without modularity—which researchers in this area generally eschew—it's completely unclear what they are trying to say. Second, and related, if all the mind does is process information, then somehow "motivation" must refer somehow to some kind of information processing.[9] Otherwise, we're back in the land of Buzzy. It's no good saying that self-deception is Buzzy's way—or "the self's" way—of feeling good. What does that mean? What could it mean?

I think there is one way to explain this in language that connects to something physical, which would be nice, given that we're supposed to be living in a post-Enlightenment world and all. Let me put it this way. Is a thermostat "motivated" to keep the temperature of my house at 68 degrees? Sort of. It behaves that way, turning the heater on when the temperature dips sufficiently. If thermostats could feel and speak, they might talk about their singular drive to keep the temperature constant, feeling grim determination to turn the heat on when it was too cold, and placid contentment when the temperature was just right.

Without a doubt it makes sense to say that a thermostat is *designed* to keep the temperature within some particular range. In the same way it probably makes sense to talk about mechanisms of the mind being *designed* to bring about certain states of affairs. Design to bring about goals—whether concrete or abstract—seems to be a good way to understand what "motivation" means.

So, let's forget about the wifty world of "motivation" and return to the physicalist world of design. Dropping the whole notion of motivation avoids the vexing problem of what it means to talk about Fred—the whole of Fred's brain—being "motivated." After that, the next question we can ask is, given this idea of motivation as simply design to bring about some goal, is "protection" of the "self" a reasonable goal for which a set of modules might be designed? Is the mind, or any part of it, designed to bring about good feelings—or avoid unpleasant ones?

Evolution doesn't care how happy you are

The argument that self-deception is to "protect the self" is something like the following.* Suppose human brains have systems designed to avoid pain and systems for thinking about the future. Taken together, it might be tempting to think that some of Fred's modules—"knowing" that other modules will produce a sensation of feeling sad if they adopt the belief that he's about to die—will avoid adopting that belief. That is, if some modules know that other modules will feel sad if they adopt the belief that death is imminent, and those modules "want" to prevent this, then they can simply maintain the representation in those modules that all is fine and dandy.

This same sort of reasoning applies equally to all sorts of things beyond one's impending death by cancer, including things discussed in the previous chapter. It would make me sad to think that I'm not as smart as others. So, maybe the modules that can predict the effect of believing any of a number of different things anticipate this and generate beliefs that I'm smart, friendly, honest, and a good driver, even though I just hit a stationary object at high speed and wound up in a hospital.

As with most intuitively appealing explanations for psychological phenomena that find their way into psychology journals, it's worth slowing down for a moment and looking these ideas squarely in the eye.

---

*The way I'm putting it here is not how this argument is usually put. I'm putting it this way because I genuinely don't understand how this argument is supposed to be taken. This version of it is supposed to be the physicalist version of what seems to me like a dualist argument, in which the "self" is Cartesian mind-stuff.

There are, in particular, at least two very basic issues these explanations have to address. The first one comes back to the discussion of Frogger and the value of being right. Everything else being equal—and holding aside arguments like the ones that I've made in the last couple of chapters that have to do with social strategizing—when it comes to making good decisions, *being right is always going to beat being wrong.* As we've seen, being wrong is useful in certain circumstances, such as when it can help convince others of things you want to persuade them about.

But being wrong isn't going to be useful because it makes you feel better for a very simple reason:

Evolution doesn't care how happy you are.[10]

Natural selection works because of reproductive outcomes. Modules are designed to bring about outcomes that contribute to reproductive success. No modules are designed to bring about feeling good for its own sake. When modules bring about certain outcomes, yes, often you feel pleasure—evolution's way of telling you,[11] hey, that was a Good Thing, and wouldn't you like to do appropriate things to bring about that outcome again? But the *feeling good* in itself isn't the outcome that the system evolved to bring about. That's not something the system might *plausibly* be designed to do.

This is not something that psychologists, on the whole, have thought much about. Indeed, psychologists have talked almost obsessively about how people are motivated by the desire to feel good, usually about themselves, in the literature on self-esteem. So, we can ask, as an empirical matter, just how important the supposedly all-important motive to maintain one's self-esteem really is.

In 2004, Thomas Scheff and David Fearon published a paper summarizing reviews of research on self-esteem. They wrote: "At this point there have probably been at least *fifteen thousand studies.* This amount of effort probably represents the largest body of research on a single topic in the history of all of the social sciences."

Wow. The largest body of research in social science history. It would be a shame if it was mostly a waste of time.

So, they ask, "How has this effort paid off?"[12]

That's a good question. We should probably know if the diligence of social scientists and the incalculable wealth in grants and research time have given the tax-paying public value for their money. To give you a sense of how much more we know about the crucial, central role self-esteem plays in life, Scheff and Fearon summarize the relationship between self-esteem and some key variables. With social class, findings regarding the relationship with self-esteem are "competing, inconclusive, and inconsistent." Does low self-esteem predict crime? The findings in that area are "rife with contradictory or weak findings."

One finding is relatively reliable. Men have higher self-esteem than women—by a little bit. Well, by a tiny bit. Actually, in the words of the authors, an amount that is so small that it is "perilously close to zero."[13]

Scheff and Fearon quote Roy Baumeister and some of his colleagues from a review that came out around the same time their paper did. Baumeister *et al.* reported: "Self-esteem is thus not a major predictor or cause of almost anything. . . . people with high self-esteem seem sincerely to believe they are smarter, more accomplished, more popular and likable, more attractive, and so forth, but some of those apparent advantages are illusory."[14] It's worth repeating that they find that *self-esteem isn't a cause of almost anything.* That's not so good for self-esteem. It's hard to argue that it's a good idea to pursue self-esteem for it's own sake if it turns out that it doesn't *cause* anything else. This leaves self-esteem as a kind of a dead-end street. Yeah, you can get there, but it doesn't get you any further than that.

One thing that Scheff and Fearon were trying to point out is how crazy it is that psychologists have been running after this particular will-o'-the-wisp, unconcerned with the fact that it's basically fruitless. Robyn Dawes, in his wonderful book *House of Cards*, quotes from an edited volume about self-esteem. Dawes found this delicious line: "One of the disappointing aspects of every chapter in this volume (at least to those of us who adhere to the intuitively correct models sketched above) is how low the association between self-esteem and its consequences are [*sic*] in the research to date."[15] The author of this little gem is saying, hey, never mind that the evidence is telling us over and over that self-esteem doesn't have the kind of effects we think it does, because—not that we're scientists or anything—we *already know* how the data ought to turn out because it is *intuitively correct* that self-esteem has important effects. We're not going to stop just because it turns out that it doesn't.

So, pretty much the jury has come back, and self-esteem is, as an empirical matter, a poor theoretical construct for predicting anything interesting in psychology, and this has been known for years and years. So, of course, practitioners in psychology—scientists, responsive to evidence and data—have all but abandoned this idea, right?[16]

In a recent book that acts as a kind of gold standard for the state of the field, the *Handbook of Self and Identity*, the chapter on self-esteem begins this way: "It is almost axiomatic in social psychology that people seek to maintain, enhance, and protect their self-esteem."[17]

I think the choice of the word "axiomatic" is interesting here. *Axiomatic.* As in, assumed, taken for granted, *not to be questioned.* This is not a subject open to, you know, *falsification*, which one might expect of people doing science.

As a psychologist myself, I'm very reluctant to call my community bullheaded, stubborn, foolish, impervious to evidence, and so on, but. . . .

Since Dawes's book came out in 1994 things haven't changed much, at least not as far as I can tell. If anything, psychology has become *more* obsessed with self-esteem. Just to give you a sense, a search of psychology's major database shows 2,450 journal articles with "self-esteem" as a key word in 2008. This number was 836 in 1998. There seems to be no closing off the taps.

The fetish for self-esteem has accompanied a similar infatuation with happiness more generally. A twin torrent has emerged, with a deluge of treatises on happiness offered at bookstores and academic colloquia.[18]

Don't get me wrong. I think people should be happy. I'd love for everyone to be happy. Nothing would please me more.

But if the question is how to explain all of the really interesting findings we've discussed to this point, then the answer is probably not going to turn out to be self-esteem or happiness. This is potentially important because by and large the most popular explanations among social psychologists for why people are wrong and inconsistent have to do with the idea that people need to "protect their selves" or "maintain a positive self-image" or more generally safeguard their self-esteem.

With Scheff and Fearon's work in mind, we can see why psychologists think positive illusions and self-deception are explained by the need for self-esteem. It's because psychologists think the need for self-esteem explains basically *everything*. The evidence suggests, in contrast, it explains almost *nothing*.

With a few moments' reflection on the fact that the brain evolved to *do* stuff, one might have reasoned right from the start that it was going to turn out that way. Self-esteem just isn't the sort of thing the mind should be designed to bring about (i.e., "be motivated" to do). The mind's systems might evolve to bring about fitness-relevant states of affairs, such as satiety, popularity, and sex, but not "self-esteem."

On bear-food brains

So, what does evolution "care" about?

The brain is designed to generate all of the many, many feelings that we feel. It's wired the way it is for all the reasons we've discussed to this point. We have brains that are very much like the ones that led our ancestors to do adaptive things.

One can at least imagine brains that are wired up very differently.

Here's one kind of brain design. Your brain could be designed so that no matter what is going on in the world, you experience euphoria.

That would be a fun brain to have, I suppose. Always euphoric. Nice. Sign me up for that.

The basic problem with such a brain is that, evolutionarily speaking, euphoria isn't all that useful.

To be clear, it's obvious that evolution works because of what people do (or, really, did), not because of what they *feel*. Evolution can "see" the effects of behavior—that is, what people do can have an effect on the different rates at which different genes get passed on. In contrast, evolution can't "see," in any direct way, the effects of being happy. The experiences of happiness or sadness or whatever else we're talking about have no effect *in and of themselves* on the rate at which genes make it from one generation to the next. Genes that make brains that cause a person to be completely happy— but don't cause them to do anything (reproductively) useful—are going to lose *every single time* to genes that make someone miserable but do things that are (reproductively) useful.

This is, of course, why experiences like pain are the way they are. Pain is evolution's way of motivating you to take appropriate corrective action— get your hand out of the fire, spit out the fetid meat, take the pencil out of your nostril—or whatever. *Evolution's interest in your happiness is—has to be—purely instrumental.* It's not interested in making you happy for its own sake. Evolution works by leading to the development of systems that motivate you to do adaptive things—and avoid maladaptive ones like sticking pencils up your nose—with no regard for how happy or miserable that makes you on balance.

In short, good explanations in social science—and it's odd that this has to be said—must refer, ultimately, to effects *outside the body*. For any given module to function, it has to, eventually, cause a change in the world. The design of the visual system has to do with making it possible to walk around without bumping into trees and falling off cliffs. You can't explain why people eat fruit by saying that "fruit tastes good" any more than you can explain being strategically wrong by saying that doing so "protects the self." Whatever the pain or pleasure associated with the way a module works, that pain or pleasure is itself something in need of an explanation, not the stopping point.

Humans are the only creatures for whom we accept these types of "explanations" for behavior. Imagine if someone tried to tell you that pigs nurse their young because it fulfills their sense of value as porcine mothers. Yes, you might say, it might *feel that way to the pig*, but that's not a scientific explanation for her behavior. It probably has something to do with delivering calories to baby pigs and all that, and to do that the sow has the appropriate bits of anatomy and a nervous system to make her appropriately inclined.

Evolution is, sad to say, greedy and mean when it comes to the experience of happiness. Consider the so-called "hedonic treadmill." Briefly, suppose you reach some really important goal that you've been striving for over a long period of time. Say you've been in the same career path for, oh, fifteen years, and you get promoted in your job, and even given a lifetime appointment. (You might be, say, a judge who comes under Article III of the United States Constitution. Or maybe you have some other job in which tenure is a possibility [*whistling innocently*].) You might think that having reached your goal, you would be happy for pretty much the rest of your life. You might do the bare minimum you need to keep your job, happy as a clam, getting your mail every morning from your mailbox standing right there on Easy Street.

Not so much. It turns out that even though reaching such goals makes one happy for a time, people relatively quickly return to the level of happiness they were at before the milestone, and begin looking longingly for the next big goal, whatever that might be. The classic finding in this literature is that paraplegics and lottery winners are roughly equally happy after some time had passed since their very good, or very bad, fortune.[19]

My interpretation of this and similar findings is that it is evolution's way of keeping the carrot just out of reach, motivating you to continue to do more useful and adaptive things. If you imagine an evolutionary history with two different mind designs—one complacent, in which once a goal is reached people rest on their laurels and whistle a happy tune all day—and one mind design that is never quite satisfied, in which each victory motivates further achievement—it's easy to see that the second one, while being less fun, would do more useful things.

This, I take it, is why Alexander, who ought to have been pretty darn happy ruling the known world, "wept, for there were no more worlds to conquer" and all that.[20]

There's an upside to this, which is that people who have bad things happen to them don't wind up permanently sad.[21] I think the reasons for this are similar, and straightforward.*

Our experiences are the way that they are because of how the modules that generate them lead to adaptive behavior. There is no reason that paper cuts have to "hurt." It's possible to imagine a mind that experiences cuts as enjoyable, though of course this would do the owner of such a mind no particular good.

We can even imagine a brain that could activate its own pleasure centers if it wanted to. There's no reason in principle that one module couldn't activate modules involved in experiencing pleasure. Heck, people do this

---

* Not obvious? OK. When bad things happen, evolution does best if you make the best of it rather than give up. People who give up leave fewer offspring, on average.

indirectly with the use of various drugs and, more indirectly still, through, er, stimulation of the parts of the anatomy that are hooked up to the pleasure centers, often with help from audiovisual inputs, especially, these days, I hear tell, from the Internet.

Indeed, there are various ways in which some modules indirectly affect the pleasure generated by other modules, including through keeping them ignorant. Anyone who has studiously avoided finding out the result of a football game until she could get home to watch her recording of it knows what I'm talking about.

But our minds don't seem to be designed so that one module can simply and directly activate the modules that make us experience pleasure. I like Marvin Minsky's view of this. I think he hit the nail right on the head with this brief but profound insight: "If we could deliberately seize control of our pleasure systems, we could reproduce the pleasure of success without the need for any actual accomplishment. And that would be the end of everything."[22]

It's not clear it would be the end of *everything*, but the point is well taken. Science fiction author Larry Niven sort of had the same idea, only he explored the issue of what would happen if we could seize control of *someone else's* pleasure system. In his novels in the "Known Space" series, some characters carry around a "tasp," a weapon that does just what Minsky was afraid of—it activates another person's pleasure center, rendering him momentarily helpless in the intensity of the experience.

It's crucial to note that explanations that refer to motives "protecting the self" or "building one's self-esteem" *completely miss this point*. It makes no sense to design a mind that has some modules whose job it is to try to make some *other set of modules* feel good. Because selection can't see these experiences, *at the very best* such modules are useless. At worst, they are actually undermining the function of the modules they're making "feel good" for no objective reason.

In short, and I can't emphasize this strongly enough, a fundamental issue that any theory of psychology ultimately has to face is that brains are *useful*. They guide behavior. Any brain that didn't cause its owner to do useful—in the evolutionary sense—things, didn't cause reproduction. The notion that we systematically adopt false beliefs to "protect the self" is illogical when you consider that whatever the mind is designed to do, it must be to get things done, not to make us happy.

Imagine a brain that, when faced with a bear, instead of feeling all those unpleasant things like fear and terror, bathes itself in contentment. *A bear . . . I think I will experience "flow," and be in the moment, me and this bear . . . I am one with the bear . . . ahhhh . . . AAAHHH! . . .* This is not un-like the solution offered by Douglas Adams's blackout sunglasses, which we encountered earlier. Such a brain, one that is content and at peace when a bear is attacking, is the kind of brain that those of us in the business like to refer to as "bear food."

The bear food brain is no more plausible than the brain that arrives at various facts—like Fred's belief that he's not going to die of cancer—be-cause doing so is "protective" or "feels good." *Mechanisms whose function it is to make someone feel good per se have no real function at all as far as evolution is concerned*, since the feeling itself is invisible to selection.

I want to be clear that I'm *not* saying that as a by-product of *other* rea-sons for being wrong—which I've now discussed at length—one might not, as a side effect, feel better. That is, if a module is designed to be strategically wrong, and the strategically wrong belief happens to be something that makes some module or other generate positive feelings, well, fine.

And none of this is to deny that people care a great deal about self-esteem. Having low self-esteem really does feel bad, and high self-esteem is, I'm told, a nice feeling indeed. So what is self-esteem, if not something for which people strive?

Mark Leary and Deborah Downs[23] had, I think, the right idea. They de-veloped what they call "sociometer theory." They liken self-esteem to a mea-surement tool, like a fuel gauge. When your gas tank is empty, they reason, you don't want to solve that problem by taking your finger, sticking it in the gas gauge, and moving the meter from empty to full.* Just manipulating the gauge wouldn't do much. Rather, you want to, you know, *fill the tank*. This will have the effect of moving the gauge because it measures how full the tank is.

---

*For those of you too young to remember a time before digital readouts, gas gauges used to be physical needles that pointed to a dial. Quaint, yes.

Self-esteem, they argue, is like a gauge. It's measuring how well you're doing, socially. Do people like you? Do they value you? Are you included in different social groups? Are they ones you want to belong to? Do you have a lot of Facebook friends? Do they comment on your status message? Leary and Downs argue that self-esteem is a measurement tool that is keeping track of the state of your various interpersonal relationships. When you're not valued, the meter is low, and you feel bad. When you are valued, the meter is high, and you feel good.

On this view, the reason it looks like people are trying to raise their self-esteem is that they're really trying to do something else (having to do with the world outside rather than inside one's head)—in particular, to become more valuable to others—which, if successful, will have that effect. Recent refinements of this idea, which resonate closely with the idea of modularity, suggest that instead of just one gauge, there are many, monitoring how one is doing in various domains of social life.[24] (Another consequence of this view is that artificially raising people's self-esteem is probably not going to be particularly useful. Putting the gauge on "Full" isn't going to make the engine work.)

So, while being wrong can be *helpful* for solving adaptive problems, particularly social ones, because of the effect of these (wrong) beliefs on others, believing things that aren't true *just to feel better* makes no evolutionary sense, as the bear example illustrates. But the same is true for cases less extreme than avoiding bears. The person who is more and more wrong, leading to more and more bad decisions, but feels better and better, is *always going to lose* the evolutionary race to the person feeling worse and worse but making good decisions.

When trying to explain how brains work, instead of focusing on how people feel, it's important to focus on functional consequences, since it's consequences that matter for evolution. And, very generally, being wrong—holding aside, again, all the arguments I've made here—leads to bad consequences. Arguments that suggest that people are motivated to believe things that aren't true about themselves have a particularly vexing hurdle to overcome: One has to explain how the incorrect belief offsets the cost of being wrong.

Not only that, but if you back up a bit further, it's easy to see that the argument itself is sort of odd. Why postulate that people are willing to believe false things in order to feel good about themselves, rather than suggest that people will believe true things about themselves, but just not feel bad about it? *No one likes me. Hooray! I don't need to mail out a ton of holiday cards!* Why not feel good that way instead of taking the tortured route of more complex beliefs: *Everyone really likes me . . . yeah, that's it. . . . It's just that they're just too busy to call, so . . . so, yeah, I'll feel good about myself. . . .*

In some ways, it's sort of easy to say people believe false things because they want to feel good about themselves. It's a powerful intuition, and certainly psychologists have been selling this general idea for a long time. But good intuitions aren't good psychology. As a theory, such motivational ideas are suspect when they're held up to scrutiny with an eye to function. What good, evolutionarily, would being wrong in order to feel good, be? As a matter of the evidence, as we've seen, the data on self-esteem aren't looking so good.

If it turns out that you can't explain much with a quest for self-esteem, then it's time to move on and try new ideas.

Lie to me . . .

So what *is* going on with Fred?

Fundamentally, all the bewilderment surrounding self-deception stems from the same basic mistake. In all these cases, instead of thinking about parts of the *mind*, which is after all the only thing that can have beliefs, people have talked about *the person* having this belief, that belief, or both beliefs. It's as though everyone keeps forgetting that whatever the person, as a whole, does, it's the brain that's doing the actual work. As soon as you wonder how "the person" can have two contradictory beliefs—or motives—you're already in trouble.

I find all the confusion about this a little perplexing. People don't worry excessively about this when they talk about *other* information-processing devices, like computers. Browse computer forums, and you'll find posts like this one (which I created by merging several different posts into one):

I hooked up my new external hard drive and my computer and it went through the installation process. But now the drive doesn't show under My Computer.

Does the computer "believe" the hard drive is there? It seems to know it's there, having gone through the installation process, but at the same time it seems to deny that it knows it's there, not acknowledging it under the all-important "My Computer." Should we worry?

I can't help imagining what philosophers and psychologists might make of this. Is this a paradox because the computer both believes and doesn't believe that the hard drive is there? Maybe the computer is *motivated* not to acknowledge the hard drive. Maybe acknowledging the hard drive would, in some way, threaten the computer's self-esteem. (*Only 40 gigs? Such a storage device is beneath me!*)

Psychologists and philosophers keep writing as though they want you to take seriously the idea that it makes sense to say things like "John was motivated to convince himself that his wife wasn't cheating on him." When you consider that whatever is doing the convincing and whatever is being convinced must both be John's brain or some part of it—what else could they be? —then you can see that we're being asked to say that John's brain was motivated to convince his brain that his wife wasn't cheating on him. It's enough to give me—all of me—a headache. I mean, if it's the same thing doing the convincing and being convinced, why not just *be* convinced and be done with it?

Psychologists and philosophers will usually respond to this question with something about "consciousness" or "awareness." They'll say they mean that some *unconscious* part of the brain is doing something to the *conscious* part, and I think that's fine, just as long as we talk clearly about bits of the brain doing things to other bits of the brain. I think of this as a kind of Buzzy explanation—various bits of the brain are feeding Buzzy only particular kinds of information, often to "protect" Buzzy's self-esteem or what have you. And even *that's* all fine, as long as you think of Buzzy as just another set of parts of the brain, rather than the little guy watching TV in Dennett's Cartesian theater.

Recall the philosophical worry about how two contradictory beliefs "can be 'separated' in a way that keeps them from 'clashing' when P comes to mind."[25] Notice here that beliefs "come to mind," a notion that makes a lot of sense if there's a central Buzzy, doing the "thinking." But this worry evaporates if we think of the brain as having a bunch of systems, all doing various things at the same time. They're *all* "thinking," in the sense of processing information. Some of them are conscious, some not, but there's no reason to worry overmuch that the "thoughts" might conflict. They can just do what they're going to do in their own modules. The notion of "clashing" only makes sense if beliefs more or less come together by default. It could be—and I think it is, as illustrated by the discussion of Vehicles—just the opposite, such that connections among various systems need to be built.

So, my view of what's going on with Fred, which is probably clear by now, is that a strategically wrong belief is in his public relations modules and a contradictory belief is in modules that guide his behavior. The public relations system is putting out propaganda that he'll get better—just as it is designed to do—to persuade others that he's still a good investment. These systems even caused him to put down $50 for a cruise he was unlikely to be able to enjoy: a small price to pay for fighting a propaganda war. That's not to say people would have completely abandoned Fred if they thought his death was imminent, like the fabled Eskimos left on ice floes. But in a highly competitive world, people can be expected to spend their limited resources on people who will be around to give something back, one way or another; Fred's PR system is designed to make some marginal difference.

Other modules are, just as one might think, designed to do the best job they can distilling truth in the service of making good decisions—and ignoring information in the public relations system. For example, some modules might well be designed to follow advice of people who have good information. Like doctors, in this case. To reconcile word and deed, I've argued that the public relations modules are designed to explain behavior in the most plausible, positive light. Such a system might well reconcile saying "I'm going to recover without treatment" with getting treatment by generating a plausible reason to get treatment, like doing it for the good of someone else. But there's nothing *forcing* some or all of these beliefs to be reconciled.[26]

So, did Fred "believe" he was going to die from cancer? The question is like "Did you stop beating your wife?"—it presumes something contrary to fact, that it's sensible to talk about what Fred—*all* of Fred—believed. Fred, as a whole, didn't believe anything, because brains aren't built like that, and there is nothing at all particularly worrisome about explaining the sad story about Fred in this way. Fred's conflicting representations are no more mysterious than the simple Müller-Lyer illusion or any other similar case. As long as one isn't wedded to answering the question of whether Fred "really and truly believed" he was going to die of cancer—a question with no answer—then there's nothing all that puzzling or mysterious about Fred's behavior.

Having contradictory beliefs seems like an intuitively odd thing, but modularity finesses the issue. In the case of the optical illusion, often one system, the visual system, is designed to work in a particular way according to a particular logic, taking information from the visual world and building a representation, as well as it can, of what is out there. Another system involved—and there are likely many—is designed to acquire information from others. Being told the lines in the illusion are equally long is driven by a different kind of logic from that of the visual system.*

As a general rule—though it need not always be true—a representation that is not the best estimate of what is true is more often going to be associated with the press secretary system, the one that has a persuasive function.[27] There might be other systems designed for functions other than persuasion which maintain representations that more closely track what is most likely to be true because for many purposes, being right is functional.

The conclusion from all of this is that "self-deception" *doesn't need some special explanation*. It just happens because of the way that the mind is organized, with many different compartments, strategically wrong representations in one place, more accurate representations in another.[28]

Finally, what of the conscious/unconscious distinction? Consciousness seems, in some way, to be associated with the social world, and with information that "leaks" to others. Having "conscious" representations of things that are beneficial for others to believe is consistent with the press secre-

---

*This is a case in which the answer to the question in *Duck Soup*, "Who you gonna believe, me or your own eyes?", turns out not to be your own eyes.

tary function for consciousness. This might help explain why it seems to be the "strategically wrong" beliefs that are the ones that are accessible to consciousness.

I'm not, of course, saying that this is *the* function of consciousness. What I am saying is that it might be possible to identify the functions of the systems in the brain that have consciousness associated with them in the same way that we've been able to identify a lot of the functions of systems in the brain that don't (happen to) have consciousness associated with them.

So, to the extent conscious systems are designed for public relations, it's not that surprising that a lot of the strategically wrong representations live in these systems, and, in contrast, "true" information, which might be damaging if others believed it, is kept out of the press secretary system.

Modularity allows the press secretary of the mind to be ill informed, another example of the potential advantage of strategic ignorance.

chapter 8

Self-Control

■ *Self-control is discussed in a way that mirrors the discussion of self-deception: what's controlling what? This leads to a discussion of "preferences." It turns out people might not have "real" preferences in the same way people don't have "real" beliefs. The chapter ends with a discussion of a key notion in biology, economics, and psychology, "self-interest."* ■

In the first chapter I mentioned that economist Steve Landsburg thought that there were two great Mysteries of the Universe: why there is anything at all (rather than nothing at all),[1] and why people lock their refrigerator doors at night. This chapter solves the second Mystery, using ideas surrounding modularity.*

To review, first, recall why Landsburg thinks that locking refrigerator doors is such a mystery. His and many others' view of how people make decisions is basically what I've called the Magic 8-Ball model, seeing the mind as distinctly non-modular, and it starts with the deceptively innocent assumption that people have preferences.[2] For example, I might say that I like desserts, skiing, and my sweetie. Those are my preferences, though not necessarily in that order.†

These preferences are ordered—I like some things more than others. If you give me the choice between chocolate cake and apple pie, I'll take the cake, as it were.

---

* I leave it to Landsburg to solve the first. I'm doing one, so he ought to do the other. Fair's fair.
† *Definitely* not in that order, sweetie.

Crucially, *if* we assume that I have ordered preferences, *then* when I make a decision or a choice, not only are my decisions easy—I pick the option I prefer—but predicting my behavior will be straightforward as well. Suppose it's 8:00 P.M., and I have just finished eating dinner. I know that I am going to wake up at midnight, and, when I do, that I am going to have to answer the following vexing question: Should I eat the leftover chocolate cake when I find it staring back at me invitingly in the refrigerator, or should I forgo the chocolate cake and go back to bed? So, at 8:00 P.M., to answer this question about what I should do at midnight, I shake up my own personal Magic 8-Ball, which takes into account how much I like cake, how much I like maintaining my present weight, and—voila!—it tells me whether or not I would be better off—in terms of satisfying my preferences—if I ate the cake at midnight and was a little fatter, or didn't, and stayed a little thinner.[3]

It's important to note that on this view of how the mind works, it absolutely doesn't matter when I shake the 8-Ball, or what room I'm in, or even if I'm hungry or not when I do the shaking, because only my *preferences* matter. If it turns out that eating the cake at midnight will bring me less pleasure overall than keeping to my diet, then the answer about whether or not to eat the cake is always—must always be—the same. If I like the bit of health I get from having forgone eating the cake more than the pleasure I get from eating it, then I just shouldn't eat cake at midnight, and that should be my view whether it's right after dinner and I'm full and watching the *Simpsons*, or midnight and it's been hours since my last meal and I'm really hungry.*

That's why it's puzzling (to economists and some psychologists) that people lock the refrigerator door. If I don't want to eat the cake (future tense) at midnight *given* all of my preferences, my Magic 8-Ball/brain will come up with this answer both at 8 P.M. and at midnight. At 8 P.M. I *know* that my 8-Ball/brain will come up with the same answer at midnight, so why would there be any need to lock the refrigerator? This is the case whether the 8-Ball is going to say yes or no. If it's "no," then it'll tell me to leave the cake alone when I wake up, so no need to lock the door. If it's "yes," then it'll tell me to feel free to eat the cake at midnight, so it's actually a bad idea to lock the door.

---

*It doesn't matter if I do or don't like cake more when I'm hungry. If I do, this difference can be taken into account at 8, knowing that I'll enjoy the cake more at midnight than I would if I ate it now.

I cannot emphasize enough how far this view is from the one I'm advancing here. The Magic 8-Ball view—that all the information gets integrated to come up with an answer—is the very opposite of the modular view. It says there's just a whole bunch of information getting all mashed together rather than a lot of different little modules in there, with their own little pieces of information, beliefs, and functions.

For those of you who are skeptical and think that I'm playing fast and loose with what economists believe in order to make my view seem different from theirs,* recall that *Landsburg*, not I, pointed to locking the refrigerator door as a Mystery of the Universe. He must have *some* model of the way people make decisions that makes this so über-mysterious. Just to make this point crystal clear: Some of the foremost thinkers in this research area, including Richard Thaler and Nobel laureate Danny Kahneman, put it as starkly as one might want, saying that economics generally holds that "most (all?) behavior can be explained by assuming that agents have stable, well-defined preferences and make rational choices consistent with those preferences."[†4]

This general idea, by the way, would be really, really nice if it were true. Huge portions of the scientific literature, especially economics, are based on the seemingly simple notion that people have preferences, and that they have some order—cake is less important to me than the associated small loss of health.

Theories using this idea don't bother engaging with the issue of how the brain integrates all the preferences living inside it and instead assume that the mind figures out what to do given all of my preferences. (This is often referred to with reference to the idea that people are "rational," as in the quotation above.) If this were true, then predicting human behavior would be easy—well, easier than it is, anyway—because if you knew people's preferences, you could use those to figure out what they were going to do. Nice.

---

*Heh. See chapter 6. . . .

†As an aside, even the Magic 8-Ball metaphor isn't quite as silly as it seems. Amos Tversky and Richard Thaler used a similar metaphor—book rather than a ball—suggesting that "the standard economic formulation of choice . . . assumes that, in the presence of complete information, people act as if they could look up their preferences in a book, and respond to situations accordingly . . ." (p. 209).

I don't think, unfortunately, that this is even remotely true. The fact that people do lock their refrigerator doors at night is a clue that it's wrong, but the problems are much deeper. Let's see why.

So, which do you prefer, coffee or red wine? Assuming you're not a tea drinker or a teetotaler, you probably like both to some extent, but you might find it hard to choose. Economists, thankfully, have a solution to this problem. We don't need you to introspect to figure out what your preferences are. We can simply give you the choice, observe what you do, and take that to be your "revealed preference."[5] So, which one would you choose if presented with a nice glass of red wine and a steaming hot cup of coffee?

If you're like me, it probably depends. Is it 8 A.M. or 8 P.M.? In the morning I like coffee but not wine, and at night I like wine but not coffee. Like so many people, when it comes to the last bastion of legal drugs, I like my uppers in the morning and my downers at night. So it might seem that I don't prefer coffee to wine, or wine to coffee. Or, perhaps, maybe I prefer coffee to wine *and* I prefer wine to coffee. This seems like a problem.

Well, you say, maybe I've just stated preferences wrong. Maybe my preference is "coffee in the morning" and "wine at night." All I need to do is add a time component, and we're safe saying that I have preferences. Let's rely on the saving power of subscripts. Rob_{pm} likes wine more than coffee, but Rob_{am} likes coffee more than wine.[6] Or maybe we can add subscripts to the things I'm choosing. Rob likes $wine_{pm}$ more than $coffee_{pm}$ but $coffee_{am}$ more than $wine_{am}$.

Maybe.

But maybe not. Thinking of Rob_{pm} and Rob_{am} as having preferences already gets away from the assumption that *people* have preferences in favor of the view that *people at different times of the day* have preferences.[7] And it seems funny to talk about identical items being different from one another depending on the time of day. But even if that doesn't bother you, moves like this one, subscripting people or the things they can choose, won't work to the extent that it's difficult or impossible to find subscripts that can make sense out of people's preferences.

Toshio Yamagishi and colleagues have done some nice work that speaks in interesting ways to this issue.[8] Do people like green pens or orange pens better? Simple question. Yamagishi had subjects, both American and Japanese, choose one pen from among a group of green and orange ones. We can just look at their choices to infer their preferences, right? When subjects were choosing among four green pens and one orange one, they chose a green one. Aha. People like green pens more than orange ones.

Except that when subjects were choosing among four orange pens and one green one, they chose an orange one. People prefer orange to green pens.

OK. Those can't both be right. The preference for pens is something like: People prefer pens that are part of, let's call it, "the local pen color majority." That's a little weird, but it's something like a preference. Just a little abstract.

Except that's not right either. People select the majority color if they are choosing a pen before other people are going to choose pens. But if they are the *last* of a group of people to choose pens, now, on average, people choose the *minority* color pen.[9]

In pen choice and so much else, context matters. Trying to character-ize pen preferences, given all of the factors that influence the preference beyond the pens themselves, is potentially difficult.

That is not breaking news. Of course context matters.[10] This idea doesn't necessarily tell you a lot more than, perhaps, that trying to figure out people's preferences is going to be difficult. If preferences depend on the context, maybe we can specify people's context-dependent preferences. This is no small thing, since it means that every time we find that some vari-able influences preferences, we have to redefine what people's preferences are. These factors now become ever more numerous subscripts, one for each contextual variable that is found to matter.

Not only that, but the approach of using "revealed preferences" now has a problem. If I find you like this pen over that one, I can no longer say you have a preference over that set of choices. All I can say is that you have such a preference *in the context in which you did the choosing*. And it's even worse than *that*. What, exactly, *is* "the context"? Without a theory about which particular aspects of the choice matter, I can't even say what your context-specific preference is because I can't define the context.[11] As Yamagishi and others have shown, the context can be any number of non-obvious factors, like the presence of a certain number of other pens. And with each contextual variable that matters, surely we're asking a great deal of our "preference books," specifying what is preferred to what across all contextual variables that surround a given choice.

If we take this seriously, then even very mild notions of what it means to have a preference might be in trouble. If we say that John likes orange pens when they're in the minority when no one else will choose a pen after him on a Tuesday afternoon in 2006 when it's nice outside . . . , this preference won't be able to predict anything about John's behavior *even if we assume John has stable preferences*. This is because the next time John makes a decision, the context—whatever the relevant variables might be, which we might or might not know—is different. The more we specify the context of John's choices, the less we can generalize them. And the less we specify the context of John's preferences, the more likely we are to miss something about how John decides.[12]

I hastily add that all this doesn't by itself mean that making the assumption, whether it is right or not, that people have stable preferences won't ever be useful. I think for certain purposes it is. As a psychologist, however, I want to know how decisions are made, and this analysis suggests that construing people as having a book of preferences might not be correct.

At a bare minimum, these findings illustrate that it really is important to take lots of context into account, even counterintuitive parts of it. Suppose someone prefers apples to blueberries, and also prefers both apples and blueberries to cherries. Clearly if we now offer such a person a choice between apples and blueberries, or a choice among apples, blueberries, and cherries, the presence of cherries as one of the options shouldn't affect the person's choice of apples, the most favored of the three options.

There's a "joke" about this that, starring the late philosopher Sidney Morgenbesser, goes like this:

> After finishing dinner, Sidney Morgenbesser decides to order dessert. The waitress tells him he has two choices: apple pie and blueberry pie. Sidney orders the apple pie. After a few minutes the waitress returns and says that they also have cherry pie at which point Morgenbesser says "In that case I'll have the blueberry pie."[13]

In one experiment investigating this issue, some people were given the option to select between $6 and a fancy pen. About a third of the subjects in this study chose the pen over the money. A different group of people were allowed to select between the $6, the pen, and an obviously inferior pen.

Adding the inferior pen to the choice set increased the number of people choosing the fancy pen to nearly 50%.[14]

But even if *that* weren't a problem, specifying preferences is *even worse than that*. What are we to make of the notion that preferences are meaningful if it turns out that people prefer A to B but also prefer B to A?

Research in this area, including so-called "preference reversals," has investigated pairs of gambles.[15] We can measure preferences over different options by asking how much people would pay for these options.[16] Consider the following two gambles. How much would you pay for each one?

H: 8 out of 9 chance of winning $4.
L: 1 out of 9 chance of winning $40.

Most subjects put a higher price on the second gamble than the first. (This makes sense to an economist, since, given the odds and the payoff, the expected value of L is greater than that of H.)

We can also measure preferences by simply giving people a choice between them. Give people the choice between L and H, and they choose . . . H. People will pay more for L than H, but prefer H to L in a direct comparison.

Which option, then, do people prefer? It seems that there is no answer to this question. If the preference depends on how one measures it, then it's awkward to say that there's a "real" preference.

Probably the best known effect of this general type is the so-called "Asian disease" problem. Suppose you learn that there is going to be a disease which will kill 600 people if nothing is done. You have to choose between two programs to fight the disease. The first one will result in exactly 200 of those people being saved for sure, and the second one will result in a one in three chance of everyone being saved and a two in three chance of no one being saved. Most people prefer the first one.

Now choose between a program in which exactly 400 people will die for sure and a second program in which there's a one in three chance that nobody will die and a two in three chance that 600 will die. Most people choose the second of those two.

The trick is, of course, that these two sets of choices are identical. People's choice of program depends on whether it's phrased in terms of how many will be saved or how many will die.

The fact that "preferences" depend on the way that the choice is put is also seen in how people choose between present versus future rewards. Suppose you had a choice of the following:

L: $2,500 five years from now.
S: $1,600 one and a half years from now.

As before, we let people make the choice by either (a) selecting one or the other or (b) indicating the smallest amount of money they would take, right now, in exchange for the option. Asked to choose between the two options, people choose S. But when asked to price the two options, they give a higher value for L than for S.[17]

There are many similar examples, and entire books have been written about the many fun ways in which people deviate from economists' expectations that people are perfectly rational in their decision making.[18] I never cease to be surprised that people are surprised by this, but maybe that's because I'm less rational than most. In any case, my concern here isn't the fact that people don't do what economists expect them to do. My concern is with explaining inconsistencies using the tools of modularity.

If context changes preferences, and even the means of measuring itself changes preferences, then there seems to be no sense in which people "really" have preferences, in much the same way that there frequently is no sense in which people "really" have beliefs. As Tversky and Thaler put it, "the context and procedures involved in making choices or judgments influence the preferences that are implied by the elicited responses."[19]

Context matters. A lot.

Modularity informs how and why context matters

Why? That is, why do our minds work like this? Wouldn't it be better to construct a brain that wasn't subject to context effects and framing effects? Wouldn't a Magic 8-Ball–type brain be a better one, integrating all one's preferences and goals, holding aside the context it found itself in and the state it happens to be in? Maybe. I'm not sure it would be, but I think the evidence strongly suggests that, whether or not brains would work "better" that way, they don't.

Modularity informs how context matters. Understanding the design of modules, and the features of the environment—internal and external—that they respond to can help explain patterns of choice. Here's how the modular view goes.

Some modules are designed to get you to satisfy immediate needs. These are important modules. Some of the needs I have in mind are things associated with the basic necessities of survival and reproduction. In biology, you might hear these referred to as the "four F's": feeding, fleeing, fighting, and having sex. Organisms that didn't have mechanisms that caused them to do the things that enabled survival and reproduction didn't leave offspring.

These modules cause you to do things that often get put under the heading of "instantaneous gratification." They're the ones in charge when you eat sweet and fatty foods, stay warm in bed (conserving calories), and have sex with your cute co-worker whom you'll see nearly every day for the foreseeable future which will be really awkward since you don't actually want to have a substantial relationship and after you've had sex everything is different . . . you get the idea.

An easy way to think about these modules is that they're the modules, by and large, that make you do things that would make a lot of sense if the world were going to end tomorrow. It's like the Dennis Miller bit about the guy on an airplane that's about to crash. The flight attendant is going around taking orders for final beverages: "I'll have a Diet Coke . . . heck, make that a *regular* Coke."*

For convenience, I'm going to talk about these modules as being *impatient*. They are, roughly, designed for *consumption* rather than *savings*. Again, these modules drive behavior toward the basic elements of survival and reproduction—high-calorie foods, sexual activity, and other stimuli for which the human reward system evolved.

---

*Even with all the power of the Internet age, I wasn't able to track down the source of this. If the line wasn't Dennis Miller's, I apologize to whoever did say it. If the line *is* Dennis Miller's, then, Dennis, I have to say that this joke seems to have been buried deeper than a trilobite from the Early Cambrian period.

Quantitatively, these modules have what is known as a high "discount rate." A discount rate indicates how much more you value a reward sooner, as opposed to later. A small, or shallow discount rate means that I don't mind waiting for my reward very much. A high discount rate means that I like to consume stuff now, that I'm impatient. My colleague Joe Kable at Penn likes to use the example of putting off drinking a wine that's going to improve with age. How much better would the wine have to get in a year's time for me to forgo drinking it tonight? The answer to that question gives you my discount rate with respect to that issue.

Different modules, I claim, can be thought of as having different discount rates. Some systems are designed to cause us to consume things now. Others, the more patient modules, cause us to forgo consumption now to reap the rewards of patience later.[20]

Many modules are impatient because being impatient makes sense in a competitive world. Putting off eating means that I might not get the benefits of the calories in question if I die, if someone else gets them first, and so on. Any forgone benefit now might be lost forever. These modules tend to exert more control over behavior when the world is presenting high-value fitness opportunities—big calorie packages, very appealing mating possibilities, risky but high-return gambles, and so on.

But, to return to Dennis Miller, the world isn't going to end tomorrow. Humans have other modules that are more farsighted. These are the modules that cause you to forgo the regular Coke because the sweet taste now is not worth the extra calories you'll have to contend with later. They cause you to get out of bed in the morning to get your run in, sacrificing snoozing now for feeling better and healthier later. And they cause you to politely decline your co-worker's blatant sexual advances, forgoing tonight's pleasures for many workdays' worth of non-awkward small talk.

Many people think that this capacity—inhibiting immediate reward in favor of deferred benefits—is something that is special about humans, and have made a great deal out of the brain structures that seem to play a role in this sort of thing. In keeping with my tradition, I'm going to ignore all of that very interesting work and just add a couple of references in the endnotes.[21]

I will mention one interesting finding comparing humans to nonhumans. In one study, cotton-top tamarins were presented with the option of two food pellets now, or six food pellets later. The experimenters changed how much "later" the six food pellets would come, and in this way measured how patient these monkeys' decisions were. That is, how long could they hold out to triple their food reward? Before I tell you, suppose I ask you if you want $100 now or $300 at some time in the future; how long could you wait for the $300? People who put $100 in a savings account are basically saying that they'll wait *years* for their $300. Tamarins could wait about 8 seconds. (Marmosets managed a more impressive 14 to 15 seconds.)[*22]

The long and the short of it

Life often seems to consist of short-sighted modules battling it out with long-sighted modules.

These conflicts are common. Here's how you can tell you're doing something that your short-term modules prefer. Fill in the following sentence in a way that makes it true. *I really like to* _____ *but afterwards I wish I hadn't.* In contrast, you can tell that you're doing something that your long-term modules prefer if the sentence goes like this: *I don't like to* _____, *but afterwards I'm glad I did.*

The first sentence can be filled in with things like "eat a pint of ice cream," "get drunk," and "gamble." The second sentence can be things like "get up at 6 A.M. to work out," "do my homework," and "wear a condom." The first sentence verbs relate to your impatient modules. The second sentence verbs relate to your patient modules.

Why are different modular systems designed to operate at cross-purposes?

Well, it should be clear that being impatient all the time is a bad idea. Eating everything that tastes good, taking advantage of every sexual opportunity, and splurging on satisfying one's senses is costly in the long run. As members of a long-lived species, we put ourselves at a disadvantage to the extent that we do not reap the gains of patience, keeping ourselves healthy,

---

[*]Having said that, in some experiments, George Ainslie reminds us, humans' decisions imply that they are not satisfied with even an annual 5 billion per cent interest rate, so it won't do to feel too haughty.

investing in ourselves by doing unpleasant things like learning and practicing useful skills, and so on.

Being patient all the time isn't a good idea either. Ultimately, modules designed to inhibit reaping rewards that gathered immediate fitness gains can't *always* get their way. There's no sense investing if you're not going to cash in on opportunities eventually.

So, the brain, with all of its patient and impatient modules, somehow has to make many trade-offs. The impatient module that "likes cake" (i.e., is designed to motivate the consumption of dense calorie packages) is driving behavior toward consumption, while the patient module that "likes being fit" (i.e., is designed to inhibit behaviors with long-run costs) is driving behavior away from it. These somehow must be reconciled.[23]

Reconciling these inter-module fights is no doubt a complicated business. Having modules in the same head that perform such different functions—really, nearly opposite functions—requires ways to arbitrate that might be complex. How is it done?

First, a good design for working out these tensions requires taking many variables into account. Whether or not one should consume a dense calorie package—e.g., a piece of cake—depends on calculations about the details. When there are "good" opportunities—dense calorie packages, easily available, with little need for processing, such as a fresh brownie just sitting there on my desk with no one around to see my gluttony*— the impatient modules have a better chance of winning the conflict with the patient modules because they are designed to respond to and take advantage of such high benefit/low cost opportunities. For this reason, we should expect that preferences are going to be *context-sensitive*. The details of the immediate opportunities should matter.

Second, a good design should also respect the current state of the organism. If I'm way low on calories, then it's not a bad idea for the impatient calorie-acquisition modules to have more weight in decision making. The long-term benefits of forgoing food matter much less as my system gets lower and lower on resources. For this reason, we should expect that prefer-

---

*By "good" here I mean evolutionarily speaking. The issue is what stimuli these evolved impatient modules are designed to prefer.

ences are going to be *state-dependent*. This has very close parallels in the nonhuman animal literature—when organisms are near death, they tend to take greater risks in foraging.[24] It makes sense to discount the future when there might not be much more of a future left.

Third, a good design should respond to reward/effort ratios. Given that time and attention are limited resources, to the extent my patient modules are guiding me toward behavior that, as it turns out, isn't, in fact, leading to anything useful, I ought to give up whatever it is I'm doing. This is in some sense how nonhuman animals solve the problem of optimal foraging: When do I stop exploiting one particular food patch and go off in search of another one? I monitor the return I'm getting from it, and move on when it's too low.[25] For this reason, we might expect that preferences will be *history-dependent*.

When push comes to shove, some behavior must, of course, be chosen. The way this seems to be implemented in the brain is that different modules gain and lose influence on behavior depending on the context, one's current state, and the recent history, an idea that should remind you of Braitenberg's Vehicles. There, too, there were conflicts among the sensor-motor pairings. Vehicles had mechanisms that caused movement toward (or away from) various things in the environment. In the same way, the argument here is that cues in the environment activate certain on-board systems. Other modules might inhibit these systems, but the idea is that seeing cake gives the cake-liking system an advantage.

A multi-module, Vehicles-like account finesses the seemingly insurmountable problem of keeping a list of preferences in a book or magic ball. Instead of listing all possible things in some order of preference, with all the seemingly limitless number of subscripts, decisions can be made on the fly.[26] Because different modules will be more or less active depending on the context, one's state, and one's history, these decisions might well not be mutually consistent. They'll obey the logic of the design of the modules in question, not necessarily economic axioms.

To return to our cake example, here's how this works. At 8pm, I'm full from dinner and I'm watching the *Simpsons*. The context is not one that will activate my impatient food-consumption modules, and my state isn't either—because I'm satiated, that module is deactivated. In contrast, nothing is inhibiting the modules that like to be healthy. The balance of power in the food domain now strongly favors the patient modules.

Further, because some modules are quite good at building representations of the future—i.e., planning—they know that at midnight the battle will be tilted in the other direction, and patient modules are also the ones that can plan. (This might explain why the impatient modules don't undermine the patient ones, but the reverse is true.) Being hungry and faced with a tempting sweet will give the impatient modules the edge. So, the module with the shallow discount rate can implement *its* preference by making cake-eating hard or impossible later. The module with the steep discount rate is at a disadvantage because it has to contend with the earlier machinations of the more patient module. Here, then, is the answer to Landsburg's mystery. Long-sighted modules have different preferences from short-sighted modules; and, as they are able to move first and are capable of planning, they can limit the choices of short-sighted modules.

There is, of course, nothing new about this. When Odysseus had his men tie him to the mast, he was recognizing that there are profound context-effects that drive behavior—in this case the Sirens' song—and the planning modules can short-circuit this by changing the rules of the game in the future.

The modern equivalents of Odysseus's strategy take various forms. People who know they find it difficult to resist spending money when they have it put it in hard-to-reach places and use instruments like automatic deposit from their paycheck. People who have difficulty getting up in the morning place their alarm clocks far from their beds so they have to get up in order to shut them off.

Inevitably, there is even a web site that helps people give their far-sighted modules an advantage over their impatient ones. stickK.com, founded by economist Dean Karlan, allows you to make a contract with yourself (or the future you, in some sense). You specify some goal (run a marathon, quit smoking, etc.) and choose some amount of money that you will forfeit if you don't obtain it. If you don't reach your goal (you're on the honor system, pretty much), stickK hands the money over to whomever you designated in the case of failure. To give yourself a strong incentive, you can name as recipient an organization that supports a cause you really don't like—such as the NRA if you're a gun control advocate—to give your long-term modules an extra edge.

Which is not to say that your patient modules always have an advantage because they're the ones that seem to plan for the future. These modules are probably the ones that cause people to buy the large quantities of exercise equipment that gather dust in the corners of rec rooms.

Hot or not

Instead of thinking about some modules being designed to be more or less patient, some people consider "self-control" to reflect two modes of thought. One type is "cold"—deliberative, rational, controlled—while the other is "hot"—emotional, automatic, intuitive. Cold cognition is associated with more recent evolutionary areas of the brain, while hot cognition is associated with evolutionarily more ancient areas.

Along similar lines, some like to think of there being two "selves" who are in control at different moments,[27] sort of a Dr. Jekyll and Mr. Hyde kind of thing. Thaler and Sunstein, in *Nudge*, suggest that it's useful to think "about an individual as containing two semiautonomous selves,"[28] one that is patient and one that is impatient.

While I'm very sympathetic to the idea that one self is not enough, I'm not fond of the notion that *two* is going to be enough either. I don't think it's quite right to say that people have two "modes," patient and impatient, or two selves. I'm *not* saying that at any given moment, one is *either* acting "emotionally" or "impulsively" on the one hand *or* "rationally" or "patiently" on the other. I think it's better to say that one's context and state act as inputs to modules that have different discount rates with respect to different kinds of choices. By understanding what activates or deactivates these modules, we can do a better job predicting behavior. I'm *not* saying that seeing cake will make one impatient, in general, and therefore more likely, say, to favor a risky gamble or drink that bottle of red wine now rather than waiting until next year. I'm saying that *different modules are sensitive to different context cues*, and these influence which modules win and which modules lose in the conflicts that occur all the time.

People themselves seem to have pretty good intuitions about this. The advice about not going to the grocery store when one is hungry is a case in point. When you're hungry, the impatient food modules have more influence, and they are likely to cause you to buy more food, as well as items that more closely fit with our evolved short-term preferences, such as those high in sugar and fat. But note that people don't tell you to avoid the grocery store when you're sexually aroused.

In contrast, at least some people believe that you shouldn't go out on a date when you're aroused. This idea found a place in popular culture in *There's Something About Mary*. Dom, played by Chris Elliott, is counseling Ted, played by Ben Stiller, about the importance of masturbating before going on a date. Dom compares going out on a date without first having masturbated as the equivalent of "going out there with a loaded gun." He similarly opines that after having had sex one is particularly honest because "you're no longer trying to get laid." Dom has a good sense that the impatient modules that like to have sex can interfere with the goals of other, more patient modules.

That was in 1998. Since then, the science has caught up to the media. Dan Ariely recruited a couple dozen male MIT students and had them answer a series of questions about sex, such as "Can you imagine being attracted to a 12-year-old girl?" and "Would you slip a woman a drug to increase the chance that she would have sex with you?" Ariely had his experimental subjects answer the questions under two conditions: a relatively normal one, and when the subject was sexually aroused by looking at erotica and masturbating.

Sexually aroused subjects were more likely to say yes to both the first question (46% vs. 23%) and the second (26% vs. 5%). A large battery of items showed similar results. When sexually aroused, the short-sighted modules designed around sex tend to get the upper hand relative to the long-sighted modules, probably some of which are designed to compute how to avoid punishment for things like rape.[29]

Ariely says that the results show that people "in a cold, rational, superego-driven state"—a not uncommon case of non-psychologists harkening back to the good old days of Freud—"respected women," but: "They were simply unable to predict the degree to which passion would change them."[30] He might be right about this, but it's worth noting that in the studies reported, people weren't asked questions about nonsexual matters. Would people be more likely to have another piece of cake when they're sexually aroused? Or are modules specific, with the impatient sexual modules getting activated in this case, with relatively little effect on the impatient eating modules? My guess is the latter, but we'll need more data to figure it out.

We have a little. If the modular view is right, then knowing the functions of the modules in question should allow you to make very textured predictions about what stimuli will activate the modules, and what the effect on measured preferences will be.

Evolutionary psychologists Martin Daly and Margo Wilson investigated the hypothesis that seeing attractive women would cause men to become economically impatient, preferring money now rather than later. They predicted no such effect for women. To investigate this, they showed one set of men and women pictures of attractive and unattractive opposite-sex people, and another set of pictures of more or less attractive cars. Subjects were then given a task measuring how impatient they were on a money task like the ones described above—did they want $15 now, or $35 later? As predicted, men, but not women, became impatient when they saw the attractive people, but they did not when they saw the cars. No such effect was found for either sex when they saw pictures of attractive cars.

In another recent investigation, Elsa Ermer and her collaborators looked at risky decision making when students thought they were being evaluated by people who were of lower, equal, or higher status. Students at Franklin and Marshall College had to decide between two options, one risky and one safe. They were led to believe that their decisions would be evaluated by people at one of three different institutions of higher learning: Gettysburg College, Swarthmore, or some place called "Princeton," which, apparently, people at Franklin and Marshall consider "high status" despite the fact that it is—and I looked it up just to be sure—undeniably in *New Jersey*.

Ermer predicted that when men (but not women) were being observed by people of similar status—but not higher or lower status—they would choose the risky option. This is what they found, with men choosing a 33% chance of $60 over a sure thing of $20 when they thought they were being evaluated by people at Swarthmore, and only in that case. Interestingly, these same people did not prefer the risky choice when it came to a medical decision. They only were risk-seeking in the case of money.[31] People don't play it safe or take risks *in general*, but they change depending on the context and the content of the decision, illustrating rich texture in decision making.

I prefer not to have preferences

The evidence reviewed here suggests that we shouldn't think of preferences as being things that are recorded in people's heads. Decisions are the result of the operation of different subroutines of the mind being brought to bear on individual decision problems. For this reason, far from being consistent, choices change depending on the way different modules operate. Because modules work differently depending on context, state, and history, changing any of these things might change the decisions we observe.

Importantly, this includes the way problems are worded or framed, either of which can change which modules are activated. That is, "framing effects" are likely due, in part at least, to the fact that superficial differences between problems recruit different modules. What a theory in economics considers to be "the same" might or might not be "the same" in terms of which modules get activated. When economic theory says that two problem contents ought to be the same—because economics looks only at the mathematics—but the modular system treats two problem contents as different—saving lives versus losing lives—this comes out as a "framing effect."

This view raises the same problem with preferences that we saw for beliefs. Is there a sense in which we even *have* preferences? In some sense, there might be. For example, broadly, we prefer having more money to having less. But once decision problems get even a little more complex, because different modules are getting involved with decisions, it's much less clear that we do. As Sarah Lichtenstein and Paul Slovic recently put it: "The variability in the ways we construct and reconstruct our preferences yields preferences that are labile, inconsistent, subject to factors we are unaware of, and not always in our own best interests. Indeed, so pervasive is that lability that the very notion of a 'true' preference must, in many situations, be rejected."[32]

In their review of preference reversals, they come to a conclusion very much like the one I come to. They prefer to use "tools" as a metaphor rather than the information-processing language of modularity, but the idea is the same: "Different tools in our toolbox will require different explanatory theories. . . ."[33] So, because different modules will become more or less active depending on the individual's context, history, and state, the individual might seem very short-sighted in one area but long-sighted in another. It's not all that hard to imagine that, say, people who can't resist brownies—being impatient in the realm of food—nonetheless can save for retirement—patient in the realm of money. Indeed, substantial evidence suggests that patience in one domain is imperfectly related to patience in another. So, just as John—as a whole—doesn't have beliefs, in similar fashion, John—as a whole—shouldn't necessarily be thought of as either patient or impatient. Instead, John's mind consists of modules, each of which is patient to a greater or lesser degree.[34]

Economics has, in some sense, come full circle on this issue. In an excellent review, Shane Frederick and colleagues, including George Loewenstein, pointed out that back in the old days, economists thought that these sorts of decisions were "the joint product of many conflicting psychological motives,"[35] which is not unlike what I'm saying. Then along came Paul Samuelson, who, in 1937, proposed the opposite, that people didn't have lots of motives, but that each person had a single "discount rate"—how impatient, as a whole, he was—which was "the same for all types of goods and all categories of intertemporal decisions."[36] They remark of this model, which is still widely used, that "[v]irtually every assumption underlying [it] has been tested and found to be descriptively invalid in at least some situations."[37] That is, as an empirical matter, it's wrong. So, in line with the view that modules have different "preferences" and exert more or less influence depending on the context, they conclude that "intertemporal choices reflect an interplay of disparate and often competing psychological motives."[38] I couldn't agree more.

Economist David Laibson has argued in similar fashion that consumption is "cue-based"; how much I want to consume something varies with the cues in the environment. As he puts it, "if the sound of ice cubes falling into a tumbler has reliably predicted ingestion of Scotch in the past, then that sound will elevate the current marginal utility of Scotch (i.e., will increase one's desire for a glass of Scotch)." [39] Laibson hangs his account on classical learning theory, drawing on behaviorism—ice cube sounds paired with drinking Scotch is just like bells paired with dog food in Pavlov's famous studies—but the general idea is not unlike the modular view: The strength of preferences depends on important elements of the person's history and context.

Neither Loewenstein nor Laibson begins with the functional, modular approach I've built here, but it's gratifying that different traditions seem to be moving in similar directions—or, at least, *away* from the same place, the unitary ideas of the past.

Indeed, various threads across different fields have been converging on the view that far from preferences being listed in a book in one's head, they are constructed on the fly as one is faced with different decisions.[40] In any case, if choices are the result of the activity of different modules, each of which operates by its own evolved logic, then it's no wonder that people's choices look so inconsistent, even reversing themselves: It's because there's no particular reason that they *would* look consistent. If the context one's in, or the state one's in, turns certain modules on, then the preferences *in those modules* will drive one's performance. In a different context, the very same options will be evaluated by different modules, leading to the possibility of a different choice being made.

So, when you ask what pen I want, you can't think that you're just asking "me" what pen I want. You're asking the modules that are active in the particular context in which you ask me. Add something to the context—such as information about who will decide after me—and as long as that's relevant to some other module, you can't be sure you'll get the same answer. So, the same way that context can affect whether patient or impatient modules are active in some decision, context can affect all kinds of decision making.

There is a kind of tension when people make decisions. The conflict between modules takes place in the here and now, when preferences are constructed as a decision is being faced, and over time, as people organize their lives—with help from refrigerator locks and stickK.com. Patient modules "know" that as the context changes, they will not necessarily be able to inhibit impatient modules. In short, they "believe" that "willpower" is not always enough, the issue we turn to next.

On the importance of ignoring marshmallows

The term "self-control" is odd, and it's odd in a way that's not all that much unlike the way "self-deception" is odd. It's not obvious what is doing the controlling or what is being controlled. When I leave the cake in the refrigerator, is my "self" being "controlled"?[41] If it is, what's doing the controlling? And what is this "self" people are so fond of talking about? Is it Buzzy?

The intuition seems to be that self-control is something like this. Being "out of control" is doing the thing that is rewarding or gratifying in the near term. Being "in control" seems to refer to being patient, doing the thing that carries long-term benefits.

Studying this type of thing—whatever you might want to call it—has a distinguished history, and has recently undergone a bit of a renaissance. History first.

In the sixties, psychologist Walter Mischel developed what is now affectionately known as the marshmallow task. Four-year-old children were presented with a marshmallow. They were told that they could eat the marshmallow if they wished. However, if they waited for fifteen or twenty minutes—details of the method varied a little—without eating the marshmallow, then the experimenter would give them a second marshmallow when he came back. In economic terms, children were being given a choice between consuming now or saving at a very attractive interest rate of 100% over twenty minutes, which means that if children were allowed to "save" over the course of a year, with compounding, this interest rate would produce a marshmallow yield equivalent to more marshmallows than currently exist, ever have existed, and quite likely ever will exist up until the heat death of the universe.

Performance on the marshmallow task, measured by how long the child delayed before eating it, varied substantially. Some children ate the marshmallow right away, others waited the full period. Mischel and his colleagues carried out a large number of follow-up studies asking if a child's ability to resist marshmallows was telling us something important about the child. In particular, does resisting marshmallows when a child is four years old predict how well she will do down the road?

Surprisingly enough, it does. Delays correlated with parents' evaluations of these children when they were adolescents on items such as "responds to reason," "is able to concentrate," and ability to deal with stress. Mischel summarized the results of one published study reporting that "children who were able to wait longer at age 4 or 5 became adolescents whose parents rated them as more academically and socially competent, verbally fluent, rational, attentive, planful,* and able to deal well with frustration and stress."[42] Perhaps most concretely, being able to resist marshmallows predicted how well children performed on the SATs.[43] The skill or ability that allows a child to resist marshmallows is apparently pretty important.

It is possible to help (or hurt) children when they are trying to avoid succumbing to the temptation of eating the marshmallow. If you get children to think about how yummy the marshmallow is going to be, they get even more impatient to eat it. But when they think about the *shape* of the marshmallow, they are able to wait longer.

Hiding the marshmallow from view also helps, doubling the amount of time young children can hold off,[44] a finding that obviously makes a great deal of sense if you think that impatient modules can be activated or inhibited depending on the immediate context. Hiding the marshmallow keeps the modules designed to take advantage of local food opportunities quiet.

From the results of the marshmallow task, we can see that people vary in how much self-control they can exercise; that the ability to exert self-control can be increased or decreased depending on the circumstances; and that the ability to exercise self-control matters, with more, generally speaking, being better than less.

---

*"Planful" was not a word then, and continues to be an unword today.

This is as true for adults as it is for children. Roy Baumeister and his colleagues developed a scale to assess self-control in adults, and found that people with greater self-control as measured by this scale engaged in less binge drinking and eating and also had better relationships and higher GPAs.[45]

Baumeister and colleagues have recently been exploring self-control in some creative ways. In one experiment, subjects who hadn't eaten in at least three hours came into the lab to participate in a "study on taste perception."* Subjects came into a room next to one in which chocolate chip cookies had recently been baked, so "the laboratory was filled with the delicious aroma of fresh chocolate and baking."† A table had cookies, candies, and radishes on it. Some subjects were allowed to eat the cookies, and some poor subjects were told to eat only radishes. Subjects in both conditions were then given a task with problems that were impossible to solve.‡ Four subjects worked on the impossible task for half an hour before the mercy rule kicked in and they were allowed to leave.

The question was this: If one's "willpower" is exhausted by the challenge of not eating the cookies, does one work for less time on the impossible problem? Yes, a lot less. Subjects in this condition worked about eight and a half minutes on the impossible problem, while subjects who ate the cookies worked for nearly 21 minutes, on average.

A similar effect was obtained when subjects were asked to suppress their emotions watching film clips (Robin Williams, or *Terms of Endearment*). Subjects were asked to solve some anagrams (this time, ones that could actually be completed), and those who suppressed their emotions solved an average of about five, while those who could laugh or cry solved seven.

---

*We've moved from economics research back to social psychology, so we're lying to subjects again.

†We've moved from economics research back to social psychology, so instead of the stilted technical language of economics, we're reading about "delicious aromas."

‡No one told to eat only radishes cheated, though some subjects "did exhibit clear interest in the chocolates, to the point of looking longingly at the chocolate display and in a few cases even picking up the cookies to sniff at them." So, half of the subjects in this study were told not to eat anything before the study, brought into a room that smelled like chocolate chip cookies, told to leave the cookies alone and eat radishes, and then asked to complete an unsolvable problem, all the while being lied to about what was really going on.

In this early work, Baumeister and colleagues laid out the reasoning behind the study. They posited that there is some "part of the self" that is used for "overriding responses"—sort of like when Buzzy tells his adrenal gland to quiet down. But Buzzy gets tired when he does this "overriding," working on hard word problems, making important decisions, and otherwise exerting "self-control." Buzzy, just like any little person, has only a limited pool of "mental energy." These tasks deplete his inner resources, and when he just can't go on, the "automatic" systems—the body, rather than the soul, you see—have to take over. This leads to less "effort," less attention to difficult tasks, and less "willpower."[46]

These ideas all make perfect sense just as long as you're living in the days before the Enlightenment.[47] If you think there's "mind stuff," separate from the brain, then maybe some of your mind stuff—willpower, which has no actual physical existence—gets "used up" when you don't eat cookies.

Well, maybe there is some physical explanation. In a recent study, Masicampo and Baumeister[48] had subjects come in and drink either regular lemonade or artificially sweetened lemonade. Subjects then watched a video in which words were displayed. Half of the subjects were told to ignore the words—something that requires "control"—and half were not. They were then all given a variant of the task described earlier in this chapter in which a third option influences the choice between two others, just like in the joke about choosing blueberry pie for dessert. Those who had to ignore the words on the screen were more affected by the irrelevant third option when they drank diet lemonade. The authors conclude that the effort of ignoring words on the screen drains the brain of glucose, which in turn is the engine of self-control. Replenish the glucose with lemonade, and self-control is again possible. Lemonade is to Buzzy as spinach is to Popeye. The glucose view is like saying that if you run Microsoft Excel for five minutes on your laptop, then the battery gets drained, and now your web browser will be slow.

The resource view is driven by misleading intuitions, picturing poor Buzzy trying to direct the show in the head, but, alas, getting tired. I like the way that the glucose model was put recently by some researchers in the area, who wrote that this sort of notion "is based on the assumption that, since glucose is the major source of fuel for the brain . . . alterations in plasma levels of glucose will result in alterations in brain levels of glucose, and thus neuronal function. However, the strength of this notion lies in its common-sense plausibility, not in scientific evidence."[49] They conclude that "behavioural effects of glucose ingestion should not be seen as resulting from simple fuelling of neural activity."[50] A very nice recent review of the state of scientific evidence on glucose and brain function similarly notes that the idea that "sugar-rich foods induce . . . an acute improvement in mood and mental function," while often asserted by popular writers, is "muddled" and constitutes an "appealing but apocryphal notion."[51]

These sorts of very critical views about the role of glucose are common among people who know something about how the brain works. Clarke and Sokoloff remarked way back in the nineties that a "fashionable" view "equates concentrated mental effort with mental work," but that "there appears to be no increased energy utilization by the brain during such processes."[52] A more recent review concluded that it is "unlikely that the blood glucose changes observed during and after a difficult cognitive task are due to increased brain glucose uptake."[53]

Now, I'm not an expert on the brain's consumption of glucose, but you don't actually have to be an expert physiologist to notice something is amiss. Subjects in this literature who do a few minutes of a "self-control task" are referred to as "depleted." What, precisely, is missing? Consider that in the radish/cookie experiment, subjects' brains in both conditions have very similar sets of modules that are active. Basically, everything brains normally do is still going on—the senses, memory, monitoring autonomic activity, and so on. In the radish condition, some modules are, presumably, inhibiting others from causing the subject to indulge in the cookies. I don't really know if it is possible to estimate what *fraction* of modules differ between these two conditions. My guess is that this number would be small. Could these extra modules be draining the brain of glucose?

Consider that *the entire brain* uses about .25 calories per minute.[54] If we suppose that the "self-control" task increases *overall* brain metabolism by 10%—a very large estimate[55]—then the brains of subjects who do one of these tasks for five minutes, who are categorized as "depleted," have consumed an extra 0.125 calories. Does it seem right that you need 100 calories from lemonade to compensate for a tenth of a Tic Tac?[56] Even worse for the glucose model, performance on "self-control" tasks should be much lower after exercise, which consumes orders of magnitude more glucose. However, research in this area shows exactly the reverse.[57]

Really, the idea that glucose is "depleted" because of what's going on in the brain during "self-control" tasks can't be right. Now, it could very well be that the amount of glucose in one's body affects performance on many tasks. It would be surprising if it didn't. Lots of organisms make decisions based on their present caloric state.[58] As mentioned above, if you're low on calories, it makes sense to take more risks in foraging. But when a bird takes foraging risks when it's hungry—but not when it's satiated—the inference from this isn't that glucose suppresses risky behavior. Glucose levels might act as an important *input* to modular decision-making systems. That is, some modules might use the current reading on blood glucose levels as information relevant to their function. But that does not mean that glucose is the substrate of willpower.

So much for the glucose-as-resource model.[59] What about the more general notion that "willpower" is a "resource" that gets consumed or expended when one exerts self-control? First and foremost, let's keep in mind that the idea is inconsistent with the most basic facts about how the mind works. The mind is an information-processing device. It's not a hydraulic machine that runs out of water pressure or something like that. Of course it is a physical object, and of course it needs energy to operate. But mechanics is the wrong way to understand, or explain, its action, because changes in complex behavior are due to changes in information processing. The "willpower as resource" view abandons these intellectual gains of the cognitive revolution, and has no place in modern psychology.

That leaves the question, of course, about what *is* going on in these studies.[60]

Let's back up for a moment and think about what the function of self-control might be. Taking the SATs, keeping your attention focused, and not eating cookies all feel more or less unpleasant, but it's not like spraining your ankle or running a marathon, where the unpleasant sensations are easy to understand from a functional point of view. The feelings of discomfort are probably the output of modules designed to compute costs. When your ankle is sprained, putting weight on it is costly because you can damage it further. When you have been running for a long time, the chance of a major injury goes up. These sensations, then, are probably evolution's way of getting you to keep your weight off the joint and stop doing all that running, respectively.

There's nothing obviously analogous for not eating cookies or doing word problems. Why does it feel like something, *anything at all*, to (not) do these things? As we've seen, lots of other stuff happens in your head, all the time, and it doesn't *feel* like anything. Further, given that it seems as if exerting self-control is a *good thing*, that is, that it generally leads to outcomes that might be expected to yield fitness benefits, you might expect that exerting self-control would feel good and easy. Why does it seem hard, and feel even harder over time? What is the sensation of "effort" designed to get you to do?

One reason it seems hard might derive from that fact that "exerting self-control" entails incurring immediate costs in various forms, and "effort" is the representation of these costs. Consider not eating a cookie. There are probably modules in your mind that are designed to compute the benefits of eating nice calorie packages. They're wired up to the senses, designed to calculate just how good (in the evolutionary sense) eating the calorie package is. *From the point of view of these modules, not eating the cookie is a cost*, in particular, the lost calories in the cookie. So, *the sensation of the effort of not eating it—"temptation"— is probably evolution's way of getting you to eat the cookie*, just as the sensation of pain is evolution's way of getting you to stay off your sprained ankle. In both cases, the experience is the output of a module designed to compute costs.

The same argument applies to other opportunities, and they take various forms. In some experiments, subjects are told to ignore words flashing on a computer screen, something that feels quite effortful. Why? Well, not reading words on a screen carries a loss of information: What did those words say? A similar argument applies regarding Ariely's work on decision making during sexual arousal, which we looked at earlier in this chapter. The reason that subjects respond to those survey questions when they are aroused is probably because the mechanisms designed to take advantage of mating opportunities are computing benefits in the environment, though they are being fooled by the fact that the images they are getting are pictures rather than actual people.

Is it also a cost to solve word problems? Sure, but the cost isn't *caloric*. Solving word problems requires the use of certain fancy modules, and when one is doing one of these tasks, these modules are kept busy.[61] This means that doing these tasks carries real (opportunity) costs: *all the things that these modules could be doing but are not because they are engaged*. It's not unlike what happens when you start up some big piece of software on your computer: Other things suffer, necessarily.* Starting up software carries these costs. Working on word problems, similarly, prevents you from using important modular systems from doing other tasks.

So, instead of a resource view, my view is that the issue is more of an effort monitor—an "effortometer"[62] in the mind. My guess is that the reason it *feels like something* to pay close attention to something, solve hard problems, or avoid eating cookies is that doing these things is costly from the perspective of certain modules.[63] The feeling of "mental effort," on this view, is like a counter, adding up all these opportunity costs to determine if it's worth continuing to do whatever one is doing.[64] As these costs get higher—either because one is doing the task for a while, or for some other reason—the effortometer counts higher, giving rise to the sensation of effort, and also giving the impatient modules more and more of an edge.

If I'm working on word problems—but not getting anywhere—using my modules in this way isn't doing much good, so maybe I should stop. Interestingly, as illustrated by the results of the studies described above, the effect seems to extend from one task to another, even if the tasks are quite different.

This idea suggests that a mechanism is needed that performs these computations, weighing the costs and benefits of doing tasks that make use of certain modules. Some modules are counting up these costs, and when the effortometer increases, there is less suppression of the short-term modules—it's time to move on. So, it's not "willpower" that's exhausted—it's that the ratio of costs to reward is too high to justify continuing. As Baumeister himself indicated, "it is adaptive to give up early on unsolvable prob-

---

* One of the first applications I got for my new smartphone was one that lists, and allows me to kill, most or all of the applications that are currently running, which frees up memory for whatever it is I want to use the phone for right now.

lems. Persistence is, after all, only adaptive and productive when it leads to eventual success."[65]

The effortometer view suggests a way to "reset" or at least reduce the count. Suppose we give subjects a reward, such as a small gift, or even light praise; this ought to "reset" the counter, just as when a foraging animal's time is rewarded by finding food morsels. Diane Tice and colleagues conducted some work in which some subjects were told not to think of a white bear,* and others were not. The idea was that not thinking of a white bear takes some "willpower," and when you've just used your willpower, you have less of it left to use in the next task, which was drinking an unpleasant beverage. They found that if you have to suppress thinking of a white bear, you can't drink as much of the awful Kool-Aid. So, that looks good for a "resource" model. Your willpower sponge has been squeezed out.

Some subjects were, however, given a small gift after suppressing thinking of a white bear. These subjects were able to drink just as much of the nasty stuff as those who were at liberty to think of as many white bears as they wanted. That is, their "willpower" seems to have been restored, making them able to endure the foul-tasting beverage.

These findings are very hard to accommodate with a "resource" model. If my self-control sponge is squeezed dry by not thinking of a white bear, a gift shouldn't help me exert willpower—I'm all out of it. (And certainly the gift didn't increase the amount of glucose in my body.) In contrast, this finding fits very well with the effortometer model.[66] If the effortometer is monitoring reward, then a gift resets it, and ought to improve subsequent self-control tasks.

"Self-regulation" was recently defined as "the self altering its own responses or inner states."[67] In a word: Huh? Without the concepts of modularity and function, sentences like this take the notion of self-control down the rabbit hole and into conceptual incoherence. What, exactly, is this "self"? What would it mean for an information-processing mechanism to "alter its own responses or inner states"? The "self" is presumably not the whole mind, so it must be a subset of it. This subset is doing something to that same subset? The whole thing is changing the whole thing? These sorts of

---

* Go ahead and try it. But first . . . white bear white bear white bear . . .

ideas continue to be popular in social psychology in spite of the fact that they make little sense. A modular view, however, has the potential to sort things out nicely.

Review

There are a few basic ideas to be taken from the modular view of self-control.

First, it's best to be clear by what we mean by "self-control." Most people seem to mean making choices in a way that is long-sighted rather than short-sighted: saving rather than spending, working out rather than sleeping, wearing a condom, and so on.

At its core, the issue of self-control derives from the interaction of modules of the mind that are designed to satisfy immediate fitness goals—e.g., conserving calories and heat, consuming food, taking advantage of sexual opportunities—with modules that inhibit these short-sighted modules in the service of reaping long-term gains, like health, status, and wealth. These sets of modules, because they have different functions, often are in conflict.

By thinking about what modules are designed to do, we can predict what will affect them. Once we understand a module's function, we can make good guesses about what will dial it up and what will dial it down. Seeing sexually appealing images, unsurprisingly, dials up the modules designed for sex, and sets these modules at an advantage, at the expense of the modules whose design keeps one out of jail. Similarly, hiding the marshmallow keeps the food-seeking modules in check, allowing the patient modules to maintain an advantage. Out of sight, out of module.

Just as in the discussion of self-deception, some researchers investigating self-control have come to the view that resonates closely with the thesis of this book. In the same way that some psychologists are ready to take the "drastic step" of thinking of the mind as something other than unitary, Dan Ariely says that the results he discusses suggest that "our models of human behavior need to be rethought. Perhaps there is no such thing as a fully integrated human being. We may, in fact, be an agglomeration of multiple selves."[68]

Similarly, the ideas here echo Dan Wegner's worries, which I think are very well founded, that much of this business about "self-control" consists of positing some Buzzy-like little guy in charge.[69] As Wegner says, we should be very sure that the answer to the question "Who is the controller of controlled processes?"—an excellent question—isn't something like Buzzy.

It's very encouraging to find that researchers in different fields are closing in on a view so nicely consistent with the modular view advanced here. That I begin and they end with similar basic ideas I take to be a good sign. Convergence in science is good evidence that all involved are getting closer to the truth. My hope is that in the future, researchers will begin with modularity, and see where it takes them.

Self/interest

I want to make a brief detour to drive past the notion of "self-interest." In previous chapters, I tried to suggest that "self-deception" was a suspect term. In this chapter, I suggested that "self-control" isn't any better. My sense is that most self-[something] terms are going to be trouble, since I don't think there's a "self" in there in any interesting sense, just a lot of modules. So, I want to pause to consider one of the biggest "self" terms out there, self-interest.

People use this term all the time. Economists in particular seem to like it a lot, but everyone uses it. What do we mean by it?

People seem to use it in at least two different ways. One has to do with being "selfish," but first let's tend to the other meaning, which seems to refer to something like doing the thing that advances one's long-term, as opposed to short-term, goals. To return to our cake example: When I eat a piece of cake at midnight, even though I'm on a diet, people would say that I'm acting against my self-interest. Am I?

Well . . . sort of. I mean, I think it's reasonable to argue that eating cake hurts my long-term goal of staying healthy and keeping weight off. That seems right. On the other hand, we know that I like to eat cake. How can doing something I like not be in my self-interest? Or, to put it another way, why do we think that staying healthy is in my self-interest, but eating something yummy is not?

We can reasonably ask, hey, what's so special about my long-term self-interest rather than my short-term self-interest? Why do long-term modules get to be the "self" that is "interested"? If one takes Tennyson's view—"better to have loved and lost" and all that—then maybe it's better to have gotten drunk and had a hangover than never to have drunk at all. Who is to say that the short-term pleasure I get from eating cake doesn't "offset"—in some abstract currency of happiness—the long-term costs of the extra calories? Saying that something is in someone's self-interest if—and only if—that something is in one's long-term self-interest seems, to me anyway, unjustified.

My sense is that the term has come to have this meaning because we often emphasize the importance of our long-term goals. It seems to me that this undersells the importance of our impatient modules. At a minimum, it's worth reflecting on exactly what we mean when we use the term in this way.

But what about another sense of "self-interest," meaning, what we pursue when we are being selfish? To act in one's "self-interest" is roughly the opposite of behaving altruistically. Now, we know that people do things that seem to be altruistic all the time. Mothers feed their young, soldiers throw themselves on grenades, and I always let a Certain Someone sit on the aisle. When you take your friend to the airport—which can really be a pain—are you "really" being altruistic, or selfish, indulging in the pleasure you get from the extra few minutes with your friend and saving her the outrageous $30 fare it costs to get from downtown to Philadelphia International by cab?

Some argue that such seemingly altruistic acts aren't "really" altruistic—that is, are "really" self-interested—because the giver gets pleasure from it. If I like to see my friend happy, donating my kidney to him isn't altruistic—it's selfish. Other than the fact that this meaning of "self-interested" labels acts that seem to be obviously altruistic as self-interested—and I'm quite willing to hold that aside—there's the additional problem that now *every* act can be understood to be self-interested, and we're led down the path that so many have worried about in economics and other disciplines in which labeling acts self-interested becomes tautological.

Compare the confusion that these uses of the term "self-interest" generates compared to the modular view. Consider first an example from nonhumans, which often makes things easier to think about. When momma bear breast-feeds baby bear, is this self-interested? The view I'm advancing here focuses only on the *design* of the (physiological) modules in question. Are mammary glands designed to deliver benefits to others? You bet. The reason for this has to do, of course, with the way evolution works, but the fact that we can *explain why* some parts of organisms are designed to benefit other organisms doesn't change the fact that mammary glands are designed to do exactly that: deliver benefits, at a cost, to another individual. This is the essence of altruism.

Now what about humans? First, it should be obvious that adaptations designed to help kin are just like the she-bear case. Is nepotism "really" altruistic? Once we know what we mean by "really," we can answer that question. On the modular view, something is "really" altruistic if the function is to deliver benefits to another individual at some cost. Again, *why* the design is there is an interesting question, but irrelevant to the issue of whether or not helping others is the function of the module.

What about non-relatives, like friends? There is a lot of debate about why humans form friendships, but one reason might be that friends can help one another when they need it.[70] If I help my friend today, she might be able to help me in the future, and so on down the road. So, when we aid our friends, is that "really" self-interest because the reason we do so has to do with reciprocal benefits down the road? Again, the modular view makes this clear. Just as with kin, the module in question functions to deliver benefits to another person, making it "really" altruistic.

The nice thing about this analysis is that it does away with the primordial and distracting question, "Are people fundamentally selfish?" The answer is that the question is bad. Some modules are designed to gather benefits, others are designed to deliver benefits, and they exist in the same head, sometimes in conflict. In the same way, this analysis does away with the question of whether individual acts are "really" self-interested. Different kinds of acts advance the goals that some, but not other, modules are designed to bring about.

So, both meanings of "self-interest" seem to be a problem because different modules have different designs, and are therefore built to bring about different outcomes. I'm not saying we ought to do away with the term (as I think we should in the case of "self-deception"), but I do think we should be careful about how we use it.

Psychology as sculpture

This ends our exploration of modularity as it relates to economic concepts like self-control and self-interest. Before moving on to the next and last broad topic—morality—I want to pause to reflect on a deep difference between the modular view of why people do such odd things and the view from economics and related disciplines.

Both economists and psychologists are, broadly, trying to explain human behavior. To do that, they are trying to explain the thing that gives rise to human behavior, the mind. But they go about it in different ways that I think of as very much like the difference between two sculptors trying to capture form.

Michelangelo is famously quoted as saying, "I saw the angel in the marble and carved until I set him free." Some economists are, in some sense, like this. They start with theories in which agents—people—have some idealized, rational mind *minus* the stuff that the economists carve away—thus we see terms like "biases," "heuristics," and "irrationality." They document departures from (supposed) perfection—rationality—much as a sculptor chips away marble, hoping that when they are done, human nature is left, like Michelangelo's angel.[71]

I see no reason at all to proceed this way, as though human psychology is perfection minus shortcomings. My view, the modular view, is more clay than marble. Like sculptors who add bits of clay, one after another, until the product is done, natural selection added—and changed—different bits, giving rise to the final product. We'll get done with psychology not by chiseling away at human shortcomings, but by building up a catalog of human capacities working together—or in opposition—in various contexts.

Instead of thinking of minds as a marble block with chips removed, I think it's better to think of minds as collections of large numbers of computational bits and pieces, woven together by the relentless if chaotic process of evolution by natural selection.

The mind is the product of modules working together, often managing to look so good that, yes, they can be confused under certain conditions for something that conforms to some definition of rational. But it's best not to be confused by this illusion. There is no reason, in principle, to start with monolithic perfection and rationality when studying human cognition and behavior. The mind is not a machine that evolved to some sort of idealized neo-classical economic perfection, with a few wrenches in the works. The mind evolved, bit by bit, over time, and the scientific study of the mind ought to respect this fact.

chapter 9

Morality and Contradictions

■ *Should sex be banned? It seems obvious why it should not be—because people ought to be able to do as they please, barring some reason to the contrary. However, the same argument could be applied to many areas of morality, but is not. Some modules, for reasons that are not yet known, appear to be designed to try to curb other people's freedoms.* ▪

If all sexual activity—literally all of it—were banned completely in the United States of America, we might be a lot better off.

In a stroke, a ban on sex—effectively enforced—would send the rates of the transmission of sexually transmitted infections (STIs) plummeting. Not only that, but poetic justice would be done: Only lawbreakers would be getting any new cases. Treatment costs for STIs would take a tumble, as it were.

Consider that all the time people spend on trying to get someone else to have sex with them—which is, I'm told, a lot of time indeed—could be put into more noble pursuits, like art, science, and reading books like this one.

To the extent that people smoke after sex, just like that, bam, we've cut down on smoking, still one of the leading causes of death in America.

Because abortion would no longer be an issue (except, again, in the case of criminal sex-havers), Democrats and Republicans would stop fighting and a new era of bipartisanship would be ushered in.

The United States' moral authority would immediately rise: the country would no longer be contributing to worldwide population growth.

The immigration "issue" would be resolved. No sex means no babies, which means the country would need immigrants to stem population loss. Another political wound healed.

Productivity would increase. Sexual activity results in lost sleep, which in turn leads to reduced productivity. If Americans were to give up sex, we would all be $18,000 richer within two months.[*]

The boundary between homosexuals and heterosexuals would blur. If no one is having any sex at all, we would be united in our common asexuality. California and Mississippi could finally learn to get along. In a Platonic way, of course.

Fights about the frequency, duration, quality, and details of sex would no longer divide couples. A few psychologists would be out of work, but relationships would be stronger, and couples could focus on the important things, like which movie star Aunt Sadie most resembles and who took the trash out last time.[†]

Would it have some other consequences or side effects? Yes, probably. I should think that there would be more travel to Canada and Mexico. Some stores would close, like the ones selling novelty condoms and so on. (On second thought, those stores might do better, depending on what else they carried.) But in any case, people would find other pursuits, giving other industries a bump. As it were.

Sadly, yes, there would be an underground sex industry—special clubs where people could find others willing to break the law and have consensual sex.

Probably the War on Sex could take care of that.

Give me liberty, or give me . . . no, wait. Just give me liberty.

Why shouldn't we ban sex?

Most people probably think that we shouldn't ban sex because (1) a general moral principle is that people ought to be allowed to do what they

---

[*] I obviously just made all of that up.
[†] Julia Stiles, and I did, respectively.

would like to do provided it doesn't hurt anyone, (2) consensual sex between two people doesn't hurt anyone, and so (3) people ought to be allowed to have consensual sex. This analysis suggests that we ought to have a reason to prevent people from doing something they would like to do. That is, most people thinking about this argument don't ask if there are reasons that we *shouldn't* ban sex, but rather if there are any good reasons that we *should*.

For things like sex—which many people want to do—people are very happy to apply *moral principles*. They think that decisions about what is right and what is wrong, what should be permitted and what should be banned and punished, should derive from principles. In this case, the principle is freedom or liberty: People ought to be allowed to do what they want as long as it doesn't hurt others. We'll return to this.

But that's not the way people make all moral judgments, and by moral judgments here I don't mean how people decide what *they themselves* should do—what their conscience tells them. I mean how people decide what *other people* ought *not* to do, what *other people* should be punished for.[1]

In deciding what other people shouldn't do, people don't necessarily start with some principle and go from there. It *could have been* that moral reasoning was not unlike mathematics—start with a few axioms, and see what follows from them. If people did that, then their moral reasoning would be consistent. Everything follows from the assumptions.

But they don't, or at least, not always.[2] Recall the story about consensual incest in chapter 4. People are quite happy to condemn things as morally wrong independently of being able to give any justification for it, let alone a *principled* justification.

In this chapter, we'll visit a number of activities that, for some reason, people want to prevent other people from doing. For these issues, my point is going to be very simple. *People won't always be able to say what the reasons are for their judgments and opinions* because of the nature of the mind. Just like split-brained patients, and just like all the examples we've seen in which the press secretary of the mind doesn't know what's going on elsewhere in the brain, people are not always going to know the reason why they morally condemn certain acts.[3]

Many modules seem to cause people to find certain things wrong and to work to prevent others from doing them. Often, people can't actually tell you the real reason behind those judgments, any more than they can tell you why they think they're among the best drivers in the country. Further, because these judgments are made by different subroutines, there is an inordinate amount of inconsistency. With no one principle, or even set of principles, guiding moral condemnation, moral judgments don't necessarily cohere in any meaningful way.[4]

So, the reasons you give about what you think is wrong, or should be illegal, aren't very often the causes of your moral judgment. That's not to say that your moral judgments aren't reasonable ones. It's just that the reasons you give for them aren't the real ones. Your press secretary modules don't really know what your moralistic modules are up to.

Who are you calling a victim?

One way you can tell people make their moral judgments based on non-conscious intuitions is that they can't explain their own moral judgments, as we've seen with Jon Haidt's work on "moral dumbfounding." People will say that incest is wrong without being able to give any justification for it. Incest is *just wrong*.

Another way you can tell moral condemnation isn't based on a principled analysis is that people often give reasons for their moral judgments that just can't be right. For example, Marc Hauser of Harvard University and colleagues presented subjects with a number of variations of moral dilemmas, including the famous trolley problem (discussed in chapter 5) in which a runaway trolley is going to kill five people unless it is diverted or stopped. In these scenarios, diverting or stopping the trolley will cause the death of one person who otherwise would not be harmed. For example, in one scenario, the only way to stop the trolley is to pull a lever that drops someone onto the track, slowing the moving trolley. In another, pulling the lever diverts the trolley to another track . . . with someone on it.

It's possible to determine what people think is morally relevant by comparing scenarios like these. Can people explain these judgments? In one set of studies, subjects were given two different variants of the trolley problems and, in cases in which they gave different answers—saying it's OK to kill one to save five in one case but not OK in another—they were asked to provide a justification for why. The researchers used a very loose criterion: They counted a justification as "sufficient" if subjects were simply able to indicate a fact that differed between the two scenarios and were able to imply that this difference accounted for the differences in their judgment. Even with this loose standard, for some pairs of scenarios for which people gave different judgments, less than a third of participants were able to meet it.[5]

We've been studying moral intuitions in my lab as well. Peter DeScioli, Skye Gilbert, and I have done some work looking not at moral justifications, but rather intuitions about victimhood. You might think that when people make moral judgments, they first determine if there's anyone who is a victim—anyone made worse off by the act in question—and use that when they're making their moral judgment. But we think that for at least some offenses, it's the other way around.

We presented people with a set of "victimless" offenses—things like urinating on a tombstone, burning a flag, cloning a human being, and so on—and asked our subjects if the act was wrong or not. After that, we asked if anyone was harmed by the action. What we found was that almost anyone who said an act was wrong also indicated a victim. But the victims included entities like "humanity," "society," "the American people," "friends of the deceased," "the clone," and so on.

Now, of course it's possible to argue that somehow these entities really are worse off as a result of the actions. So in a follow-up, we changed the scenarios to get rid of these potential victims. We had a story in which someone urinated on the tombstone of someone with no living family or friends, or a scientist cloned a human being, but the clone was never alive, so couldn't ever have suffered, felt pain, or worried that she was a clone.

Doesn't seem to matter. People still judged the acts wrong, and, when they did, they searched for a victim. If the clone wasn't ever alive, fine, the clone wasn't the victim: the scientist (somehow) was. If the dead person had no family or friends, "society" was worse off.

People seem to judge acts first, and search for justifications and victims afterwards, which strongly suggests that one coherent set of principles isn't driving moral judgments.

I'm not, by the way, saying that this is an "explanation" for moral judgments. To say that people's moral judgments are driven by intuitions is more of a negative claim than a positive one. It means that the moral judgments *aren't* driven by a set of consciously accessible general principles that are applied to particular cases. It remains to be explained precisely what the intuitions are, as well as the function of the modules that generate the intuitions.

In similar fashion, it's not complete to say that these judgments are driven by "emotions." That might be true, but that's also not an explanation. By itself, this idea makes no predictions. It would be necessary to say something quite a bit more complex about what these emotional systems are doing.

The remainder of this chapter is about a small number of issues that are controversial. For each one, I'm going to argue that people on both sides—or all sides—are inconsistent in their reasoning. Because different (nonconscious) modules are causing different moral judgments, there's nothing that keeps them from being inconsistent.

Abortion

In 2000, Larry King moderated a debate between George Bush, Alan Keyes, and John McCain, at the time the remaining candidates running for the Republican nomination for President. In the course of that debate, McCain dramatically took a campaign leaflet out of his jacket pocket, asking Bush if, as it said on the leaflet, he supported the pro-life plank of the Republican Party platform, which makes no exception for rape and incest because "the unborn child has a fundamental individual right to life which cannot be infringed." Bush agreed that he supported the plank . . . and then also indicated that he favored an exception for rape and incest.

Holding aside the fact that Bush both agreed and disagreed with the exception for rape and incest[6]—a contradiction itself—these exceptions are inconsistent with the reason pro-life advocates give—and the reason in the Republican Party platform—for banning abortion. Opposing abortion on the grounds that a life is being protected—that what is being protected has a *fundamental* right which *cannot be infringed*—has to mean, well, that it can't be infringed, even if the life was the result of rape or incest. If the right can't be infringed, then the fact that one's parents are closely genetically related can't justify violating that right, whether one is inside or outside of the womb. Claiming that embryos have an absolute right not to be aborted is inconsistent with the idea that the identity of the parents can void that right.[7]

The Democratic position on abortion isn't inconsistent with Democrats' stated reason for their position, but that's because, as far as I can tell, they don't actually *have* a reason for their position.[8] The 2004 platform* says:

> Because we believe in the privacy and equality of women, we stand proudly for a woman's right to choose. . . .

The Democrats base their position on abortion on "privacy" and "equality of women." Taking the second point first, with all due respect, it's silly. It would make sense if men had a right to an abortion but women didn't; then the principle of equality would require that one be pro-choice for women. Men don't have the right to an abortion, since they can't, actually, have an abortion.[9]

Returning to the first point, how does a right to *privacy* justify a woman's right to choose an abortion? It seems like the right to privacy might be relevant to a woman's right for no one, in particular the government, to *know* if she had an abortion, but its relevance is obscure with respect to whether she ought to have a right to *choose*.

Well, it's not really obscure. The reason the Democrats base their position on "privacy" doesn't have to do with a *moral* basis for their belief that abortion ought to be legal: rather, they're using a legal case to find a moral basis. The legal justification in the Supreme Court case *Roe v. Wade* reads in part that "State criminal abortion laws . . . violate the Due Process Clause of the Fourteenth Amendment, which protects against state action the right to privacy. . . ." It is in this sense that Democrats are using the term "privacy."

Because of *Roe v. Wade*, the Democratic justification for their position on this issue is nearly always "privacy." The National Organization for Women

---

*The 2008 platform, from my reading, offers no justification, just reiterates support for *Roe v. Wade*.

(NOW), however, makes the argument that one suspects one would hear if it weren't for the Democrats having to defend *Roe* (one does in fact read it in blogs and elsewhere). NOW claims that women should be able to "make decisions about their bodies and sexuality free from government interference. . . ." I think most pro-choice advocates might agree that their defense of abortion rests on this idea: People should be able to do with their bodies as they please.

But if one takes this position seriously, that women "should be able to make decisions about their bodies without government interference," then it's hard to simultaneously hold that other things that a woman might want to do with her body ought to be illegal. This principle ought to make people oppose the government's banning of everything from prostitution to pornography to surrogate motherhood. These are all things that a woman might decide to do with her body, and it seems very difficult to reconcile the view that these things ought to be banned or heavily restricted with the justification for being pro-choice.[10]

To give equal time to the pro-life position, in addition to the issue of exceptions, there's the issue of punishment. In November of 2007, Chris Matthews on *Hardball* interviewed David O'Steen, executive director of the National Right to Life Committee.

> MATTHEWS: I have always wondered something about the pro-life movement. If—if you believe that killing—well, killing a fetus or killing an unborn child is—is murder, why don't you bring murder charge[s] or seek a murder penalty against a woman who has an abortion? Why do you let her off, if you really believe it's murder?[11]

I've wondered about this for a long time, too, just one of doubtless many things Chris Matthews and I have in common.

O'Steen, who says that abortion is "the killing of a human being," responded, "We have never sought criminal penalties against a woman," which is not a reason, but rather a restatement of the basis for the question, and then he says that one doesn't know "how she's been forced into this," which is just bizarre and certainly not an answer to the question. He finally lands on "civil penalties, aiming at the doctors, taking away their financial incentives."

This still doesn't answer the question. If you think that abortion is killing, then you think that a woman who goes to a doctor is paying the doctor to murder. If you're pro-life because you think a fertilized egg is a human being, then you ought to think that the laws about doing away with one ought to apply to such cases. We have rules and laws about paying someone to commit murder. We also have many plot lines in movies and television about this, like *Grosse Pointe Blank*, with John Cusack, which I thought was pretty good.

Even if one doesn't worry too much about that, isn't it odd that the way that we're going to prevent murder is to take away *financial incentives*? This reminds me of the old *Doonesbury* cartoon in which cops with their guns on a mugger, who has just clubbed a victim, tell him to put the money back because he's facing a stiff fine. (I think the cartoon was supposed to be poking fun at the idea that we impose fines for white-collar criminals. Stealing a little money gets you a jail term; stealing a lot of money gets you a fine. . . .)

In Mexico, abortion came before that country's Supreme Court in 2008. The *New York Times* reported:

> Magistrate Mariano Azuela, who was one of two justices to speak against the law, declared that life begins at conception. "I feel that a woman in some way has to live with the phenomenon of becoming pregnant," he said. "When she does not want to keep the product of the pregnancy, she still has to suffer the effects during the whole period."[12]

If life begins at conception, and the issue is about protection, then the next part of that should be about *protecting that life*, but it's not. It's about the woman *having to suffer*. This strikes me as extremely revealing. It's *almost* as if the magistrate is more interested in punishing women for having sex than saving lives. Hm.

This is particularly interesting in the context of exceptions for rape. Should a woman have to "suffer" through pregnancy for having sex voluntarily, but not for having sex involuntarily? If that's what's driving moral judgment in this case, then it's *almost* as if intuitions about abortion are actually about women's *sexuality*, and not about saving lives at all.

Let me be clear. I don't think that when people take a pro-choice position the cause of that position has much to do with privacy or the very basic principle that women should be able to do whatever they want with their bodies without government interference, and they're just applying this basic principle to abortion. I think people are pro-choice for other reasons, and they are justifying their position this way.

I also don't think that (most) pro-life people are pro-life because they begin with the idea that a fertilized egg is a life and that it's wrong to kill. I think people are pro-life for other reasons and they are justifying their position this way.

What are those other reasons?[13]

Good question. Psychologists ought to be trying to figure out the answer to this question, which is at the core of one of the most important political debates of our time.

Drugs

Drugs really weird me out.

With the notable exceptions of caffeine, alcohol, and nicotine, the United States prohibits the sale and use of countless drugs, including uppers, downers, hallucinogens, and so on. Drug policy doesn't seem to reflect the wishes of a small number of politically powerful soulless dullards who want to make sure no one is having any fun. Drug policy gets broad support, with candidates often competing to be perceived as the "toughest on drugs." This apparently plays well with the electorate.

Why do people think that drugs are bad and want laws preventing their use? The easy answer is that using drugs is harmful and we should take a moral stand against harmful things, and the government should prevent people from doing them.

Can't possibly be. First of all, if that were the main argument for the war on drugs, people would be jumping up and down about nicotine and cigarettes. Various estimates put cigarettes as among the biggest killers, if not the biggest killer, of Americans. If we're really concerned about harm, then cigarettes would have been banned a long time ago. That's definitely not it.

Not only that, but people do any number of things every day that are dangerous. I'm going to go out on a limb and say that anyone trying to organize a "war on downhill skiing" would be seen to be joking, crazy, or on some mountain-saving eco-rampage.[14] Really, the "war on drugs" has nothing to do with the beneficence of the electorate interested only in preventing other people from hurting themselves.

People in the medical profession will tell you that's why they're opposed to recreational drugs, with an ominous "I've seen what drugs can do." They've seen what mishandling a kitchen knife can do, too, but you don't see them crying out for a war on cleavers. Not only that, but that's not the point. If you think recreational drugs are harmful, and you want to reduce the harm they do, then the argument you want has to be that banning drugs will *reduce* the harm they do. If that's the argument, then you're forced to say that you're not opposed to drugs *in principle*. You have to say that if people would be harmed less by recreational drugs, overall, if they were legal than if they were illegal, then you would be in favor of legalization. In my experience, no one says they're in favor of legalizing drugs as long as everyone is better off that way. Drugs are just *bad*. OK, you say, it's not doing the drugs themselves. It's the crime and violence that *surrounds* drugs. Well, that's reasonable - except that's not it either.

There are basic economic principles that explain why violence surrounds transactions that are illegal. Because people engaged in illegal trade can't count on the courts and the police to enforce contracts, they have to enforce their own. They can't rely on the police to protect them from robbery because filing a stolen property report for a brick of cocaine might raise suspicions that you're, I don't know, somehow involved with the drug trade. So, they have to protect themselves with more than just a locked door. With these problems, violence, or at least the threat of violence, is a necessity for people engaged in illegal activities. The fact that drugs are illegal *creates* the atmosphere of violence.

Don't believe me? Probably the best experiment ever that answers the question "Is there more or less violence when you make a drug illegal?" was conducted between 1920 and 1933 in the United States. This experiment was called the 18th Amendment to the Constitution of the United States of America. Alcohol is bad. Let's get rid of the evils of alcohol by using the highest law of the land to stop people from drinking. How did that work out?

With Prohibition in place, a black market was created for alcohol, with predictable results: Crime went up, quality of the product went down (who was going to complain?), and criminals like Al Capone made money beyond the dreams of avarice. Of course many factors influence national crime rates, including economic conditions, but the fact that the murder rate in the United States increased right as Prohibition took effect and went down again right after repeal seems pretty telling.

I'm not saying Philip Morris and Coors aren't doing quite well, thank you. I'm saying that you don't see these guys fighting turf wars with tommy guns.

Another reason people give for being opposed to drug legalization is along the same "threat to society" line. The argument goes something like, "If drugs were legal, people would be high all the time and no one would get any work done."

I just don't know how to reply to that. The first part of it, the notion that it's reasonable to be opposed to drugs because if they were legal everyone would use them, makes no sense. If you don't think using drugs is bad or wrong for some *other reason*, then the fact that many people would use them if they were legal is irrelevant.

Besides, certain drugs *are* legal, like alcohol, and people seem to do work. The reason—well, one reason—is that there are more incentives in life than getting high. Not only that, but there are lots and lots of things people like to do—go on vacation, have sex, watch TV, have sex while watching TV on vacation—and somehow society pushes onward. This is not the reason people are opposed to drugs.

I'm not saying that these arguments should convince you that the United States should legalize all drugs. I'm saying that the explanations people give for being in favor of prohibiting drugs are like the explanation split-brain patients give when they say "the shovel is for cleaning the chicken coop." It's a reason fabricated by the press secretary of the mind that is not the real reason for the view.

But whatever the real reason is, it's strong. How strong? Well, one argument in favor of drug legalization that to me seems particularly compelling is that legalizing drugs would have profound effects on the war on terror. To the extent that high drug prices are filling the coffers of terrorists, people should at least be *talking* about the possibility of legalizing drugs to reduce prices. Arguments of this sort get made from time to time, but few people seem to take these ideas very seriously.

Why are people so opposed to drugs? Which modules hidden beneath consciousness are generating this particular judgment, and what is their function?

Good question. Psychologists ought to be trying to figure out the answer to this question, which is closely related to one of the most important national security issues of our time.

Immoral markets

James Surowiecki's recent and very popular book *The Wisdom of Crowds* explains how surprisingly good large numbers of people can be at answering questions. For example, on *Who Wants to Be a Millionaire?* when a contestant facing a tough question looks for help to a room full of people with nothing better to do than sit in the studio audience of *Who Wants to Be a Millionaire?*, 91% of the time the most common answer the audience gives is the correct one.

One way crowds are wise is more practical than answering game show questions. Crowds can predict the future. Imagine that people could place bets on things like, say, who is going to win the next U.S. presidential election. The bets work like this: you can buy a "share" of either (or any) candidate for some price, and if that candidate wins, you get $1 on election day. If the candidate loses, you lose the money you paid.

When large numbers of people can make this sort of bet, the price shows what people, as a whole, think each candidate's chance of winning is. If people think one candidate is a shoo-in, the price for that candidate will be very high. Prices, then, show us what people think is going to happen.

To see this, take the extreme case. Suppose you knew, for sure, that Fred was going to win the election. (Say you really *could* predict the future.) You would be willing to pay—holding aside the issue of interest—anything up to 99 cents for a "share" of Fred because each share would eventually be worth $1. You would earn one dollar minus the price you paid for each share you bought on the futures market. The result of this is that the price of the share would eventually rise to $1.

In effect, by bidding in this way, you would be "telling the market" that you know for sure that Fred was going to win. The result of this market would be that you would make some money—$1 minus the price you paid for each share—and people observing the market, seeing the price rise to $1, would know that participants in the market were essentially sure Fred was going to win. The price allows people to predict the future.

The same reasoning applies for any other price.[15] As people buy and sell shares on futures markets, prices "gather" everyone's guesses about what's going to happen. If some futures market share is selling at 50 cents, then we know that, overall, people think it's a coin flip as to whether or not whatever they're betting on is going to happen. As the price gets higher and higher, we're learning that people, overall, think it's more and more likely that whatever it is will actually happen. As the price goes down, we're learning that people think it's less likely to happen.

You can watch this process in real time. Sites like TradeSports* have markets during sporting events. As one team pulls ahead, you can watch the price of the share go up. This means that bidders participating in these markets, quite reasonably, are more confident that team will win. In this way, information is fed into markets in the form of bids, which then tell you what others think will happen.

And they're right. These markets have been in place for years, and they do a good job—better, even, than polls—at predicting what's going to happen.[16] Prediction markets have come within a percentage point or two of predicting results of national elections, for example. That they're better than polls isn't too surprising (to economists). Paying for shares on a market means that you

---

*I should really use the past tense here. TradeSports closed its virtual doors. The legal status of betting on such sites is murky. Some people argue that it is illegal for people in the United States to bet using these sites, in which case, as in the difference between pornography and prostitution, it's legal to watch, but you don't get to play.

have an incentive to "tell the truth." That is, if you buy an expensive share of someone you don't really think will win, you're throwing your money away. It costs you to inject false information into the system. Not so with polls. It costs as much to lie to a pollster as it does to tell the truth: nothing.

On web sites like Intrade, people can place bets on a bewildering array of events that might take place, ranging from who will win major political elections to scientific issues, such as whether or not the Higgs Boson particle will be observed by a certain date. These markets collect a lot of information from a lot of people and convert this information into an easy-to-understand summary: a price.

These prices are valuable because they are like crystal balls. And they're relatively easy to get. Compare this to what happens across all the various intelligence agencies in the United States—the CIA, FBI, NSA. . . . We constantly heard after 9/11 that information flow and inter-agency barriers were an impediment to gathering together all the information various agencies had.

Wouldn't it be great if we could harness the knowledge of experts in these agencies using the power of markets? What if we could *use* the wisdom of crowds, allowing people to enter a market for events we care a great deal about, and then use the prices on those markets to help our intelligence communities to focus efforts in a sensible way?

Would that be an intelligent and efficient way to bring everyone's opinions together? Or would it be useless, grotesque, offensive, and unbelievably stupid?

In July of 2003, the "Policy Analysis Market" was introduced. It was a futures market, just as I've described here, designed to gather information about geopolitical trends, such as whether or not countries in the Middle East would be stable. It had the potential to use the wisdom of crowds to help the United States with important policy decisions.

Two United States senators thought it was "useless," "grotesque," "offensive," and "unbelievably stupid."[17]

Maybe the senators have good reasons for their views. I have no idea.

What I do know is that there was moral revulsion over this idea, and no one knows if lives might have been saved if this tool were available to the intelligence community.

I'm not sure why people think it's wrong to have futures markets. For that matter, I don't really know why people feel the way they do about gambling, either.

What I do know is that markets make people better off. Economists, who disagree on so much, pretty much agree on this. Markets allow people who have something that they don't want—are willing to part with for some price—to get together with people who need something—are willing to pay a price for it. Markets leave buyers and sellers better off. The sellers now have money, which they value more than the item they just sold, and the buyers have something that they value more than the money they just paid. Everyone's better off.

Everyone is better off. The beauty of markets is that—I really think it's worth repeating—*everyone is better off.*

In fact, people make people *way* better off. Markets are a great way to ensure that the people who want something the most get it. The laws of supply and demand see to it that prices rise and fall in such a way that the people who are willing to pay the most for goods get those goods, and the people who are willing to part most easily with goods do so.

Not only *that*, but *not* having markets stinks. In the case of drugs, without markets—that is, legal markets, backed by things like police, lawyers, and the 82nd Airborne—people who still want to make exchanges do so illegally, and that leads to things like organized crime and bootlegging, which make for really good movies but not such good actual real life.

Don't take my word for it. Ask people from the former Soviet Union how much they enjoyed the shortages endured in their non-market economies.

Or don't ask them. The point is that markets—free trade of goods and services—allow people to find ways to make themselves better off. I'm not saying that all government regulation is bad. I'm saying that the intuition that some mutually beneficial transactions are "wrong" harms the people who otherwise could engage in those transactions.[18]

Why, exactly, are people opposed to markets like this? Why is it a moral issue at all?

Good question. Psychologists ought to be trying to figure out the answer to this question. If we could answer it, not only would we know more about human nature, but we might be able make a lot of people a lot better off.

Things you may give away but not sell

Perhaps you are enlightened and you're in favor of futures markets. Why, then, do you think that people shouldn't be allowed to sell their kidneys?

Tens of thousands of people need kidneys, with the waiting list in 2006 topping 65,000. A substantial number of people—around 10,000 or so each year[19]—take perfectly good kidneys (and livers) with them when they're buried even though, given their particular mode of death, they would have been good candidates for donation. Imagine if these people could have sold their organs for use after they died. Many of them would, perhaps, have rather had more money while they were alive and been buried without their kidneys than had less money when they were alive and taken their kidneys with them.

However, there is no market for kidneys in this country. I can, somewhat perversely, *give* my organs away—and I have a little notation on my driver's license to do just that, potentially making an event that's really bad for me turn into an occasion that's really good for someone else. But I can't sell them, leading to the somewhat odd policy that it's OK to donate your kidney but not to charge for it, making kidneys, like sex, among the very few things that you can give away but not sell.

Never mind selling your kidney for use after you're dead. Why not be able to sell it while you're alive? Ask yourself this: Would you rather have (a) both your kidneys or (b) one kidney and $15,000?[20] True, if you lose your second one after you've donated the first, that's a little awkward,* and it's true that donating a kidney means an operation. But shouldn't people be allowed to decide if they want to take that particular risk? If we're going to prevent people from taking risks in exchange for money, we're going to have to put an end to the mining industry and disband the military.

The stakes are high. In a recent analysis of the possible benefits of organ markets, two prominent scholars concluded that giving people incentives (money) to be organ donors "would eliminate all the suffering and deaths of individuals who now must wait in long queues to receive organs."[21]

---

*It's much less awkward if there's a market for kidneys. You just hope that they don't change the law after you're a seller but before you're a buyer.

Most arguments against organ markets are moral arguments. True, some people have made political or economic arguments. For example, some worry that organ markets will lead to a disproportionate number of organ donations from poor people, who need money more. I think these arguments are easily dealt with, but I won't address them, since I'm interested in the moral objections. (The answer to that particular objection is that, yes, people who need money are willing to do unpleasant, risky, or embarrassing things to get it, like carry heavy boxes, work on oil rigs, or dress up in a hamburger costume and hand out coupons on a street corner; it doesn't seem to me that this means these things should be *banned.*)

The core of the issue seems to be that people say that buying and selling bits of bodies is just *wrong*. Some part of their brain generates this judgment, and then people justify it with arguments after the fact. As Richard Thaler and Cass Sunstein recently put it in their book *Nudge,* "Although the idea [of organ markets] has obvious merit, it is also spectacularly unpopular for reasons that are not well understood."[22]

"Not well understood. . . ." It seems to me that psychologists ought to be trying to understand these reasons.

The moralistic mind

In November of 2007, a British schoolteacher was arrested, tried, convicted, and imprisoned for allowing her class in Khartoum, Sudan, to use a particular word when referring to a particular toy. The clause she was charged under carries a possible penalty of forty lashes. This was far below the penalty sought by street protesters, who shouted, according to the Associated Press, "No tolerance—execution."

In a country in which tens of thousands of unarmed civilians, men, women, and children, were being mutilated and killed, hundreds of thousands displaced, and acts of unspeakable violence being perpetrated at astonishing rates, what brought people to the streets—and attracted international media attention—was the air passing through the lungs of a few children making certain sounds when referring to a stuffed bear, who, presumably, didn't care all that much.

Why are people pro-life, pro-choice, anti-drug, anti-prostitution, anti-markets, anti-nude beaches, and anti-people-naming-teddy-bears-Mohammed?

Those are good questions.

From my perspective—that of an evolutionary psychologist—one of the most peculiar things about humans is just how much they care about what other humans are up to. In essentially all of the rest of the natural world, unless one organism's fate is intimately tied to another organism's decision—such as when one is a potential meal or mate of the other—organisms typically ignore one another. This makes a great deal of sense, biologically. Spending time and energy worrying about what others are up to is costly. Organisms should be designed to monitor what is going on with kin, allies, and enemies. Better to pay attention only to those things that are directly relevant.

We're different. We seem to care *a lot* about what other humans are up to. And when other people ignite a leaf and inhale, say some particular magical words, or try to sell (or rent) a body part to someone else, not only do we care, but we insist that they be punished.

This is a biological mystery of the first order. No one has yet solved this mystery, though a lot of people have claimed to. Most explanations of why people are "moral" are really explanations of why people are generous, which is a completely different thing. [23]

There are two important lessons to take from all this. First, and in line with one of the central arguments of this book, we don't know the reasons we morally condemn various acts. We just think they're wrong, and say they're wrong, and try to justify this view. The problem is, of course, that the justifications we give are so inconsistent that it's easy to show the justification must have come after, rather than before, the moral judgment. What I've been calling the press secretary doesn't have access to the reason generating the moral judgment, so it's forced to generate a reason.

The second point returns us squarely to modularity. It could have been that people adopted some set of very basic moral principles and derived their views from them systematically. I alluded to something along these lines in the first chapter with the help of a hypothetical moral robot. But that doesn't seem to be how we operate. It looks like moral judgments are generated by nonconscious modules, and then the press secretary justifies them, often quite poorly. This isn't all that surprising. People are condemning some things and not condemning others in a way that admits of no consistent set of principles, leaving the press secretary with an impossible job.

This, then, is the reason for human moral inconsistency. Because different parts of the mind, with different functions, are generating different moral judgments, there is nothing that keeps them mutually consistent.

Consistency is not a default. It takes careful engineering to keep systems consistent. In some cases, the human mind is engineered that way. But in many cases, it is not. If consistency doesn't improve the functioning of the system overall, there's no particular reason to expect it. To the extent that there's no advantage to consistency in moral judgments, it's not all that surprising that they are mutually contradictory.

It's actually quite a bit worse than that.

To return to the distinction between conscience and condemnation, the modules that seem to be designed to prevent other people from doing certain things—using birth control, naming teddy bears, and such—are not the same modules that guide our own behavior. I do not have to bring up certain former governors of New York and South Carolina to convince anyone that whether or not someone conforms to a particular moral rule about what is forbidden is not necessarily closely related to whether or not he endorses the rule.

The modules that guide conscience are no doubt influenced by many factors. To return to poor Mr. Spitzer, when he was deciding whether or not to have sex with a prostitute, some modules were probably responsible for weighing the costs and benefits. Sure, one cost was the risk to his political career, particularly because of his well-known anti-prostitution stance, but this was just one factor. Set against the modules that compute these potential costs were the (impatient) modules that are designed to seek sex. Apparently, these sex-seeking modules had an advantage.

The modules that cause behavior are different from the ones that cause people to voice agreement with moral rules. Because condemnation and conscience are caused by different modules, it is no wonder that speech and action often conflict.

Taken together, these ideas make it clear that the modular design of the human mind guarantees hypocrisy.

What remains to be explained is why you think this doesn't apply to you.

chapter 10

Morality Is for the Birds

■ *We reflect on a population of birds in which different individuals do better or worse, in terms of their fitness, depending on the rules surrounding mating that are imposed on them. In such birds, there could be selection for modules designed to impose these rules, even though they might well not know that this was the origin of their "moral intuitions" about behavior in the sexual realm.* ■

It's easy to explain why people don't, by and large, *commit* incest. Because of the genetic costs of inbreeding, people who avoided mating with close relatives left more offspring than those who did not, and the genes associated with incest aversion spread over evolutionary time.

This is a very good, convincing argument.[1] However, it most certainly, by itself, does not explain why people care that *other people* don't commit incest.

I don't pretend to know the reasons for the existence of the moral intuitions surrounding incest or the other areas I discussed in the previous chapter. Instead, my interest in this chapter is to try to sketch one kind of answer to the question of why people condemn others for certain behaviors. It's a different type of explanation from what one sees in most books and papers about moral psychology lately, where the focus is on trying to understand how evolution made us nice, kind, generous, and so on. I think that these are interesting parts of human nature, but they are not what generate such mind-numbing inconsistencies in the moral domain. My musings here are intended to give a sense of what the right answers might look like, broadly, to the question of why people judge others' actions and condemn them. Good explanations of moral condemnation should account for the basic phenomenon: *stopping other people from doing various things*.

In order to do this, I'm going to talk about birds. Why might birds have modules that cause them to control what other birds get up to in the privacy of their own nests?

The moralistic animal

I've often found that perfectly logical arguments about how evolution works are subject to all sorts of very strange errors and misconceptions if they happen to be about people, especially about social relations between people. People seem to *insist* on evolutionary explanations when they are trying to understand what non-humans are up to, but reflexively reject such explanations when it comes to people.

Some stories from the world of animals are sad. When male lions take over a pride, they kill all the cubs who are not their own. This brings the lionesses into a state of "receptivity," as it is frequently called, and they then copulate with the murderous male lions. The narrator explains that this behavior in males and females has been selected because males and females who do this leave more offspring than those who don't. Males who don't kill the cubs sire fewer offspring because the females in the pride don't become receptive. Females who don't copulate with these murderous males leave fewer offspring because, well, it's hard to get pregnant without having sex. It's a straightforward explanation, and it's sad, I suppose, but rarely do people *object* to the explanation and insist on counter-explanations. "Maybe the male lions do that because they *learned* to do it." "Maybe the female lions copulate with the male lions who just killed their offspring in order to raise their self-esteem, which has been damaged after the trauma of losing a child."

You never hear that.

Some stories are happier. Among my favorite accounts of evolution in action are from Jonathan Weiner's *The Beak of the Finch*, which relates Peter and Rosemary Grant's research on the finches on the Galápagos Islands. One interesting little observation is that as water becomes more abundant, the finches start reproducing at younger ages. This makes a lot of evolution-ary sense. Birds that are designed to use times of plenty to gain reproductive advantage by starting their reproductive career early out-reproduce birds who don't. The logic is relentless, the data are excellent, and readers' first impulse is never to blame the parents for setting a bad example or to blame the state for not funding abstinence-only education or anything.

You never hear that either.

So, I'd like to talk about birds. Forget humans for a moment, and when I'm done you can worry a lot about whether the kind of explanation I favor doesn't apply to humans for some reason that you'll make up but is wrong.

I'll use birds because the mating pattern of certain bird species illus-trates what's known as the "polygyny threshold model," which has to do with how female birds choose a mate in certain complex environments. As we'll see, one result of the model is that it makes it easy to think about how changing the rules of the mating game leave some birds better off and other birds worse off. This is important for thinking about morality.

Imagine a bird species in which males set up territories and females choose which male to mate with. High-quality males can defend bigger, richer territories. Low-quality males have to settle for smaller, poorer territories.

Suppose I'm a female bird and I'm in the market for a mate. I come to the nesting grounds a little late, and I find that that many of the best males are already taken: Other females have already set up housekeeping with the males with the biggest territories. So, I'm faced with a choice. I can either nest with one of the remaining single—but lower quality—males, or I can nest with a male who is already paired, becoming the second female on the patch. Is it better to be the only mate of a poorer male or share a better one?

The polygyny threshold model focuses attention on the answer to this question: Depending on the details, there will be some monogamously mated pairs and some polygyny. When the payoff to being the second fe-male on a patch is greater than the payoff to being the only mate of an inferior male, there will be polygyny.

Now we add the key ingredient: Somehow, we make these birds moral-istic. They judge certain kinds of behavior "wrong," and they have the intu-ition that any bird that does something "wrong" should be punished. This, of course, deters these "wrong" acts. Now what happens?

Is morality for the birds?

Suppose that our moralistic birds have to make a decision about whether polygyny—two female birds nesting with one male bird—is "wrong," and suppose that the modules in the bird minds that make this decision are subject to the forces of natural selection. What kind of modules should we expect to find?

To figure this out, we have to ask which birds stand to gain reproductive advantage when polygyny is prohibited. Clearly, female birds with the best male mates will do better: Their mates won't be able to acquire secondary females whose offspring would compete for the male's resources. *Enforced monogamy is a strategic win for monogamously mated females.* Over time, one would expect a moral module regarding monogamy would be very active in females that find themselves in such a situation.

What about the males? Which males gain when polygyny is prohibited? Well, you might think that the low-quality males benefit, since they now might get mates who would otherwise wind up as secondary mates of high-quality males. That's probably right. So, in some sense there's a natural alliance between monogamously mated females and low-quality males because they both gain by enforced monogamy. Will they ally against the high-quality males? Maybe. But remember that we're just talking about the module that morally condemns polygyny. Which males benefit from *all other males* being monogamous, even if they themselves are not? That's nearly *all* males. From the point of view of any given individual, it's best to constrain *others'* sexual behavior. We're all in favor of moral rules that prevent others from doing things that harm our own interests. Just look at the Seven Deadly Sins, a list of all those things we don't want *other people* to do, though we might well have an interest in doing them all ourselves. (Symmetrically, "virtues" are traits you want *other people* to possess—altruism, modesty, chastity —even if you yourself are better off avoiding them.)

If a high-quality male could prevent some males from polygyny *while simultaneously being polygynous himself*—having one monogamous mate, and then having illicit but unpunished affairs—that would be the best of all possible worlds in terms of fitness. To the extent that high-quality males can protect themselves from punishment for having extra-pair matings, the rule prohibiting them is less of a problem.

Who stands to lose if monogamy is enforced? Single females do, since they'll be forced to mate with the lower-quality males. Basically, they've lost all the advantages of having the choice described in the polygyny threshold model because they can no longer select a potentially better option, becoming the second female on a high-quality male's patch.

Suppose that selection acted on this bird species, and they came to be designed to favor the arrangement that benefited them, *even if they couldn't say why*. In the same way that our birds might very much like to have sex without having to understand the relationship between sex and reproduction, they might have preferences for monogamy and polygyny in line with their reproductive interests *without knowing the ultimate cause of these preferences*. One can easily imagine what would happen if high-quality males got to make the rules, or, if there were some sort of democracy instituted, how these birds would vote.

The point is that in *a species in which individuals can constrain others' behavior with rules, you'd expect evolution to act to cause members of the species to favor rules that serve their reproductive interests even if they don't know this is why they're endorsing these rules.*

Crucially, consider what these birds would say if they could talk. Perhaps the ones in favor of monogamy would talk about things that sound "good," like love, family, and the "naturalness" of a two-parent nest. They might even refer to a very special magic book where *other birds* pursing *their fitness interests* wrote down rules that took on a sort of mystical quality.[2]

On the other side of the debate, those in favor of polygyny might talk about individual freedoms to do as a free bird will. They might cite moving passages of Declarations and Constitutions, and quote famous birds of times past.

It should be clear that any bird social scientists would have a serious problem trying to figure out the true cause of moral intuitions if their only tool was asking other birds to justify their moral stance. Without Darwin, of course, these bird scientists would be in trouble because they wouldn't know how to think about what the modules designed to generate moral judgments were up to. They would wind up spinning explanations based on introspection, or perhaps a historical riff based on recent events in the local bird population. They would be explaining bird psychology in terms of what it felt like to be a bird, rather than in terms of the logic of design.

That probably would lead them down a lot of blind alleys, and leave many, many mysteries.

The scramble for eggs

As the lives of our birds get increasingly complex, selection would cause the modules designed to manipulate others' sexual behavior to become more sophisticated. To add another wrinkle, suppose there are two kinds of male birds. Some males make nice nests and bring back nice worms for the whole family to enjoy. These are investing males, and we'll call them "dads." Another kind of male doesn't set up house at all. Instead of the domestic life, these males offer females a different commodity: good genes. We'll call the good-genes guys "cads," not to prejudge the moral issue, but just for the rhyme with "dads."[3] We assume that cads, on average, have better genes than dads do, but that dads invest more in offspring than cads. In many species—including many bird species—females choose to mate with males on the basis of how they look because how they look reveals their genetic quality. The reasoning behind this has been discussed elsewhere—most notably perhaps in Darwin's second great work, *Descent of Man*—so I won't rehash it here.[4]

Who wins and who loses (in terms of evolutionary fitness) with different rules in a population that includes both dads and cads? Which birds want promiscuity? The cads do. They can't win if the battle is being fought over who brings in the most worms. They only win in a world in which being sexy matters. Without promiscuity, sexy males can't make the most of what they've got.

Dads, however, win if the sexy males can't be promiscuous. (They also benefit from keeping their females at home, rather than searching for the good-gene cads.) The good females, if they're unable to get good genes from cads, will go with the dads. If you can't get the genes, get the worms.

So, *promiscuity on the part of other birds is bad for dads*.

On the female side, mated females are potential losers in a promiscuous world because their mated males might be tempted to stray, potentially diverting precious worms away from her children.

So, *promiscuity on the part of other birds is bad for mated females*.

If these birds could vote, then *birds in monogamous pairs would cast their ballots for policies*—and, in a republic, for the birds who favor policies—*that prevent other birds from engaging in practices like sex outside of mateships and anything else that went along with promiscuity*.

Again, they probably wouldn't know *why* they were opposed to these practices. They would be insensitive to arguments about freedom and individual choice. They would probably be "pro-family" and interested in "traditional values" and so on. Further, because they didn't *know* why they wanted to constrain other birds' sexual behavior, they would be forced into contradictory positions.

They might be opposed to abortion—the availability of which, by reducing the costs of sex, might well be linked to promiscuity[5]—and say that their opposition is based on the principle that a new life begins at conception, even though their intuition is really that a female bird who is promiscuous ought to be punished. These birds would be "pro-life," "pro-family," and other platitudes, but basically their minds would be designed to prevent other birds from having sex.

OK, enough with the birds, since at this point it should be clear that my point is that humans, just like these hypothetical birds, have moralistic modules designed to favor rules that promote their fitness interests.

This might be difficult to believe. But suppose, just for a moment, that opposition to abortion really doesn't have *anything to do* with saving the life of the embryo. People's stance on abortion might then really be a stance based on the output of certain modules designed to limit other people's promiscuity.[6]

In this, abortion isn't all that different from many other ways in which people try to control other people's sexuality. Fathers have been sequestering daughters and older women have been curbing younger women's sexual expression and behavior for millennia. From an evolutionary point of view, sex is fundamental, and if there were going to be some area in which people wanted to set the rules, this would probably be among the first.

Organisms are better or worse off, in terms of reproductive success, depending on the rules of the mating game. Suppose that humans, like some of our primate relatives, are, potentially at least, somewhat polygynous, with the "best" males getting more than one mate, meaning some males will be left with none. Low-quality males would have a deep, abiding, even *crucial* interest in rules that force everyone into monogamy—in such a world, the low-quality males do a lot better. Similarly, some women are better off with enforced monogamy. This implies that—at least the possibility that—*some modules are designed to try to impose certain sexual rules on other people.* I think the way this works is through moral intuitions surrounding behavior like abortion, prostitution, and much else that might be associated with promiscuity or mating patterns. The key is that some people win and some people lose in the evolutionary sense under different regimes. I think this explains the large differences in views on sexual behavior.

The issues surrounding sex and morality are, no doubt, going to turn out to be more complicated. My main purpose here has been to sketch what an argument might look like for explaining why people are inclined to constrain other people's behavior.

This type of explanation won't be adequate for all moral intuitions, some of which don't have a clear link to fitness interests. For example, moving from sex to drugs, people have a very strong intuition that many, indeed, most, recreational drugs should remain illegal. This intuition runs afoul of the principle of freedom that most people in liberal democracies endorse. To return to the example of banning sex, most people would agree that we ought not do that because people should be allowed to do what they want. Make no mistake, some people really, really want to do drugs, perhaps in a way that mirrors the way people really, really want to have sex.

For whatever reason, we seem to have modules designed to work very hard to prevent people from doing the things they want to do.

This is arguably one of the greatest inconsistencies of modern times, given that our press secretary modules, at least in the West, are always going on and on about our deep, fundamental abiding commitment to liberty, the point with which I close the book. But first, a moment to ensure I've explained to your satisfaction *why everyone (else) is a hypocrite.*

Why everyone (else) is a hypocrite

Modularity explains why everyone is a hypocrite. Moral(istic) modules constrain others' behavior. The mob's moral sticks can be used to prevent an arbitrarily wide set of acts. At the same time, other modules advance our own fitness interests, often by doing the very same acts our moral modules condemn. In this sense, the explanation for hypocrisy lies in the rather quotidian notion of competition. Organisms are designed to advance their own fitness interests, which entails harming others and helping oneself and one's allies. Hypocrisy is, in its most abstract sense, no different from other kinds of competition.

So, if hypocrisy is nothing less—but nothing more—than a manifestation of competition, then why does it seem so offensive? And it is offensive: It ranks 8 out of a possible 9, using the circles of Dante's *Inferno* as a metric.

The answer lies in the nature of morality. One might wonder why morality evolved in the first place,[7] but a key feature of morality is that humans seem designed to accept—even create—rules that constrain their own behavior, *as long as these rules constrain others' behavior as well.* Morality can be seen as the informal equivalent of a justice system. I'll agree to rules that specify that *I* can be punished for various deeds, but only as long as *everyone else* is subject to the same rules. This makes sense; we shouldn't expect evolved creatures to be designed to consent to limit their own options, but not others'.

This means that a key—perhaps *the* key—feature of moral cognition is that morality, to be stable, must include *impartiality*, the idea that rules apply equally to everyone. Impartiality is crucial because without it, rules become nothing more than a way from some people to coerce others. As one might expect, humans *don't* tend to want to accept rules that bind them but not others.[8] Imagine the fate of one of our fictional birds that agreed to a rule that prevented him, but no other birds, from mating; such a rule would be, from this bird's (genes') perspective, an evolutionary disaster. Such complacent designs would be quickly selected out.

So, if we think of morality as rules that bind behavior, then we might expect that, by and large, people might be designed to favor rules that bind everyone equally. This is not unlike John Rawls's idea that good principles are those that everyone would agree to if they did not know their particular place or role in society until after the rules were made. This leads people to rules that apply more or less equally to all.[9]

Impartiality, then, implements a kind of Rawlsian morality. People will accept the threat of punishment, as long as the sword of justice is poised over the heads of everyone. Rawlsian morality, more or less, equalizes costs and benefits across individuals. Everyone is willing to play soccer under the rule that imposes penalties for using one's hands—as long as both teams play by the same rule. A key part of moral cognition is that it is designed to oppose violations of impartiality because impartiality prevents morality from being a net cost to disfavored individuals.[10]

Hypocrisy undermines impartiality. A rule that says *anyone* who does X will have costs imposed on them, for a surpassingly large number of X's, is something that one might expect evolved creatures to get behind: Such a rule might prevent me from doing X, but I'm no worse off than anyone else, who is similarly constrained, as in soccer. If you think of morality as all of us holding sticks that we beat rule-breakers with, then when the rules apply to everyone, no one is, to a first approximation, worse off. But if we use our sticks on some people but not others, that's just naked aggression.

So, when Spitzer condemns prostitution but then avails himself of it, he is, obviously, doing the thing that he says others must not do. The rules do not apply to him. The human mind seems designed to object strongly to this; if the mob's moral sticks are applied unequally, then these sticks become instruments of coercion, a way to impose costs on some to the benefit of others. Evolved creatures should not be designed to favor such a state of affairs (unless they are the advantaged individuals). Indeed, they ought to have strong intuitions against it, which they do.

The hypocrisy embodied in contradictory moral positions amounts to the same thing. Because people are affected differently by moral rules, as illustrated by the example of the birds, people have different interests in which rules are in place.[11] This makes the notion of moral principles from which rules are derived important: People might well be willing to agree that certain principles—such as individual liberty—should determine which rules can be put in place. Applied uniformly, this, more or less, prevents individuals from gaining advantages.

However, when a moral principle is applied in one case but not another to which it is relevant, people are, in essence, trying to get those and only those moral rules good for them (or bad for others) while excluding rules that harm them (but help others). Once morality is seen for what it is—a group of people's decisions about what acts will result in punishment—then it is clear that evolved systems ought to be designed to try to prevent others from using these moral sticks differentially to their own advantage. The uniform application of moral principles prevents this; hypocrisy undermines it.

At its core, then, hypocrisy really amounts to *favoritism*.[12] When rules apply to you but not to me, I'm better off. Our intuitions surrounding hypocrisy are designed to prevent others from using the mob's (or the headman's or the police's) moral sticks in a way that benefits themselves, their family, and their allies.

The uniform application of moral principles in deriving moral rules makes buffet morality—picking and choosing rules—more difficult. And, again, we would expect people to be on the lookout for such inconsistencies in others.

There is, then, an advantage in detecting others' hypocrisy. Identifying and pointing out hypocrisy helps to recruit others in suppressing the attempts of hypocrites to gain advantage. It would not be surprising to find that humans have modules whose job it is to detect inconsistencies in others.[13] Detecting and pointing out such inconsistencies would be of substantial value in recruiting allies against the inconsistent individual.

What about our own hypocrisy? As we've seen, people think themselves less biased than others, and in the domain of hypocrisy, this has been known since biblical times: "Why do you look at the speck of sawdust in your brother's eye and pay no attention to the plank in your own eye?"[14] Why are people blind to their own moral inconsistencies?

First, moral inconsistency can often be hard to notice. The inconsistencies in the abortion debate are infrequently mentioned, for instance. It seems that we're just not all that good at noticing these sorts of inconsistencies, which is an asset for hypocrites. Given this fact, that many inconsistencies remain unnoticed, one can exploit the advantages of hypocrisy without worrying, in every case, about the costs of detection. That is, *we need only be as consistent as others notice and hold us accountable for*. In this sense, inconsistency is a little like the joke about the two hikers who come across a bear. One starts to put his sneakers on, while the other points out that he can't outrun the bear. "I don't have to outrun the bear; I have to outrun *you.*"

This might be one reason that politicians appear to be such hypocrites. My guess is that—and maybe I'm just naïve—politicians, despite appearances, aren't actually all that much more hypocritical than the rest of us. It's just that the rest of us skate by without anyone noticing. Politicians are unlike the rest of us because (1) they frequently have to make their moral stands public—how many people know your position on gay marriage?—and (2) they are tempted in ways the rest of us are not—when was the last time someone offered you $50,000 for preferential treatment on a municipal waste-disposal contract? Because politicians have to express moral condemnation publicly, when they commit immoral acts they can be found to have condemned them, on the record, in the *New York Times.* Having to say that many things are wrong, combined with public scrutiny, makes hypocrisy among politicians and other publicly visible moralists, such as religious leaders, easy to spot.

For the rest of us, well, hypocrisy is part of the modular design. We condemn because our moralistic modules are designed to constrain others but there is nothing that keeps our behavior consistent with our condemnation. And we can get by with a great deal of inconsistency because it's not always easy for others to notice it. We can be as inconsistent as others allow us to be. Because being caught in inconsistency is damaging, it makes sense not to call attention to it, and one way to do that is for our own modules simply not to be designed to notice. When it comes to seeing our own hypocrisy, just like crossing the street in Philadelphia, remaining strategically ignorant can be advantageous.

epilogue

American independence from England began with the self-evident truth that people had certain "unalienable Rights, that among these are Life, *Liberty* and the pursuit of Happiness." When Americans pledge allegiance to the flag, it is to a republic with *liberty* for all. In our national anthem, we celebrate living in the "land of the *free*." Other nations highlight their commitments to liberty as well; the French, for example, put *liberté* first in their top-three list.

I don't know what else "freedom" and "liberty" might mean if not the idea that I should be able to do as I please as long as it doesn't harm your ability to do as *you* please.

Our brains—our press secretary modules—are good at broadcasting that we are in favor of liberty—but an army of other modules work in the other direction at every turn.

Our moral psychology is a many-headed beast. For reasons that science has not yet explained, we want to prevent people from doing any number of things. The mind's subroutines work to prevent other people taking certain kinds of drugs, doing certain acts with their bodies, and selling their livers.

It's true that we psychologists are partly to blame. We don't yet understand where these systems of moral condemnation come from.

But one thing we do understand—which I hope to have persuaded you in this book—is that these systems in your head are acting separately. This means that while there is an important sense in which some of your modules "believe in" *promoting* others' liberty and freedom, other modules simultaneously "believe in" *restricting* other people's liberty. This is one of the challenges of coming to terms with having a modular mind.

We can simply accept these inconsistencies. We can say that it's OK to claim to be in favor of freedom but to think, vote, and act in ways that restrict other people's freedoms. As long as you don't mind being a hypocrite, then that's fine.

My own view is that while hypocrisy is the natural state of the human mind, it makes for bad policy. If people say that they are in favor of liberty, failing to hold them accountable for the view that others' liberties should be constrained on pain of punishment gives them a blank check to use authority in any way at all. The whole point of agreeing on the principles that should guide rules is to limit the rules. To allow unchecked exceptions and inconsistencies is to undermine the agreements that we have made on the rules that govern us.

Moral judgments are sticks, and a moral rule is just a way to say that people who do something should be punished for it. When we all have the same view—particularly in a democracy—we are saying that we as a group will use our sticks to stop people from doing various things.

In many cases, it's hard to argue against the application of our moral sticks. People who harm others for their own gain ought to be subject to punishment.[1] But if we are allowed to make rules, using our sticks for whatever we want, then we're allowed to prevent people from whatever our modules come up with, whether it's certain kinds of sexual acts, market transactions, or even clothing choices. Failing to use moral sticks in a way that is constrained by principles allows us to use them as, well, *sticks*, aggressively controlling others. In my view, if a moral rule can't be justified as *consistent with the set of moral principles,* then it shouldn't be allowed.

When I talk about these ideas, I often have Emerson quoted to me. *A foolish consistency is the hobgoblin of little minds.* Yes, a *foolish* consistency is. Indeed, in this book I've documented a great deal of inconsistency in people's minds, and I think it's just fine. I'm certainly not going to worry about or fault anyone for seeing two lines as unequal yet saying that they are equal.

But morality is not perception. In morality, consistency matters. When moral rules are allowed that are inconsistent with moral principles, those principles are compromised. When moral rules are applied to some individuals but not others, we are using our moral sticks for inter-group oppression, also something that many of us would like to work against.

Moral consistency is hard. It *really, really* feels to many people that those who commit incest should be punished. I don't know why we have modules that cause us to think that, but we do.

As Walt Whitman wrote, we are large. We contain multitudes. Modules make us conflicted, and inconsistent.

But by the same token, they make us flexible, and different modules exert more or less control under different circumstances, in more or less conflict depending on the circumstances. Awareness of these conflicts gives us the opportunity to appreciate the conflict, and to change the balance of power.

Moralistic modules often win the battle in their struggle with the principle of liberty in many areas of our personal lives and our political discourse.

There is a deep inconsistency between what these modules do and the principle of liberty that we supposedly hold so dearly.

This is one kind of inconsistency which, in my view, we would be better off without.

notes

Chapter 1
Consistently Inconsistent

1 Gazzaniga & LeDoux 1978.
2 See Hirstein 2005 for a nice recent book about "confabulation," or, less technically, "just making stuff up."
3 This apparently has legs. Walton (1999) claims that a variant of this question dates back to Greek philosophers in the 4th century B.C.
4 Ramachandran & Blakeslee 1998, p. 43.
5 Ibid., p. 45.
6 Biran et al. 2006, p. 565. See also Biran & Chatterjee 2004.
7 Biran et al. 2006, p. 567.
8 See Wegner (2002), who uses these and some of the other examples I also like in order to illustrate some similar points.
9 Pegna et al. 2005; Morris et al. 2001.
10 Gelder et al. 2008.
11 Frith 2005, p. 767.
12 Davidson (1998) makes a similar move, suggesting that normal minds are like "a brain suffering from a perhaps temporary self-inflicted lobotomy" (p. 8).

13 Others have used this example to illustrate various points about the nature of visual experience (e.g., Pinker 2002). My point is slightly different from the usual one, which focuses on the implications of the fact that two mutually incompatible representations exist in the same mind, independent of issues associated with consciousness, experience, or representational format.

14 This famous image is by Richard Gregory. Again, it has been used by other authors to illustrate a similar principle. Ramachandran, in *A Brief Tour of Consciousness*, says of it that "you can sense your visual brain trying to solve a perceptual problem" (p. 48). There's something odd about that idea that *you* can sense *your visual brain* (I address this later, in chapter 3). Whatever the "you" is in that sentence, it must be some bit of your brain, so the sentence has to mean something like: One part of your brain can sense another part of your brain.

15 Note that not everyone experiences this illusion. For a recent discussion of the implications of this fact for arguments about what I'll refer to as informational encapsulation, see McCauley & Henrich 2006. The authors, in their conclusion, say, in part, that "*informational encapsulation is not comprehensively specified in the human genome*" (p. 20, emphasis original). For my views on "specification" of traits "in the human genome," see Barrett & Kurzban 2006.

16 Vokey & Read 1985, p. 1237.

17 This term is sometimes used in computer science to refer to a related concept, and also is referred to as "information hiding" (Parnas 1972). The basic idea is that I can write a subroutine that others can use without their having to know anything about how it works. The details of the procedure are "hidden" from view.

18 Landsburg 2007, p. 177.

19 The large number of recent books about how people are "irrational" illustrates how thinking is changing about this. I address this in more detail in chapter 8.

20 Having said that, this example isn't quite as fanciful as it seems. Computer scientist Ronald Arkin produced a report of "recommendations for the implementation of an ethical control and reasoning system potentially suitable for constraining lethal actions in an autonomous robotic system" (Ronald C. Arkin, "Governing Lethal Behavior: Embedding Ethics in a Hybrid Deliberative/Reactive Robot Architecture," http://www.cc.gatech.edu/ai/ robot-lab/online-publications/formalizationv35.pdf).

21 See Parnas 1972 for an interesting discussion of modularity in computer science, in which he talks about "modularization as a mechanism for

improving the flexibility and comprehensibility of a system" (p. 1053). From my (admittedly very limited) reading in computer science, it does not seem controversial that modularity *increases*, rather than decreases, flexibility. It is unclear why this idea is, in contrast, so controversial in psychology.

Chapter 2
Evolution and the Fragmented Brain

1 Braitenberg 1984.
2 Ibid., p.12.
3 Braitenberg uses the term "instinct" a little differently from the way I do here.
4 This use differs from the way Fodor (1983) used the term in his landmark book. For a discussion of the Fodorian view compared to my own, see Barrett & Kurzban 2006. Other important pieces on modularity that inform the material here include Barrett 2005; Coltheart 1999; Cosmides & Tooby 1994b; Sperber 2005.
5 See especially Minsky 1985.
6 Pinker 1999.
7 Dawkins 1976.
8 Fodor 2000.
9 Tooby & Cosmides 1992.
10 Cochran and Harpending's (2009) recent book has generated a great deal of discussion about this issue. There is a crucial difference between rapid genetic change on the one hand and the evolution of complex adaptations on the other. It is important to note that they are interested in the latter. Cochran and Harpending themselves note that they "think that this argument concerning the evolution of complex adaptations is correct, but it underestimates the importance of simple adaptations, those that involve changes in one or a few genes" (p. 10), and that they "expect that most of the recent changes in humans are evolutionarily shallow, one mutation deep for the most part" (p. 12). They make a convincing case for their view. This does not change the logic of the argument presented here that human mental adaptations are designed for the past rather than the future. The adaptations I discuss here are complex and are, in that sense, quite unlike skin color and lactose tolerance, for example.
11 Cochran & Harpending 2009. See Burnham & Phelan 2000, for an excellent account of implications of human design for past environments.
12 See, for instance, Barrett, Cosmides, & Tooby 2007.
13 Cosmides & Tooby 2001.
14 Vogel 1998.

15 Burnham & Phelan 2000.

16 Brown 1991.

17 Dawkins 1976.

18 Some people don't like the word "design" to be used in the way that I am using it here. As the material in this chapter should make clear, I intend no consciousness or intention when I use the word. The process of natural selection is a causal process by which mechanisms come to be that have functions, and they have the properties they do *by virtue of the fact that they perform these functions*. Natural selection "designs" organisms' features in this sense. The eye is no less designed for seeing than cameras are for taking pictures. I therefore use the term "design" without blushing, as many others have, and use this term throughout the rest of the book. See Williams 1966, and Dawkins 1986.

19 See Williams 1966 for a discussion.

20 Ossher & Tarr 2001, p. 43. See also Baldwin & Clark 2000.

21 I was intrigued by Rasmussen & Niles (2005), who *assume* that biology— including psychology—is modular, and use the evolutionary success of modular systems—including humans—as a basis for arguing for the value of modularity in human-engineered systems. This was the first time I had seen the argument in this direction.

22 http://en.wikipedia.org/wiki/Domain_Specific_Language (retrieved 7/1/2009).

23 Cosmides & Tooby 1994a. See also Gigerenzer & Selton 2001.

24 Reynolds & Tymann 2008, p. 59.

25 Pinker 1994.

26 Weiner 1994.

27 See Marr 1982.

28 Symons 1979; Tooby & Cosmides 1992.

29 Pinker (2005) uses this example.

30 McElreath et al. 2008. Here I am disagreeing with an argument made in a chapter of which I myself am an author, in a book on human inconsistency.

31 Bramble & Lieberman 2004.

32 Chris Maume, "Pistorius Bounds on Despite Olympic Knockback," *The Independent* (London), March 8, 2008.

33 Cliff Gromer, "The Nine Legs of Paul Martin," *Popular Mechanics*, November 2002.

34 Nisbett & Wilson 1977.

35 Ibid., p. 231.

36 This also has an analog in computer science, in particular the principle of "information hiding," which Parnas, Clements, & Weiss (1984) describe this way:

> According to this principle, system details that are likely to change independently should be the secrets of separate modules. . . .
>
> Each data structure is used in only one module; it may be directly accessed by one or more programs within the module but not by programs outside the module. Any other program that requires information stored in a module's data structures must obtain it by calling access programs belonging to that module.

The use of the word "secrets" is an intriguing parallel with the arguments here.

37 See, especially, Trivers 2000.

Chapter 3
Who Is "I"?

1 This issue has been discussed by any number of philosophers and psychologists. I have been impressed with Danny Wegner's lucid thoughts on this topic (see, e.g., Wegner 2005). His views in certain respects resonate with those expressed here. For example, we agree that people seem to acknowledge this argument explicitly, but then introduce a cranium commando implicitly in their explanations. I think he is exactly correct that "the notions of controlled and automatic processes carry with them the implicit assumption of a kind of homunculus" (p. 21). Damasio 1994 is another good source for discussion of this issue.

2 Minsky 1985, p. 17.

3 Here and elsewhere, Gazzaniga's idea of an "interpreter" (e.g., Gazzaniga 1998) resembles the kind of view I'm endorsing.

4 Dennett 1991.

5 Ibid., p. 108.

6 Fodor 1998.

7 Wilson 2002.

8 Some of the material in this section is addressed in Kurzban 2008.

9 Dennett 1991, p. 107.

10 See, e.g., Jackendoff 1987. Note that the claim that it is only the "last" link in this chain very well might not be correct, but that issue doesn't change the structure of the argument here.

11 See Wegner 2002, p. 55, for a similar view; see also his figure 3.1, p. 68, for a nice illustration of how to think about this issue of thoughts causing one's

actions. This book, *The Illusion of Conscious Will*, addresses a number of the themes discussed here, and our views seem to be compatible.

12 Libet 1999, p. 49.

13 B. Keim, "Brain Scanners Can See Your Decisions before You Make Them," *Wired*, 13 April 2008.

14 See also Wegner 2003.

15 Weisberg et al. 2008, p. 475.

Chapter 4
Modular Me

1 "Internal Displacement," season 7, episode 11, first aired 1/15/2006.

2 Schelling 1960, p. 161.

3 Ibid., p. 38.

4 Haidt 2001, p. 814.

5 Cushman, Young, & Hauser, 2006; Hauser et al. 2007.

6 Haidt 2006, pp. 4–5.

7 Ibid., p. 5.

8 In Kurzban & Aktipis 2007, I referred to this as the "Social Cognitive Interface." Here, I'll stick with calling this system the press secretary.

9 Dennett 1981, p. 156, 152.

10 Humphrey & Dennett 1998, pp. 38–39.

11 Ibid., pp. 42–43.

12 Elements of this idea appear elsewhere. John Elster (1985) reviewed some of the history of these sorts of ideas in the introduction to his edited volume, *The Multiple Self*. Tetlock and Manstead (1985) reviewed the "impression management" literature to that point, illustrating the expansion of theories that took seriously the notion that many domains of behavior might profitably be construed in the context of goals associated with controlling and manipulating one's reputation. Rorty (1985) uses the analogy of a medieval city "of relatively autonomous neighborhoods, linked by small lanes that change their names half way across their paths, a city that is a very loose confederation of neighborhoods of quite different kinds, each with its distinctive internal organization" (p. 116); "it might seem as if the agent disappears into a loose community. . . . The *persona* who says *I* is not necessarily central, not an absolute ruler or even surveyor of the complex actions of the subsystems . . . the *I* is the entire configuration, the loosely connected system seen as whole" (pp. 130–131). The parallels ought to be obvious. See Schlenker & Pontari (2000) for a review relating to self-presentation. As mentioned above, Gazzaniga's idea of the "interpreter," a part of

the brain in the left hemisphere that digests information about the individual's behavior and generates as coherent and cohesive a narrative as possible, is similar. Other representative works by important researchers in the area include: Boyer, Robbins, & Jack 2005; Baumeister 1982; Gallagher 2000; Jones 1964; Jones & Pittman 1982; Neisser 1988; Schlenker & Leary 1982; Tedeschi & Norman 1985. See Hirstein (2005) for a very nice recent treatment of closely related issues.

13 Fiddick, Cosmides, & Tooby (2000) used a little riff like this in their title. Sue me.

14 The cognitive dissonance literature is vast, and I do not try to engage it here. I discuss it a little in Kurzban & Aktipis 2007, pp. 139–141. There, I make a few points that I will just summarize. First, it is clear that there are many inconsistencies that people maintain, perhaps the most obvious of which are commitments to intuitive theories of physics and biology along with supernatural beliefs that contradict these commitments (e.g., Boyer 2001). Second, the motive for consistency might have to do with being *perceived* as consistent, given that other people might have mechanisms designed to detect discrepancies (Sperber 2000). This suggests that the "motive for consistency" is really a motive to *appear* consistent, an idea that appears in various forms in this literature (Baumeister 1982; Tice 1992; Tice & Baumeister 2001). This idea is actually implicit even when it looks as though it is being denied. For instance, Aronson, Fried, and Stone (1991), arguing that the phenomenon has to do with maintaining consistency with one's behavior and how *one thinks of oneself*, emphasize "not practicing what you preach" (p. 1636). "Preaching" is what one says to others, not what one thinks of oneself. This locates the issue of maintaining consistency in what the social world knows, rather than one's own representational system. My arguments resonate with this view, that to the extent inconsistency needs to be corrected, it is likely to be in the context of others' perceptions.

15 Kurzban 2001.

16 Dutton & Aron 1974. I omit here the various controversies that surround this classic study.

17 Cosmides & Tooby 2000; Tooby & Cosmides 2008.

18 Ames & Dissanayake 1996, p. 6.

19 McLaughlin 1996, p. 41.

20 Stich 1983 is still a good source for arguments about doing good cognitive science with folk psychological categories. He argues that "the folk psychological concept of belief . . . *ought not* to play any significant role

in a science aimed at explaining human cognition and behavior" (p. 5, emphasis original).

21 I'm not going after the notion of belief here, as some philosophers have, but rather the notion of unitary agents. Ross (2005, p. 254) also discusses the notion of unified agency.

22 This example comes from Nosek, Greenwald, & Banaji 2007.

23 See, e.g., research in the tradition of Flavell 1970.

24 Greenwald & Banaji 1995; Greenwald McGhee, & Schwartz1998.

25 Lane et al. (2007, p. 84) write: "A person's IAT score is no more a measure of his or her 'true' attitude than that person's response to a Likert scale." See also Nosek, Greenwald, & Banaji 2007, which has a nice section called *"Does the IAT Reveal Cognitions That Are More 'True' or 'Real' Than Self-Report?"* (they essentially answer "no"). I note in passing that this is another place where "the individual" is taken to be "the part that talks." They say that "the IAT and self-report can differ because the individual is unaware of the implicitly measured associations" (p. 282).

26 DeSteno, Bartlett, & Salovey 2006, p. 522. In the original, they specify that the jealousy is coming from an "Evolved Cognitive Module," which I have replaced with "module" here, for simplicity.

27 Here, in this book on hypocrisy, it's impossible not to mention that DeSteno, Bartlett, & Salovey (2006), in the paper in which they implicitly endorse dualism, accuse *us* of positing a homunculus, the little brain in the big brain. Delicious.

28 Nagel 1974.

29 The quoted material was drawn from the script available at IMSDB: http://www.imsdb.com/scripts/Awakenings.html.

30 It's always difficult to tell what's going to have legs. "There's an app for that" was an advertising slogan Apple used to market the iPhone, meaning that the applications you could download for the phone could do whatever job it was that you needed done. This is a riff on that slogan. As an aside, Jenna Wortham ("Apple's Game Changer, Downloading Now," *New York Times*, 5 December 2009) remarked that "smartphones have become the Swiss Army knives of the digital age" and "provide a staggering arsenal of functions. . . ." This is the same analogy that Cosmides & Tooby (1994a) used to talk about their modular view of the mind, an interesting convergence.

31 I found this at http://web.media.mit.edu/~push/ExaminingSOM.html (retrieved 7/1/2009). The source is given as P. Singh, *Computing and Informatics*, 2004, vol. 22, part 6, pp. 521–544.

Chapter 5
The Truth Hurts

1 Fodor 2000, p. 68, emphasis original. Pears (1985) appears to take a similar position, suggesting: "Truth seems to be an overriding goal . . ." (p. 62). See McKay & Dennett 2009 for a recent discussion.

2 Fodor 2000, p. 67.

3 This is from Baber's (1826) memoirs, pp. 222–223. I came across this example in Stewart (2006).

4 Churchland 1987, pp. 547–548.

5 Schwartz 2004.

6 Todd 1997 is a good example. See also Todd & Miller 1999.

7 Dana, Weber, & Kuang 2007. See also Dana, Cain, & Dawes 2006.

8 For very nice discussions of this, see Schelling 1960 and Frank 1988.

9 Foot 1967.

10 See, e.g., Hauser, Young, & Cushman 2008.

11 Schelling (1960) addressed this issue as well.

12 *The Wire*, "All Due Respect," season 3, episode 2.

13 Kurzban, DeScioli & O'Brien, 2007.

14 Webber (1997, p. 267) discusses cases such as *State v. Hinkhouse* in which a man was convicted of attempted murder for having unprotected sex with women while he knew that he was HIV positive.

15 Generally, it seems to be considered to be less morally wrong to fail to act than to act.

16 Byrne & Whiten 1988; Whiten & Byrne 1997.

17 Cacioppo, Hawkley, & Berntson 2003.

18 Uchino, Cacioppo, & Kiecolt-Glaser 1996.

19 Bradburn 1969.

20 Williams 2007, p. 434.

21 Don Symons's *The Evolution of Human Sexuality*, David Buss's *The Evolution of Desire*, and Geoffrey Miller's *The Mating Mind* are excellent further reading.

22 DeScioli & Kurzban 2009a.

23 DeScioli 2008; DeScioli & Kurzban 2009a.

24 Tooby & Cosmides 1996.

25 Trivers (2000) developed a version of this idea, "hiding" potentially damaging information away in parts of the mind so that it doesn't "leak." Trivers seems to define self-deception as "active misrepresentation of reality to the conscious mind" (p. 114). I don't define it the same way, and think that

"to" is puzzling. Trivers's view of the conscious mind as "a social front, maintained to deceive others" (p. 115) is similar to my own, though I think his statement is too strong, as deception is not *all* the conscious mind does. Material in this and subsequent chapters resembles Trivers's views to a degree. See also Nesse & Lloyd 1992.

26 Ambady & Rosenthal 1992, p. 267.

27 Kurzban & Weeden 2005, 2007.

28 Baumeister 1999b, p. 8.

29 Dawson, Savitsky, & Dunning 2006.

30 The explanation for such phenomena is usually "self-protection," another one of many "self-" terms that seems to mean something like, people don't want to feel bad. See chapter 8.

31 Trivers (2000) has a similar account, although what he refers to as "self-deception" I would call "strategically wrong." See his chapters 5 and 6.

32 Krebs and Denton (1997) observed, "It is in our interest to induce others to overestimate our value" (p. 36).

33 Merton 1969; see the subsection entitled "A Sociological Parable," p. 476.

34 Which is not to discount the Greeks' stories that contained self-fulfilling prophecies.

35 James 1897/1979, p. 24.

36 Surbey (2004, p. 126) recently took a similar view: "By boosting a man's confidence and self-esteem and suppressing his faults and fears, self-deception could lead to greater attractiveness to the opposite sex."

37 I don't treat lying at length here. Lying is a bad solution to the extent that you might get caught and getting caught is costly. There are also other costs, such as the problem of having to keep track of what lie you told to whom, to try to reduce the chance of detection; this adds computational baggage to the operation. Of course I'm not saying that people don't lie or that lying isn't used effectively in social transactions. I'm saying that being wrong has advantages over lying.

38 Again, this seems to be Trivers's view. We differ in that he sees things as binary—conscious and not—rather than modular. Figure 1 of Trivers 2000 (p. 116) is illustrative.

39 Dawkins 2006, p. 77.

40 Yes, I see the irony here of the argument I'm making. My view is that some modular systems really do "police" consistency *within the modular system*.

41 See also David Sloan Wilson's *Darwin's Cathedral*, and the more recent *Breaking the Spell* by Daniel Dennett and *The God Delusion* by Richard Dawkins.

42 My views are in Kurzban & Christner (in press). They bear a certain resemblance to those of Sosis and Bressler (2003).

43 Pinker 2005, p. 18. I think it's worth pointing out that why people care which supernatural beliefs other people hold remains a mystery. Kurzban & Christner (in press).

44 Sources vary on the details of the politics surrounding Bruno.

45 Janet Elder, "Finding Religion on the Campaign Trail," *New York Times*, 7/11/2007.

Chapter 6
Psychological Propaganda

1 I don't address the issue of legal culpability here. If the mind is modular, then we're locking up a large number of modules that didn't cause their owner to do anything wrong, along with the module or modules that did. I don't see any way around this, since we can't (yet?) punish one set of modules but not others.

2 Taylor 1989, p. 157. As an aside, she resolves the problem with reference to "selective attention" and "selective memory." She claims that "it recognizes negativity at some preconscious level and then shields it from view" (p. 158). The first use of the word "it" in that sentence seems to refer to "pre-processing of information," which is a strange thing to be "recognizing" anything. As in the case of "one" discussed above, little pronouns can loom large. It is not clear what "it" is. For other "paradox" claims, see Mele 2001, chapter 1, p. 7. See also Mele 1998 and Pears 1985.

3 There is much philosophy on this topic. Nearly all of it has to do with the fact that philosophers start with the seemingly innocuous notion that you have to talk about Agents having Beliefs, rather than modules having representations. The intuitive appeal of the notion that I, as a whole, have a belief has been (and continues to be) an impediment to clear thinking about this. Those authors who notice that division in the mind completely finesses this issue don't get bent out of shape about it. See, especially, Davidson (2004), who writes that "people can and do sometimes keep closely related but opposite beliefs apart. To this extent we must accept the idea that there can be boundaries between parts of the mind" (p. 211). See, e.g., Dupuy 1998 for some authors' views.

4 Cross 1977, pp. 9–10.

5 Alicke & Govorun 2005.

6 See Dunning 2005, especially chapter 6, on this point. More generally, this book, *Self-insight,* is a good source for research on the issues I present in this chapter and indeed in this book. There is an important difference

between Dunning's book and mine. As Dunning puts it, in his volume, there is "no overarching theory of self-insight, or the lack thereof" (p. 10). This is fairly typical of social psychology: Without a theory of evolved function, the field tends to be a loose aggregation of research findings.

7 Dunning & Cohen 1992.

8 Dunning, Meyerowitz, & Holzberg 1989.

9 Mabe & West 1982.

10 Epley & Whitchurch 2008.

11 Apparently not everyone would agree with this. Van Leeuwen (2007) recently took cases like this to be paradigmatic cases of self-deception rather than being wrong. He asks us to " take the case of the abused spouse who convinces herself that her husband will stop beating her for good after this time. I am inclined to count her mental state as self-deception . . ." (p. 331). Note that the spouse "convinces herself," whatever that means. In any case, this seems—to me—to be a case in which someone is wrong, but, somehow, *ought* to be able to be right, but we need to be very careful when we try to articulate what that "ought" means. Van Leeuwen, it might be worth noting, would not approve of the model advanced here. He's worried that if I believe something (that is false) so that I can persuade others, my action is then guided by the false information, which leaves me worse off. This worry is alleviated if one system is active when deception is needed and another system is active when the "correct" action is called for; this is discussed in the next chapter.

12 The view I'm endorsing touches the large literature on "strategic self-enhancement," but is distinct in that my use of "strategic" is in the game-theoretical sense of leading to better outcomes in social games. Other authors have similar ideas. See, e.g., Leary 2007.

13 This view bears some relationship to the social psychological literature on "self-presentation," about which Erving Goffman had a great deal to say in his 1959 book, *The Presentation of Self in Everyday Life*.

14 The game here described is similar to but not quite the same as in Godfray 1991. In Godfray, baby birds are essentially competing with future siblings rather than existing siblings.

15 The idea that being strategically wrong is in the service of social propaganda is similar to a view Mark Leary and his colleagues have been advancing. Recently (Leary 2007, p. 328) he wrote that "people do not self-enhance for its own sake but rather because they are trying to increase their value and acceptance in others' eyes." It's worth noting that this view is very different from the view that people self-enhance in the service of feeling better.

16 Alicke & Govorun 2005, p. 87.

17 Preston & Harris 1965.

18 McKenna & Albery 2001.

19 Alicke et al. 1995.

20 Williams & Gilovich 2008.

21 I do, by the way, think that there are mechanisms designed to cause people to *appear* consistent to others, though this is a large issue that I don't treat in detail here. Cialdini (e.g., 2001, chapter 3), among others, has discussed this.

22 See, e.g., Schacter 2001.

23 But see Moore & Healy 2008 for arguments about how uncertainty can account for the direction of these types of effects.

24 Pronin, Gilovich & Ross, 2004.

25 Streufert & Streufert (1969, p. 146) wrote that "blame for failure is placed externally, while credit for success is ascribed to one's own group if conditions permit." See also Weiner et al. 1971. More recently, As Mark Leary (2007, p. 320) put it, "hundreds of studies have shown that people tend to attribute positive events to their own personal characteristics but attribute negative events to factors beyond their control."

26 Blaine & Crocker 1993.

27 Riess et al. 1981, p. 229.

28 See, for example, Moore 2007.

29 Compare, e.g., Kurman 2001 to Sedikides, Gaertner, & Vevea 2005. See also Mezulis et al. 2004.

30 Moore & Healy 2008.

31 See Tavris & Aronson 2007.

32 Daniel W. Reilly, "GOP: Oil Markets 'Responding' to Our Protest," CBS News, 8/8/2008.

33 See DeScioli & Kurzban 2009a, for a different presepctive.

34 Taylor (1989, p. 153) echoes these sentiments: "All of us have the creative capacity to prize the things that we are good at and to value less highly, if at all, those domains in which we lack talent."

35 James 1890/1950, p. 310.

36 Festinger 1954.

37 Tesser & Smith 1980, p. 584.

38 DeScioli & Kurzban 2009a.

39 Henslin 1967.

40 Goffman 1967, p. 193.

41 Langer 1975.

42 Bandura 1989, p. 1177.

43 Mechanisms designed to maximize *expected value* will not, obviously, always maximize percent correct (Wiley 1994). Smoke alarms are designed to minimize expected costs (see, e.g., Nesse 2005), but often err (i.e., produce a false positive) because their thresholds are set low.

44 Baumeister, Heatherton, & Tice 1993.

45 This difference was non-significant, but that's not crucial to the point here.

46 Baumeister, Heatherton, & Tice 1993, p. 148.

47 A technical aside on this important point: My friend Dan Nettle (2004) discusses this issue to try to show there are cases in which overestimating chances of success really can lead to better outcomes than using an unbiased estimate. The model he presents, however, rests on "rational" actors doing something manifestly irrational: using an estimate of the probability of success in making their decision even though their estimate is only poorly correlated with the true probability. As he and colleagues later put it, the advantage to overestimating only occurs "when the agents are unaware of noise" (Evans, Heuvelink, & Nettle, no date, p. 7). If you don't have any good information about the chance of success—meaning that a "rational" actor would simply assign a probability of .5—and the positive payoff for success is greater than the negative payoff of failure, then of course you do better ignoring the (bad) information about probability of success and attending only to the relative payoffs. See also Haselton & Nettle 2006. To reiterate, in games against Nature, in which what one communicates to others is not a factor, *a strategy that maximizes expected value simply cannot be beaten.* When the chance of success is unknown, maximizing expected value requires acting on the basis of only the payoff information. See also Kurzban & Christner (in press).

48 Fenton-O'Creevy et al. 2003.

49 John Tooby suggested it to me.

50 See Taleb 2001 for an excellent discussion.

51 Babad 1987.

52 See Markman & Hirt 2002 for a similar effect for American football.

53 Granberg & Brent 1983.

54 Weinstein 1980. See also Weinstein 1982. For more recent results, see Covey & Davies 2004. For a recent review, see Sheppard et al. 2002.

55 Van der Velde, van der Pligt, & Hooykaas 1994.

56 Williams & Gilovich 2008, p. 1122.

57 Helweg-Larsen, Sadeghian, & Webb 2002, p. 92.

58 This is an area in which my view diverges from Trivers (2000). He writes in this context that "mental operations that keep a positive future orientation at the forefront result in better future outcomes" (p. 126), which, it seems to

me, runs into the Frogger problem. Otherwise, some of the ideas here and in the next chapter overlap with his.

59 Windschitl, Kruger, & Simms 2003.

60 Rothman, Klein, & Weisman 1996.

61 Burger & Burns 1988.

62 Sedikides et al. 2002.

63 Sedikides & Gregg 2008, p. 108. For a recent discussion of these and related issues, see Sedikides & Luke 2007.

64 Martin 2002, p. 71. This kind of thing isn't as unusual as one might think. See the classic paper by Brickman, Coates, & Janoff-Bulman (1978).

65 Martin 2002, p. 12.

66 The absurd criticisms that I discuss in Kurzban 2002a continue to be leveled against the field.

67 Buller 2008.

68 For a very careful discussion of this issue, see Tooby & Cosmides 1990, especially pp. 386–388. They make the same point in Tooby and Cosmides 1992.

69 This is located at http://www.psych.ucsb.edu/research/cep/primer.html (retrieved August 2009).

70 Daly & Wilson 2007.

71 See p. 123 of Gould 2000.

72 Tooby & Cosmides 1992, p. 62.

73 Tooby and Cosmides wrote a letter to the editor to the New York Review of Books that discusses this issue. See http://cogweb.ucla.edu/Debate/CEP_Gould.html, retrieved 5/12/2010.

74 Maynard Smith 1995, p. 46.

75 Kurzban 2002a. In later reading, I found a piece by Richard Dawkins in *New Scientist* in 1985, in which he reviews *Not in Our Genes*. Dawkins writes, "Rose et al. cannot substantiate their allegation about sociobiologists believing in inevitable genetic determination, because the allegation is a simple lie." What I take to be strategic error, Dawkins takes as a falsehood. I concede my "strategic error" interpretation gets harder to support as the identical incorrect claim, rebutted forcefully, persists over three decades.

76 Marcus 2008, p. 11.

77 The quote is drawn from Tooby & Cosmides (1995, p. 1193). Elsewhere, they wrote that "while adaptations are in some abstract sense undoubtedly far from optimal, they are nevertheless extremely well engineered" (Cosmides & Tooby 2000, pp. 95–96).

78 Tooby, & Cosmides 1995, p. 1191.

79 For an extensive treatment of memory, including some material on how the design of memory intersects with "positive illusions," see Schacter 2001.

80 This position is not all that different from that taken by Humphrey (2002), who also locates the explanation in the issue of trade-offs.

81 For a very nice treatment of this, see Nesse & Williams 1994.

82 See, e.g., Wedekind & Følstad 1994. See Råberg et al. 1998 for a discussion of the issue of trade-offs surrounding the immune system.

83 McKay & Dennett (2009) discuss this (drawing on Humphrey 2002).

84 Kaptchuk et al. (2008) investigated factors that influence the effect and concluded that "the patient-practitioner relationship is the most robust component."

Chapter 7
Self-Deception

1 Sedikides & Gregg 2008, p. 102. See Batson 2008, p. 58, for another recent use of the term in referring to simultaneously held contradictory beliefs.

2 See Hirstein 2005 for a recent volume that includes ideas on self-deception, among other issues.

3 Gur & Sackeim 1979.

4 Ibid., p. 150.

5 Ibid., p. 161.

6 Greenwald 1997, p. 51.

7 Ibid., p. 55.

8 In a recent review of this literature, Dunning et al. (2004, p. 79) suggested that, regarding views of their own health, people's "unrealistic optimism is based on a need to defend self-esteem against possible threats." I think that I am not myself being "strategically wrong" about the way the field views this issue.

9 See, e.g., Tooby et al. 2008.

10 I'm using "care" here as a metaphor to make this point, but of course natural selection is a causal process, and doesn't "care" about anything. The use of the metaphor is to make a point about what does and does not affect the feedback loop between a gene's effect and the replication rate of that gene. By what natural selection "cares" about, I mean all those things and only those things that have a causal effect on the replication rate of the relevant genes.

11 See previous endnote. Obviously, evolution doesn't literally tell you anything. Reinforcement mechanisms function (roughly) to cause the organism to (re-)engage in behaviors that bring about adaptive outcomes.

12 Scheff & Fearon 2004, emphasis original, both quotations from p. 74.

13 All quotes from ibid., p. 75.

14 Baumeister et al. 2003, p. 42.

15 Dawes, 1994, p. 237. Dawes was quoting from Mecca, Smelser, & Vasconcellos 1989.

16 Recent work links low self-esteem to violence (see, for example, Donnellan et al. 2005). However, again, these effects are small and do not establish low self-esteem as the causal variable (See also Trzesniewski et al. 2006).

17 Crocker & Park 2003, p. 291.

18 For an excellent recent treatment about the epidemic of positivity, see Ehrenreich 2009.

19 Brickman, Coates, & Janoff-Bulman 1978.

20 Like so many such things, this quotation has been mangled through the years, it seems. I'm just concerned with the sentiment here.

21 Brickman, Coates, & Janoff-Bulman 1978.

22 Minsky 1985, p. 68.

23 Leary, & Downs 1995.

24 Kirkpatrick & Ellis 2001.

25 McLaughlin 1996, p. 33.

26 Very recently, Mijović-Prelec and Prelec (2010) advanced some closely related ideas, suggesting that "genuine self-deception, as opposed to mere bias, is a byproduct of this specific modular architecture. Like ordinary deception, it is an external, public activity, involving overt statements or actions directed towards an audience, whether real or imagined." They suggest this view " draws attention to the possibility of a stable state of inauthentic belief, characterized by a chronic mismatch between what a person says and what they truly believe and experience" (p. 238). Other than the notion of what one "truly" believes, there are obvious close links to my view.

27 Trivers (2000) suggests a similar view to the one endorsed here.

28 As Pinker (1999, p. 421) put it, "the truth is useful, so it should be registered somewhere in the mind, walled off from the parts that interact with other people." (p. 421). Davidson (1985) seems to favor such a view, referring to "boundaries" in the mind that sit well with the modular account. This idea is present in much of Davidson's later work as well. See, e.g., Davidson 1998. See Kurzban & Aktipis 2007.

Chapter 8
Self-Control

1 Heidegger, of course, wondered about this in his lecture "What Is Metaphysics?"

2 It is reasonable to object that economists like Landsburg don't think about the mind or modularity because economics is not really about process, but rather outcomes. Fair enough.

3 Nothing here turns on whether this decision-making process is done "rationally," whatever that means, or by heuristics, of whatever stripe. The argument turns only on the idea that however it is done, it is done the same way at both times.

4 Kahneman, Knetsch, & Thaler 1991, p. 193. Other prominent economists have portrayed the mainstream position of the field similarly: Camerer, Loewenstein, & Prelec (2005) recently wrote: "Economists currently classify individuals on such dimensions as 'time preference,' 'risk preference,' and 'altruism.' These are seen as characteristics that are stable within an individual over time and consistent across activities" (p. 32). I like the way Ken Binmore (2007) put this, saying that "economists get by with *no theory at all* of why people choose one thing rather than another. The modern theory . . . assumes that we already know what people choose in some situations, and uses this data to deduce what they will chose in others—on the assumption that their behavior is consistent" (pp. 111–112, emphasis original). Note the explicit assumption of consistency. My claim is not, however, that all economists assume that all preferences are completely stable, or that they deny the plausibility of state-dependent preferences. I also hasten to point out that my analysis here completely omits any discussion of the important issues of costs and budget constraints, and ignores the success of models that include such constraints—see, e.g., Stigler & Becker (1977)—and I thank Bart Wilson for pointing this out to me.

5 See, e.g., Samuelson 1948.

6 Gintis (2005) discussed the issue of incorporating various kinds of preferences into economic theory. See Gigerenzer 1996 for, in my view, a very nice treatment of thinking about preferences within contexts.

7 Economists do not seem to worry about coffee/wine cases (see Sen 1997).

8 Yamagishi, Hashimoto, & Schug 2008.

9 See Sen 1997 for a discussion using fruit, rather than pens.

10 See, e.g., Shafir, Simonson, & Tversky 1993.

11 Again, note that economists don't seem to care what is placed into preference functions.

12 This line of reasoning is why I don't feel that the notion that people are "rational" if and only if they are "consistent" is any more useful than previous conceptions of rationality. In the limiting case, if by "consistent" we mean that people do the same thing if they are in exactly the same state in exactly the same context, then this is just physicalism. That is, it is trivially true that someone in the same (brain) state will make the same choice. I am perfectly comfortable saying that preferences are consistent *in this sense*.

13 I drew this from Wikipedia: http://en.wikipedia.org/wiki/Sidney_ Morgenbesser (retrieved 2/29/09).

14 Simonson & Tversky 1992. This type of phenomenon could be another case of reputation management, having to do with the fact that when options are not easily comparable, but one option is clearly better than one other option, it's easier to justify to others one's choice if you choose the one that's obviously better than one other option. See, e.g., Slovic 1975, Simonson 1989, and Shafir, Simonson, & Tversky 1993.

15 Slovic and Lichtenstein 1968.

16 Ibid.

17 Tversky, Slovic, & Kahneman 1990.

18 Dan Ariely's book *Predictably Irrational* and Dick Thaler and Cass Sunstein's book *Nudge* are good sources.

19 Tversky & Thaler 1990, p. 210.

20 Steedman and Krause (1985, p. 197) remarked that "when we turn to economic (and other) theory concerned with individual decision-takers, we find that the 'individual' of the theory is represented by a single, compete, transitive preference ordering," but they worry about the possibility of "many souls" and "inner conflict and contradiction." They quote J. R. Hicks as saying "There is no reason why one person should not combine a number of distinct want-systems" (p. 197). Elster (1985), in the same volume, cites Schelling 1980, for an example of the (simultaneous) desire for dessert and long life.

21 For some recent work related to the discounting work discussed here, see, for example, McClure et al. 2004. For a review, see Miller & Cohen 2001.

22 Stevens, Hallinan, & Hauser, 2005; Ainslie 1985.

23 Elster (1985), discussing preference reversals of the kind described here, says the reason for this "is not because two parts of the person have different preferences. Rather it is because *the* person reacts to the way in which the options are presented" (p. 5, emphasis original). Obviously, Elster and I disagree, and I would argue that saying that the person reacts differently to the way things are presented is not an *explanation* for the phenomenon in question but rather a restatement of it.

24 See the literature on risk-sensitive foraging, e.g., Stephens & John 1986. Recently, Wang & Dvorak (2010) showed that discounting choices depends on glucose levels in humans, just as one would expect from foraging theory.

25 Randy Gallistel's work on computing when to switch foraging patches is excellent. For example, see Gallistel 1994.

26 See the edited volume by Lichtenstein & Slovic (2006a), which gathers together papers that relate to this idea.

27 Frederick, Loewenstein, & O'Donoghue (2002) cite several sources for models that assume that "there are two agents, one myopic and one farsighted, who alternately take control of behavior," including Ainslie & Haslam 1992, Schelling 1984, and Winston 1980.

28 Thaler & Sunstein 2008, p. 42.

29 An aside: If this is right, then when we imprison a person, we are, in effect, punishing *all* of his modules for the intentions of a *subset* of his modules, not unlike putting conjoined twins in jail for the action one twin took while the other was asleep. Because modules are intertwined with one another, all are held responsible. One could argue about the justice of this, but it is difficult to see what the alternative might be.

30 Ariely 2008, p. 97.

31 Ermer, Cosmides, & Tooby 2008.

32 Lichtenstein and Slovic 2006b, p. 2.

33 Ibid., p. 20.

34 See pp. 391–392 in Frederick, Loewenstein, & O'Donoghue 2002. I note, however, that a graduate student at Penn, Eli Tsukayama, has persuaded me that there might be more inter-domain consistency than I would have thought.

35 Frederick, Loewenstein, & O'Donoghue 2002, p. 351. Ross (2005)—who addresses a number of issues at stake here—concludes that "whole people are not straightforward economic agents" (p. 317).

36 Frederick, Loewenstein, & O'Donoghue 2002, pp. 362, 351.

37 See ibid., p. 352. This paper is strongly recommended for those interested in the history of and current thought in this research area.

38 Ibid., p. 393.

39 Laibson, 2001, p. 83.

40 Slovic, 1995. See also Lichtenstein & Slovic (2006a); also, for example, Payne, Bettman, & Johnson 1993.

41 See Wegner (2005), who wonders about the same thing.

42 Mischel, Shoda, & Peake 1988, p. 687.

43 Shoda, Mischel, & Peake 1990.

44 Mischel, Shoda, & Rodriguez 1989.

45 Tangney, Baumeister, & Boone 2004. See Schmeichel & Zell 2007 for a test of the relationship between self-report and behavior in the domain of self-control.

46 Baumeister et al. 1998; all words in quotation marks from p. 1253.

47 See Van den Berg 1986 for a very nice little piece on this.

48 Masicampo & Baumeister 2008.

49 Gibson and Green 2002, p. 185.

50 Ibid., p. 198.

51 Gibson 2007, p. 73.

52 Clarke & Sokoloff 1998, p. 673.

53 Messier 2004, p. 39.

54 Clarke & Sokoloff 1998, p. 660.

55 I have in mind here evidence from imaging (PET, fMRI), in which percentage changes are small, and of course restricted to particular regions. See, e.g., Madsen et al. 1995.

56 Note also that in this work, researchers use Splenda for the control. While sucralose, which gives rise to the sensation of sweetness, is itself not metabolized, Splenda packets contain carbohydrates in the medium in which sucralose is delivered, and so have about 3 calories. The "zero calorie control" in these studies has an *order of magnitude* more calories than this (very large over-) estimate of how many calories are consumed. Note also that performance on physically taxing tasks (riding a stationary cycle) can be improved by simply swishing a sugar solution around in one's mouth (Chambers, Bridge, & Jones 2009). It could be that concentrated sugar in the mouth acts activates reward systems, which would explain why lemonade has this effect.

57 See, for example, Tomporowski 2003.

58 See Wang & Dvorak 2010 for a brief recent discussion. See also Dvorak & Simons 2009 for some recent work.

59 Even if "self-control" tasks do reduce glucose, my guess is that this will turn out to be due to the action of peripheral systems, rather than cognitive mechanisms.

60 Maybe less than one would think; see Murtagh & Todd 2004.

61 I have in mind systems associated with executive control (e.g., Miller & Cohen 2001).

62 This is an homage to the idea of a "sociometer."

63 Boksem and Tops (2008) explain "mental fatigue" with reference to computations of costs, though they construe the costs as energetic, rather than the opportunity costs I have in mind. They write that mental fatigue "can best be considered as an adaptive signal that the present behavioural strategy may no longer be the most appropriate, because it continues to demand effort while substantial effort has already been invested and the goal evidently has not yet been achieved. Fatigue may provide the cognitive system with a signal that encourages the organism to lower present goals and/or seek lower effort alternative strategies" (p. 133).

64 This idea is not unlike the "central governor" notion in the exercise and physiology literature. See, e.g., Noakes, St. Clair Gibson, & Lambert 2005.

65 Baumeister et al. 1998.

66 Tice et al. 2007. I have not been able to figure out why this work has not led the authors to abandon the resource model. Getting a gift, which gives rise to positive feelings, or affect, clearly does not increase the amount of glucose in the bloodstream, so showing that positive affect eliminates the "depleting" effect of a self-control task—which this paper did four times over—effectively falsifies the glucose-as-resource model. It's not clear how or why positive affect replenishes any other "resource." What "stuff" in the mind could the gift replenish? If these results do not falsify the model, then it is unclear what result *would* do so. (The authors suggest that "positive emotion may help the self reassert its volitional powers" [p. 379], which sounds, to me, like nothing more than dualist mysticism.) If the resource model is unfalsifiable, then it should be abandoned. This illustrates a weakness of social psychology as currently practiced. While evolutionary psychology explicitly links the study of social behavior to the natural sciences, especially biology, social psychology eschews any such tethers, and therefore it tends to be a collection of intuitive "just-so" stories, driven by folk notions such as the one here, the idea that "willpower" is a resource to be used up. Because social psychology does not feel compelled to give accounts of its models in the language of information-processing, or provide any plausible functional account, it's frequently not recognizable as science.

67 Baumeister, Schmeichel, & Vohs 2007.

68 Ariely 2008, 105.

69 Wegner 2005.

70 See DeScioli & Kurzban 2009a for my view of this.

71 I used this metaphor in a book review of *Bounded Rationality: The Adaptive Toolbox*.

Chapter 9
Morality and Contradictions

1 See DeScioli & Kurzban 2009b for a discussion of this distinction.

2 See, e.g., Jon Haidt's (2001) work and his discussions of "moral dumbfounding," and other "intuitionist" accounts of moral judgments.

3 This view is similar to so-called intuitionist models of morality.

4 Uhlmann et al. (2009) have similarly recently argued that people invoke moral principles to justify a desired moral judgment.

5 Cushman, Young, & Hauser 2006.

6 His position elsewhere makes clear that he supports the exceptions. In April of 2000, GeorgeWBush.com included among his policy points: "pro life with exceptions for rape, incest and life of the mother."

7 Westen (2007, pp. 290–291) also highlights how difficult the issue of exceptions is for pro-life candidates.

8 I was interested to discover that Drew Westen, who knows a lot more about these things than I do, writes, "*thirty years* after *Roe v. Wade*, the Democratic Party has been unable to generate a principled stand," and says that he has "no idea where the Democratic Party *really* stands on abortion" (Westen 2007, pp. 177, 179, emphasis original).

9 Ruth Bader Ginsburg is well known for having made an equality argument about this. The argument seems to be that the state doesn't restrict men's autonomy, so it shouldn't restrict women's autonomy. Bader's key statement on this is: "I said on the equality side of it, that it is essential to a woman's equality with man that she be the decision-maker, that her choice be controlling. If you impose restraints, you are disadvantaging her because of her sex. The state controlling a woman would mean denying her full autonomy and full equality." (Retrieved 5/5/2010 from http://www.ontheissues.org.)

10 There could be countervailing reasons in each individual case. Of course moral principles can pull in opposite directions.

11 http://www.msnbc.msn.com/id/21791463/ (retrieved 2/22/2009).

12 Elisabeth Malkin, "Mexico Court Is Set to Uphold Legalized Abortion in Capital," *New York Times*, 8/27/2008.

13 See Weeden 2003.

14 See Nutt 2009, making the same point, using horseback riding as the example.

15 Wolfers & Zitzewitz 2006.

16 Arrow et al. 2008.

17 BBC report, "Pentagon axes online terror bets," 7/23/2003. http://news.bbc.co.uk/2/hi/americas/3106559.stm (retrieved 2/22/2009).

18 See Roth 2007 for a recent discussion.

19 This estimate comes from Becker & Elias 2007, p. 17.

20 This estimate also comes from Becker & Elias 2007; see p. 11.

21 Note that this quotation appears in one version of the Becker and Elias paper: http://graphics8.nytimes.com/images/blogs/freakonomics/pdf/ BeckerEliasOrgans%285-06%29.pdf (retrieved 2/22/2009). It does not, however, appear in the version (Becker & Elias 2007) that eventually was published in the *Journal of Economic Perspectives*.

22 Thaler & Sunstein 2008, p. 175. See also Roth 2007.
23 DeScioli & Kurzban 2009b. Robert Wright's *The Moral Animal*, which is an excellent book, is a good example. Wright explains why people are altruistic, not moralistic.

Chapter 10
Morality Is for the Birds

1 See, e.g., Lieberman, Tooby, & Cosmides 2003.
2 For a few remarks on this, see Kurzban & DeScioli 2009.
3 Draper & Harpending 1982.
4 See Miller 2000 regarding sexual selection in humans.
5 See, especially, Weeden 2003.
6 I have borrowed liberally from Jason Weeden here.
7 See DeScioli 2008; DeScioli & Kurzban 2009b.
8 Without getting into issues of "false consciousness," I note only that what might seem to be a willing acceptance of certain political arrangements might simply reflect the fact that when there is great power asymmetry, the choices for those who are less powerful can be between open rebellion and conformity to a system in which they are disadvantaged. Conformity can be the less bad option. See, e.g., Sidanius & Kurzban 2003.
9 Rawls 1971.
10 Of course many rules are partial, as in caste systems and Jim Crow laws. Modern institutional arrangements have led to communities of people who live under moral sticks that they neither create nor support. See also Boehm (1999).
11 For a discussion of agreement and disagreement about moral rules, see Robinson & Kurzban 2007, and Robinson, Kurzban, & Jones 2008.
12 DeScioli & Kurzban 2009b.
13 See, for instance, Sperber 2000.
14 This is one rendering of Matthew 7:3.

Epilogue

1 The ideas here have obvious ties to philosophical traditions, especially libertarianism (e.g., Nozick 1974).

references

Ainslie, G. (1985). Beyond microeconomics. In J. Elster (ed.), *The multiple self* (pp. 133–176). Cambridge: Cambridge University Press.

Ainslie, G., & Haslam, N. (1992). Hyperbolic discounting. In G. Loewenstein & J. Elster (eds.), *Choice over time* (pp. 57–92). New York: Russell Sage.

Alicke, M. D., & Govorun, O. (2005). The better-than-average effect. In M. D. Alicke, D. A. Dunning, & J. I. Krueger (eds.), *Studies in self and identity* (pp. 85–106). New York: Psychology Press.

Alicke, M. D., Klotz, M. L., Breitenbecher, D. L., Yurak, T. J., & Vredenburg, D. S. (1995). Personal contact, individuation and the better than average effect. *Journal of Personality and Social Psychology, 68*, 804–825.

Ambady, N., & Rosenthal, R. (1992). Thin slices of expressive behavior as predictors of interpersonal consequences: A meta-analysis. *Psychological Bulletin, 111*, 256–274.

Ames, R. T., & Dissanayake, W. (1996). Introduction. In R. T. Ames & W. Dissanayake (eds.), *Self and deception: A cross-cultural philosophical enquiry* (pp. 1–30). Albany: State University of New York Press.

Ariely, D. (2008). *Predictably irrational: The hidden forces that shape our decisions*. New York: HarperCollins.

Arkin, R. C. (2007). Governing lethal behavior: Embedding ethics in a hybrid deliberative/reactive robot architecture. Technical report FITVU-07-11, Georgia Institute of Technology.

Aronson, E., Fried, C., & Stone, J. (1991). Overcoming denial and increasing the intention to use condoms through the induction of hypocrisy. *American Journal of Public Health, 81*, 1636–1638.

Arrow, K., Forsythe, R., Gorham, M., Hahn, R., Hanson, R., Ledyard, J., et al. (2008). The promise of prediction markets. *Science*, May 16, 877–878.

Babad, E. (1987). Wishful thinking and objectivity among sports fans. *Social Behaviour, 2*, 231–240.

Baber, Z. M. (1826). Memoirs of Zehir-ed-din Muhammed Baber, Emperor of Hindustan. Trans. J. Leyden, W. Erskine, & C. Waddington. London: Longman, Rees, Orme, Brown, and Green.

Baldwin, C. Y., & Clark, K. B. (2000). *Design rules*. Volume 1: *The power of modularity*. Cambridge, MA: MIT Press.

Bandura, A. (1989). Human agency in social cognitive theory. *American Psychologist, 44*, 1175–1184.

Barrett, H. C. (2005). Enzymatic computation and cognitive modularity. *Mind and Language, 20*, 259–287.

Barrett, H. C., Cosmides, L., & Tooby, J. (2007). The hominid entry into the cognitive niche. In S. Gangstead & J. Simpson (eds.), *The evolution of mind: Fundamental questions and controversies* (pp. 241–248). New York: Guilford Press.

Barrett, H. C., Frederick, D. A., Haselton, M. G. & Kurzban, R. (2006). Can manipulations of cognitive load be used to test evolutionary hypotheses? *Journal of Personality and Social Psychology, 91* (3), 513–518.

Barrett, H. C., & Kurzban, R. (2006). Modularity in cognition: Framing the debate. *Psychological Review, 113*, 628–647.

Batson, C. (2008). Moral masquerades: Experimental exploration of the nature of moral motivation. *Phenomenology and the Cognitive Sciences, 7*, 51–66.

Baumeister, R. F. (1982). A self-presentational view of social phenomena. *Psychological Bulletin, 91*, 3–26.

——— (1999a). *The cultural animal: Human nature, meaning, and social life.* Oxford: Oxford University Press.

——— (1999b). The nature and structure of the self: An overview. In R. F. Baumeister (ed.), *The self in social psychology* (pp. 1–20). Philadelphia: Psychology Press.

Baumeister, R. F., Bratslavsky, E., Muraven, M., & Tice, D. M. (1998). Ego depletion: Is the active self a limited resource? *Journal of Personality and Social Psychology, 74*, 1252–1265.

Baumeister, R. F., Campbell, J. D., Krueger, J. I., & Vohs, K. D. (2003). Does high self-esteem cause better performance, interpersonal success, happiness, or healthier lifestyles? *Psychological Science in the Public Interest, 4,* 1–44.

Baumeister, R. F., Heatherton, T. F., & Tice, D. M. (1993). When ego threats lead to self-regulation failure: Negative consequences of high self-esteem. *Journal of Personality and Social Psychology, 64,* 141–156.

Baumeister, R. F., Schmeichel, B. J., & Vohs, K. D. (2007). Self-regulation and the executive function: The self as controlling agent. In A. W. Kruglanski & E. T. Higgins (eds.), *Social Psychology: Handbook of Basic Principles,* 2nd ed. (pp. 516–539). New York: Guilford Press.

Baumeister, R. F., & Vohs, K D. (2007). Self-regulation, ego depletion, and motivation. *Social and Personality Psychology Compass, 1,* 115–128.

Becker, G. S., & Elias, J. J. (2007). Introducing incentives in the market for live and cadaveric organ donations. *Journal of Economic Perspectives, 21,* 3–24.

Binmore, K. (2007). *Playing for real: A text on game theory.* New York: Oxford University Press.

Biran, I., & Chatterjee, A. (2004). Alien hand syndrome. *Archives of Neurology, 61,* 292–294.

Biran, I., Giovannetti, T., Buxbaum, L., & Chatterjee, A. (2006). The alien hand syndrome: What makes the alien hand alien? *Cognitive Neuropsychology, 23,* 563–582.

Blaine, B., & Crocker, J. (1993). Self-esteem and self-serving biases in reactions to positive and negative events: An integrative review. In R. F. Baumeister (ed.), *Self-esteem: The puzzle of low self-regard* (pp. 55–85). New York: Plenum.

Boehm, C. (1999). *Hierarchy in the forest: The evolution of egalitarian behavior.* Cambridge, MA: Harvard University Press.

Boksem, M.A.S., & Tops, M. (2008). Mental fatigue: Costs and benefits. *Brain Research Reviews, 59,* 125–139.

Boyer, P. (2001). *Religion explained: The evolutionary origins of religious thought.* NewYork: Basic Books.

Boyer, P., Robbins, P., & Jack, A. I. (2005). Varieties of self-systems worth having. *Consciousness and Cognition, 14,* 647–660.

Bradburn, N. M. (1969). *The structure of psychological well-being.* Chicago: Aldine.

Braitenberg, V. (1984). *Vehicles: Experiments in synthetic psychology.* Cambridge, MA: MIT Press.

Bramble, D. M., & Lieberman, D. E. (2004). Endurance running and the evolution of Homo. *Nature, 432,* 345–352.

Brickman, P., Coates, D., & Janoff-Bulman, R. (1978). Lottery winners and accident victims: Is happiness relative? *Journal of Personality & Social Psychology, 36,* 917–927.

Brown, D. E. (1991). *Human universals.* New York: McGraw-Hill.

Buller, D. J. (2008). Evolution of the mind: Four fallacies of psychology. *Scientific American,* December. Retrieved from http://www.sciam.com/article.cfm?id=four-fallacies.

Burger, J. M., & Burns, L. (1988). The illusion of unique invulnerability and the use of effective contraception. *Personality and Social Psychology Bulletin, 14,* 264–270.

Burnham, T., & Phelan, J. (2000). *Mean genes: From sex to money to food: Taming our primal instincts.* Cambridge, MA: Perseus.

Buss, D.M. (2003). *The evolution of desire: Strategies of human mating* (revised edition). New York: Basic Books.

Buunk, B. P. (2001). Perceived superiority of one's own relationship and perceived prevalence of happy and unhappy relationships. *British Journal of Social Psychology, 40,* 565–574.

Byrne, R. W., & Whiten, A. (eds.) (1988). *Machiavellian intelligence: Social expertise and the evolution of intellect in monkeys, apes, and humans.* New York: Oxford University Press.

Cacioppo, J. T., Hawkley, L. C., & Berntson, G. G. (2003). The anatomy of loneliness. *Current Directions in Psychological Science, 12,* 71–74.

Camerer, C. (2003). *Behavioral game theory: Experiments in strategic interaction.* Princeton, NJ: Princeton University Press.

Camerer, C., Loewenstein, G. & Prelec, D. (2005). Neuroeconomics: How neuroscience can inform economics. *Journal of Economic Literature, 43,* 9–64.

Chambers E. S., Bridge, M. W., & Jones, D. A. (2009). Carbohydrate sensing in the human mouth: effects on exercise performance and brain activity. *Journal of Physiology, 587,* 1779–1794.

Churchland, P. (1987). Epistemology in the age of neuroscience. *Journal of Philosophy, 84,* 544–553.

Cialdini, R. B. (2001). *Influence: Science and practice* (4th ed.). Boston: Allyn and Bacon.

Clarke, D. D., & Sokoloff, L. (1998). Circulation and energy metabolism of the brain. In G. Siegel, B. Agranoff, R. Albers, S. Fisher, & M. Uhler (eds.), *Basic neurochemistry: Molecular, cellular, and medical aspects* (6th ed.) (pp. 637–669). Philadelphia, PA: Lippincott-Raven.

Cochran, F., & Harpending, H. (2009). *The 10,000 year explosion: How civilization accelerated human evolution.* New York: Basic Books.

Coltheart, M. (1999). Modularity and cognition. *Trends in Cognitive Science, 3*, 115–120.

Cosmides, L., & Tooby, J. (1994a). Beyond intuition and instinct blindness: The case for an evolutionarily rigorous cognitive science. *Cognition, 50*, 41–77.

——— (1994b). Origins of domain specificity: The evolution of functional organization. In L. Hirschfeld & S. Gelman (eds.), *Mapping the mind: Domain specificity in cognition and culture* (pp. 85–116). New York: Cambridge University Press.

——— (2000). Evolutionary psychology and the emotions In M. Lewis & J. M. Haviland-Jones (eds.), *Handbook of emotions,* 2nd edition (pp. 91–115.) New York: Guilford Press.

——— (2001). Unraveling the enigma of human intelligence: Evolutionary psychology and the multimodular mind. In R. J. Sternberg & J. C. Kaufman (eds.), *The evolution of intelligence* (pp. 145–198). Hillsdale, NJ: Erlbaum.

Covey, J. A., & Davies, A.D.M. (2004). Are people unrealistically optimistic? It depends how you ask them. *British Journal of Health Psychology, 9*, 39–49.

Crocker, J., & Park, L. E. (2003). Seeking self-esteem: Maintenance, enhancement, and protection of self-worth. In M. R. Leary & J. P. Tangney (eds.), *Handbook of self and identity* (pp. 291–313). New York: Guilford Press.

Cross, K. P. (1977). Not can but *will* college teaching be improved? *New Directions for Higher Education, 1977,* issue 17 (Spring 1977), 1–15.

Cushman, F. A., Young, L., & Hauser, M. D. (2006). The role of reasoning and intuition in moral judgments: Testing three principles of harm. *Psychological Science, 17,* 1082–1089.

Daly, M., & Wilson, M. (2007). Is the "Cinderella effect" controversial? A case study of evolution-minded research and critiques thereof. In C. Crawford & D. Krebs (eds.), *Foundations of evolutionary psychology* (pp. 383–400). Mahwah, NJ: Erlbaum.

Damasio, A. R. (1994). *Descartes' error: Emotion, reason, and the human brain.* New York: Grosset/Putnam.

Dana, J., Cain, D. M., & Dawes, R. (2006). What you don't know won't hurt me: Costly (but quiet) exit in a dictator game. *Organizational Behavior and Human Decision Processes, 100,* 193–201.

Dana, J., Weber, R. A., & Kuang, J. X. (2007). Exploiting moral wiggle room: Experiments demonstrating an illusory preference for fairness. *Economic Theory, 33,* 67–80.

Davidson, D. (1985). Deception and division. In J. Elster (ed.), *The multiple self* (pp. 79–92). Cambridge: Cambridge University Press.

Davidson, D. (1998). Who is fooled? In J. P. Dupuy (ed.), *Self-deception and para-doxes of rationality.* (pp. 1–18). Stanford, CA: CSLI Publications.

——— (2004). *Problems of rationality* (vol. 4). Oxford: Oxford University Press.

Dawes, R. (1994). *House of cards: Psychology and psychotherapy built on myth.* New York: Free Press.

Dawkins, R. (1976). *The selfish gene.* Oxford: Oxford University Press.

——— (1986). *The blind watchmaker.* London: Longmans.

——— (2006). *The God delusion.* New York: Bantam Books.

Dawson, E., Savitsky, K., & Dunning, D. (2006). "Don't tell me, I don't want to know": Understanding people's reluctance to obtain medical diagnostic information. *Journal of Applied Social Psychology, 36,* 751–768.

Dennett, D. (1981). *Brainstorms: Philosophical essays on mind and psychology.* Cambridge, MA: MIT Press.

——— (1991). *Consciousness explained.* Boston: Little Brown.

——— (2006). *Breaking the spell: Religion as a natural phenomenon.* New York: Penguin Books.

DeScioli, P. (2008). Investigations into the problems of moral cognition. Unpublished doctoral dissertation.

DeScioli, P., & Kurzban, R. (2009a). The alliance hypothesis for human friendship. *PLoS ONE, 4(6): e5802.*

——— (2009b). Mysteries of morality. *Cognition, 112,* 281–299.

DeSteno, D., Bartlett, M. Y., & Salovey, P. (2006). Constraining accommodative homunculi in evolutionary explorations of jealousy: A reply to Barrett et al. (2006). *Journal of Personality and Social Psychology, 91,* 519–523.

Donnellan, M. B., Trzesniewski, K. H., Robins, R. W., Moffitt, T. E., & Caspi, A. (2005). Low self-esteem is related to aggression, antisocial behavior, and delinquency. *Psychological Science, 16,* 328–335.

Draper, P., & Harpending, H. (1982). Father absence and reproductive strategy: An evolutionary perspective. *Journal of Anthropological Research, 38,* 255–279.

Dunning, D. (1999). A newer look: Motivated social cognition and the schematic representation of social concepts. *Psychological Inquiry, 10,* 1–11.

——— (2005). *Self-insight: Roadblocks and detours on the path to knowing thyself.* New York: Psychology Press.

Dunning, D., & Cohen, G. L. (1992). Egocentric definitions of traits and abilities in social judgment. *Journal of Personality and Social Psychology, 63,* 341–355.

Dunning, D., Heath, C., & Suls, J. (2004). Flawed self-assessment: Implications for health, education, and the workplace. *Psychological Science in the Public Interest, 5,* 69–106.

Dunning, D., Meyerowitz, J. A., & Holzberg, A. D. (1989). Ambiguity and self-evaluation: The role of idiosyncratic trait definitions in self-serving assessments of ability. *Journal of Personality and Social Psychology, 57,* 1082–1090.

Dupuy, J. P. (ed.) (1998). *Self-deception and paradoxes of rationality.* Stanford, CA: CSLI Publications.

Dutton, D. G., & Aron, A. P. (1974). Some evidence for heightened sexual attraction under conditions of high anxiety. *Journal of Personality and Social Psychology, 30,* 510–517.

Dvorak, R. D., & Simons, J. S. (2009). Moderation of resource depletion in the self-control strength model: Differing effects of two modes of self-control. *Personality and Social Psychology Bulletin, 35,* 572–58.

Ehrenreich, B. (2009). *Bright-sided: How the relentless promotion of positive thinking has undermined America.* New York: Metropolitan Books.

Eisenberger, N. I., Lieberman, M. D., & Williams, K. D. (2003). Does rejection hurt? An fMRI study of social exclusion. *Science, 302,* 290–292.

Elster, J. (1985). *The multiple self.* Cambridge: Cambridge University Press.

Epley, N., & Whitchurch, E. (2008). Mirror, mirror on the wall: Enhancement in self-recognition. *Personality and Social Psychology Bulletin, 34,* 1159–1170.

Ermer, E., Cosmides, L., & Tooby, J. (2008). Relative status regulates risky decision-making about resources in men: Evidence for the co-evolution of motivation and cognition. *Evolution and Human Behavior, 29,* 106–118.

Evans, D., Heuvelink, A., & Nettle, D. (no date). Are motivational biases adaptive? An agent-based model of human judgement under uncertainty. Retrieved from www.dylan.org.uk/bias.pdf.

Fenton-O'Creevy, M., Nicholson, N., Soane, E., & Willman, P. (2003). Trading on illusions: Unrealistic perceptions of control and trading performance. *Journal of Occupational and Organisational Psychology, 76,* 53–68.

Festinger, L. (1954). A theory of social comparison processes. *Human Relations, 7,* 117–140.

Fiddick, L., Cosmides, L., & Tooby, J. (2000). No interpretation without representation: The role of domain-specific representations and inferences in the Wason selection task. *Cognition, 77,* 1–79.

Flavell, J. H. (1970). Developmental studies of mediated memory. In H. W. Reese & L. P. Lipsitt (eds.), *Advances in child development and child behavior* (vol. 5, pp. 181–211). New York: Academic Press.

Fodor, J. (1983). *The modularity of mind.* Cambridge, MA: MIT Press.

———— (1998). The trouble with psychological Darwinism. *London Review of Books.* Retrieved from http://www.lrb.co.uk/v20/n02/fodo01_.html.

Fodor, J. (2000). *The mind doesn't work that way.* Cambridge, MA: Bradford Books/MIT Press.

Foot, P. (1967). The problem of abortion and the doctrine of double effect. *Oxford Review, 5,* 5–15.

Frank, R. (1988). *Passions within reason: The strategic role of the emotions.* New York: W.W. Norton.

Frederick, S., Loewenstein, G., & O'Donoghue, T. (2002). Time discounting and time preference: A critical review. *Journal of Economic Literature, 40,* 351–401.

Frith, C. (2005). The self in action: Lessons from delusions of control. *Consciousness and Cognition, 14,* 752–770.

Gailliot, M. T., & Baumeister, R. F. (2007). Self-regulation and sexual restraint: Dispositionally and temporarily poor self-regulatory abilities contribute to failures at restraining sexual behavior. *Personality and Social Psychology Bulletin, 33,* 173–186.

Gailliot, M. T., Baumeister, R. F., DeWall, C. N., Maner, J. K., Plant, E. A., Tice, D. M., Brewer, L. E., & Schmeichel, B. J. (2007). Self-control relies on glucose as a limited energy source: Willpower is more than a metaphor. *Journal of Personality and Social Psychology, 92,* 325–336.

Gallagher, S. (2000). Philosophical conceptions of the self: Implications for cognitive science. *Trends in Cognitive Sciences, 4,* 14–21.

Gallistel C. R. (1994). Foraging for brain stimulation: Toward a neurobiology of computation. *Cognition, 50,* 151–170.

Gazzaniga, M.S. (1998). *The mind's past.* Berkeley: University of California Press.

Gazzaniga, M. S., & LeDoux, J. E. (1978). *The integrated mind.* New York: Plenum.

Gelder, B. D., Tamietto, M., Boxtel, G. V., Goebel, R., Sahraie, A., Stock, J. V. D., et al. (2008). Intact navigation skills after bilateral loss of striate cortex. *Current Biology, 18,* R1128–R1129.

Gibson, E. L. (2007). Carbohydrates and mental function: Feeding or impeding the brain? *Nutrition Bulletin, 32,* 71–83.

Gibson, E. L., & Green M. W. (2002). Nutritional influences on cognitive function: mechanisms of susceptibility. *Nutrition Research Reviews, 15,* 169–206.

Gigerenzer, G. (1996). Rationality: Why social context matters. In P. B. Baltes & U. M. Staudinger (eds.), *Interactive minds: Life-span perspectives on the social foundation of cognition* (pp. 319–346). Cambridge: Cambridge University Press.

Gigerenzer, G., & Selten, R. (eds.) (2001). *Bounded rationality: The adaptive toolbox.* Cambridge, MA: MIT Press.

Gintis, H. (2005). Behavioral game theory and contemporary economic theory. *Analyse und Kritik, 27*, 6–47.

Gladwell, M. (2005). *Blink: The power of thinking without thinking.* New York: Little, Brown, & Co.

Godfray, H.C.J. (1991). Signalling of need by offspring to their parents. *Nature, 352*, 328–330.

Goffman, E. (1967). *Interaction ritual: Essays on face-to-face behavior.* New York: Doubleday/Anchor.

Gould, S. J. (2000). More things in heaven and earth. In H. Rose & S. Rose (eds.), *Alas poor Darwin: Arguments against evolutionary psychology* (pp. 101–126). New York: Harmony Books.

Gould, S. J., & Lewontin, R. C. (1979). The spandrels of San Marcos and the Pan-glossian program: A critique of the adaptationist programme. *Proceedings of the Royal Society of London, 205*, 581–598.

Granberg, D., & Brent, E. (1983). When prophecy bends: The preference-expectation link in U.S. presidential elections. *Journal of Personality and Social Psychology, 45*, 477–49.

Greenwald, A. G. (1997). Self-knowledge and self-deception: Further consideration. In M. S. Myslobodsky (ed.), *The mythomanias: An inquiry into the nature of deception and self-deception* (pp. 51–71). Mahwah, NJ: Erlbaum.

Greenwald, A. G., & Banaji, M. R. (1995). Implicit social cognition: Attitudes, self-esteem, and stereotypes. *Psychological Review, 102*, 4–27.

Greenwald, A. G., McGhee, D. E., & Schwartz, J.L.K. (1998). Measuring individual differences in implicit cognition: The implicit association test. *Journal of Personality and Social Psychology, 74*, 1464–1480.

Gregory, R. L. (1970). *The intelligent eye.* New York: McGraw-Hill.

Gur, R. & Sackeim, H. (1979) Self-deception: A concept in search of a phenomenon. *Journal of Personality and Social Psychology, 37*, 147–169.

Haidt, J. (2001). The emotional dog and its rational tail: A social intuitionist approach to moral judgment. *Psychological Review, 108*, 814–834.

———— (2006). *The happiness hypothesis: Finding modern truth in ancient wisdom.* New York: Basic Books.

Haselton, M. G., & Nettle, D. (2006). The paranoid optimist: An integrative evolutionary model of cognitive biases. *Personality and Social Psychology Review, 10*, 47–66.

Hauser, M. D., Cushman, F. A., Young, L., Kang-Xing Jin, R., & Mikhail, J. (2007). A dissociation between moral judgments and justifications. *Mind and Language, 22*, 1–21.

Hauser, M. D., Young, L., & Cushman, F. A. (2008). Reviving Rawls' linguistic analogy. In W. Sinnott-Armstrong (ed.) *Moral psychology, Volume 2: The cognitive science of morality: Intuition and diversity* (pp. 107–144). Cambridge, MA: Bradford Books.

Helweg-Larsen, M., Sadeghian, P., & Webb, M. A. (2002). The stigma of being pessimistically biased. *Journal of Social and Clinical Psychology, 21,* 92–107.

Henslin, J. M. (1967). Craps and magic. *American Journal of Sociology, 73,* 316–330.

Hirstein, W. (2005). *Brain fiction: Self-deception and the riddle of confabulation.* Cambridge, MA: MIT Press.

Humphrey, N. (2002). Great expectations: The evolutionary psychology of faith-healing and the placebo effect. In C. von Hofsten & L. Backman (eds.), *Psychology at the turn of the millennium, Vol. 2: Social, developmental, and clinical perspectives* (pp. 225–246). Florence, KY: Routledge.

Humphrey, N., & Dennett, D. C. (1998). Speaking for our selves. In D. C. Dennett (ed.), *Brainchildren: Essays on designing minds* (pp. 31–58). London: Penguin Books.

Jackendoff, R. (1987). *Consciousness and the computational mind.* Cambridge, MA: MIT Press.

James, W. (1890/1950). *The principles of psychology* (vol. 1). New York: Dover.
——— (1897/1979). *The will to believe and other essays in popular philosophy.* Cambridge, MA: Harvard University Press.

Jones, E. E. (1964). *Ingratiation: A social psychological analysis.* New York: Appleton-Century-Crofts.

Jones, E. E., & Pittman, T. S. (1982). Towards a general theory of strategic self-presentation. In J. Suls (ed.), *Psychological perspectives on the self* (vol. 1, pp. 231–262). Hillsdale, NJ: Erlbaum.

Kaptchuk, T. J., Kelley, J. M., Conboy, L. A., Davis, R. B., Kerr, C. E., Jacobson, E. E., et al. (2008). Components of placebo effect: Randomised controlled trial in patients with irritable bowel syndrome. *British Journal of Medicine, 336,* 999–1003.

Kahneman, D., Knetsch, J., & Thaler, R. (1991). Anomalies: The endowment effect, loss aversion, and status quo bias. *Journal of Economic Perspectives, 5,* 193–206.

Kirkpatrick, L. A., & Ellis, B. J. (2001). An evolutionary-psychological approach to self-esteem: Multiple domains and multiple functions. In G. Fletcher & M. Clark (eds.), *The Blackwell handbook of social psychology, Vol. 2: Interpersonal processes* (pp. 411–436). Oxford: Blackwell.

Krebs, D. L., & Denton, K. (1997). Social illusions and self-deception: The evolution of biases in person perception. In J. A. Simpson & D. T. Kenrick (eds.), *Evolutionary Social Psychology* (pp. 21–47). Hillsdale, NJ: Erlbaum.

Kurman, J. (2001). Self-enhancement: Is it restricted to individualistic cultures? *Personality and Social Psychology Bulletin, 27*, 1705–1716.

Kurzban, R. (2001). The social psychophysics of cooperation: Nonverbal communication in a public goods game. *Journal of Nonverbal Behavior, 25*, 241–259.

———— (2002a). Alas poor evolutionary psychology: Unfairly accused, unjustly condemned. *Human Nature Review, 2*, 99–109.

———— (2002b). The human mind: Evolution's tinkering or Michelangelo's chiseling? Review of *Bounded rationality: The adaptive toolbox* by G. Gigerenzer and R. Selten, eds. *Contemporary Psychology, 47*, 661–663.

———— (2008). Evolution of implicit and explicit decision making. In C. Engel, & W. Singer, (eds.), *Better than conscious? Implications for performance and institutional analysis. Strüngmann Forum Report 1* (pp. 155–172). Cambridge, MA: MIT Press.

Kurzban, R., & Aktipis, C. A. (2006). Modular minds, multiple motives. In M. Schaller, J. Simpson, & D. Kenrick (eds.) *Evolution and social psychology* (pp. 39–53). New York: Psychology Press.

———— (2007). Modularity and the social mind: Are psychologists too self-ish? *Personality and Social Psychology Review, 11*, 131–149.

Kurzban, R., & Christner, J. (in press). Are supernatural beliefs commitment devices for intergroup conflict? Prepared for the 13th Sydney Symposium of Social Psychology.

Kurzban, R., & DeScioli, P. (2009). Why religions turn oppressive: A perspective from evolutionary psychology. *Skeptic, 15*, 38–41.

Kurzban, R., DeScioli, P., & O'Brien, E. (2007). Audience effects on moralistic punishment. *Evolution and Human Behavior, 28*, 75–84.

Kurzban, R., & Leary, M. R. (2001). Evolutionary origins of stigmatization: The functions of social exclusion. *Psychological Bulletin, 127*, 187–208.

Kurzban, R., & Weeden, J. (2005). HurryDate: Mate preferences in action. *Evolution and Human Behavior, 26*, 227–244.

———— (2007). Do advertised preferences predict the behavior of speed daters? *Personal Relationships, 14*, 623–632.

Laibson, D. (2001). A cue-theory of consumption. *Quarterly Journal of Economics, 116*, 81–119.

Landsburg, S. (2007). *More sex is safer sex: The unconventional wisdom of economics*. New York: Free Press.

Lane K. A., Banaji, M. R., Nosek B. A., & Greenwald A. G. (2007). Understanding and using the Implicit Association Test: IV. What we know (so far) about the method. In B. Wittenbrink & N. Schwarz (eds.), *Implicit measures of attitudes: Procedures and controversies* (pp. 59–102). New York: Guilford Press.

Langer, E. J. (1975). The illusion of control. *Journal of Personality and Social Psychology, 32,* 311–328.

Langer, E. J., & Roth, J. (1975). Heads I win, tails it's chance: The illusion of control as a function of the sequence of outcomes in a purely chance task. *Journal of Personality and Social Psychology, 32,* 951–955.

Leary, M. R. (2007). Motivational and emotional aspects of the self. *Annual Review of Psychology, 58,* 317–344.

Leary, M. R., & Downs, D. L. (1995). Interpersonal functions of the self-esteem motive: The self-esteem system as a sociometer. In M. H. Kernis (ed.), *Efficacy, agency, and self-esteem* (pp. 123–144). New York: Plenum Press.

Lewontin, R. C., Rose, S. & Kamin, L. (1984). *Biology, ideology and human nature: Not in our genes.* New York: Pantheon.

Libet, B. (1999). Do we have free will? *Journal of Consciousness Studies, 6,* 47–57.

Lichtenstein, S., & Slovic, P. (2006a). *The construction of preference.* Cambridge: Cambridge University Press.

Lichtenstein, S. & Slovic, P. (2006b). The construction of preference: An overview. In S. Lichtenstein & P. Slovic (eds.), *The construction of preference* (pp. 1–40). New York: Cambridge University Press.

Lieberman, D., Tooby, J., & Cosmides, L. (2003). Does morality have a biological basis? An empirical test of the factors governing moral sentiments relating to incest. *Proceedings of the Royal Society of London Series B—Biological Sciences, 270,* 819–826.

Mabe, P. A. III, & West, S. G. (1982). Validity of self-evaluation of ability: A review and meta-analysis. *Journal of Applied Psychology, 67,* 280–286.

MacDonald, G., & Leary, M. R. (2005). Why does social exclusion hurt? The relationship between social and physical pain. *Psychological Bulletin, 131,* 202–223.

Madsen P. L., Hasselbalch, S. G., Hagemann, L. P., Olsen, K. S., Bulow, J., Holm, S., Wildschiødtz, G., Paulson, O. B., & Lassen, N. A. (1995). Persistent resetting of the cerebral oxygen/glucose uptake ratio by brain activation: Evidence obtained with the Kety-Schmidt technique. *Journal of Cerebral Blood Flow and Metabolism, 15,* 485–491.

Marcus, G. F. (2008). *Kluge: The haphazard construction of the human mind.* New York: Houghton Mifflin.

Markman, K. D., & Hirt, E. R. (2002). Social prediction and the "allegiance bias." *Social Cognition, 20,* 58–86.

Marr, D. (1982). *Vision.* San Francisco: W.H. Freeman.

Martin, P. (2002). *One man's leg: A memoir.* Pine Bush, NY: GreyCore Press.

Masicampo, E. J., & Baumeister, R. F. (2008). Toward a physiology of dual-process reasoning and judgment: Lemonade, willpower, and effortful rule-based analysis. *Psychological Science, 19,* 255–260.

Maynard Smith, J. (1995). Genes, memes, and minds. *New York Review of Books,* November 30.

McCauley, R. N., & Henrich, J. (2006). Susceptibility to the Müller-Lyer illusion, theory neutral observation, and the diachronic cognitive penetrability of the visual input system. *Philosophical Psychology, 19,* 79–101.

McClure, S. M., Laibson, D. I., Loewenstein, G., & Cohen, J. D. (2004). Separate neural systems value immediate and delayed monetary rewards. *Science, 306,* 503–507.

McElreath, R., Boyd, R., Gigerenzer, G., Glöckner, A., Hammerstein, P., Kurzban, R., et al. (2008). Individual decision making and the evolutionary roots of institutions: Explicit and implicit strategies in decision making. In C. Engel & W. Singer, (eds.), *Better than conscious? Implications for performance and institutional analysis. Strüngmann Forum Report 1* (pp. 325–342). Cambridge, MA: MIT Press.

McKay, R. T., & Dennett, D. C. (2009). The evolution of misbelief. *Behavioral and Brain Sciences, 32,* 493–561.

McKenna, F., & Albery, I. (2001). Does unrealistic optimism change following a negative experience? *Journal of Applied Social Psychology, 31,* 1146–1157.

McLaughlin, B. P. (1996). On the very possibility of self-deception. In R. T. Ames & W. Dissanayake (eds.), *Self and deception: A cross-cultural philosophical enquiry* (pp. 31–51). Albany: State University of New York Press.

Mecca, A. M., Smelser, N. J., & Vasconcellos, J. (1989). *The social importance of self-esteem.* Berkeley: University of California Press.

Mele, A. R. (1998). Two paradoxes of self-deception. In J. Dupuy (ed.), *Self-deception and paradoxes of rationality* (pp. 37–58). Stanford, CA: CSLI Publications.

———— (2001). *Self-deception unmasked.* Princeton, NJ: Princeton University Press.

Merton, R. K. (1969). *Social theory and social structure.* New York: Free Press.

Messier, C. (2004). Glucose improvement of memory: A review. *European Journal of Pharmacology, 490,* 33–57.

Mezulis, A. H., Abramson, L. Y., Hyde, J. S., & Hankin, B. L. (2004). Is there a universal positivity bias in attributions? A meta-analytic review of individual, developmental, and cultural differences in the self-serving attributional bias. *Psychological Bulletin, 130,* 711–747.

Mijović-Prelec, D. & Prelec, D. (2010). Self-deception as self-signalling: A model and experimental evidence. *Philosophical Transactions of the Royal Society, 365,* 227–240.

Miller, E. K., & Cohen, J. D. (2001). An integrative theory of prefrontal cortex function. *Annual Review of Neuroscience, 24,* 167–202.

Miller, G. (2000). *The mating mind: How sexual choice shaped the evolution of human nature.* New York: Doubleday.

Minsky, M. (1985). *Society of mind.* New York: Simon & Schuster.

Mischel, W., Shoda, Y., & Peake, P. K. (1988). The nature of adolescent competencies predicted by preschool delay of gratification. *Journal of Personality and Social Psychology, 54,* 687–696.

Mischel, W., Shoda, Y., & Rodriguez, M. L. (1989). Delay of gratification in children. *Science, 244,* 933–938.

Moore, D. A. (2007). Not so above average after all: When people believe they are worse than average and its implications for theories of bias in social comparison. *Organizational Behavior and Human Decision Processes, 102,* 42–58.

Moore, D. A., & Healy, P. J. (2008). The trouble with overconfidence. *Psychological Review, 115,* 502–517.

Morris, J., DeGelder, B., Weiskrantz, L., & Dolan, R. (2001). Differential extrageniculostriate and amygdala responses to presentation of emotional faces in a cortically blind field. *Brain, 124,* 1241–1252.

Murtagh, A. M., & Todd, S. A. (2004). Self-regulation: A challenge to the strength model. *Journal of Articles in Support of the Null Hypothesis, 3,* 19–51.

Nagel, T. (1974). What is it like to be a bat? *Philosophical Review, 4,* 435–450.

Neisser, U. (1988). Five kinds of self-knowledge. *Philosophical Psychology, 1,* 35–59.

Nesse, R. M. (2005). Natural selection and the regulation of defenses: A signal detection analysis of the smoke detector principle. *Evolution and Human Behavior, 26,* 88–105.

Nesse, R. M., & Lloyd, A. T. (1992). The evolution of psychodynamic mechanisms. In J. Barkow, L. Cosmides & J. Tooby (eds.), *The adapted mind: Evolutionary psychology and the generation of culture* (601–624). New York: Oxford University Press.

Nesse, R. M., & Williams, G. C. (1994). *Why we get sick: The new science of Darwinian medicine.* New York: Vintage Books.

Nettle, D. (2004). Adaptive illusions: Optimism, control and human rationality. In D. Evans & P. Cruse (eds.), *Emotion, evolution and rationality* (pp. 193–208). Oxford: Oxford University Press.

Nisbett, R., & Wilson, T. (1977). Telling more than we can know: Verbal reports on mental processes. *Psychological Review, 84,* 231–259.

Noakes T. D., St. Clair Gibson, A., & Lambert, E. V. (2005). From catastrophe to complexity: A novel model of integrative central neural regulation of effort and fatigue during exercise in humans: Summary and conclusions. *British Journal of Sports Medicine, 39,* 120–124.

Nosek , B. A., Greenwald, A. G., & Banaji, M. R. (2007). The Implicit Association Test at age 7: A methodological and conceptual review. In J. A. Bargh (ed.), *Social Psychology and the Unconscious: The Automaticity of Higher Mental Processes* (pp. 265–292). Philadelphia: Psychology Press.

Nozick, R. (1974). *Anarchy, state, and utopia.* Oxford: Blackwell.

Nutt, D. J. (2009). Equasy—An overlooked addiction with implications for the current debate on drug harms. *Journal of Psychopharmacology, 23,* 3–5.

Ossher, H., & Tarr, P. (2001). Using multidimensional separation of concerns to (re)shape evolving software. *Communications of the ACM, 44,* 43–50.

Parnas, D. L. (1972). On the criteria to be used in decomposing systems into modules. *Communications of the ACM, 15,* 1053–1058.

Parnas, D. L., Clements, P. C., & Weiss, D. M. (1984). The modular structure of complex systems. *Proceedings of the 7th International Conference on Software Engineering,* 408–417.

Payne, J. W., Bettman, J. R., & Johnson, E. J. (1993). *The adaptive decision maker.* New York: Cambridge University Press.

Pears, D. (1985). The goals and strategies of self-deception. In J. Elster (ed.), *The multiple self* (pp. 59–77). New York: Cambridge University Press.

Pegna, A. J., Khateb, A., Lazeyras, F., & Seghier, M. L. (2005). Discriminating emotional faces without primary visual cortices involves the right amygdala. *Nature Neuroscience, 8,* 24–25.

Pinker, S. (1994). *The language instinct. How the mind creates language.* New York: Morrow.

Pinker, S. (1999). *How the mind works.* New York: W. W. Norton.

Pinker, S. (2002). *The blank slate: The modern denial of human nature.* New York: Viking.

Pinker, S. (2005). So how *does* the mind work? *Mind and Language, 20,* 1–24.

Preston, C. E., & Harris, S. (1965). Psychology of drivers in traffic accidents. *Journal of Applied Psychology, 49,* 264–288.

Pronin, E., Gilovich, T., & Ross, L. (2004). Objectivity in the eye of the beholder: Divergent perceptions of bias in self versus others. *Psychological Review, 3,* 781–799.

Råberg, L., Grahn, M., Hasselquist, D., & Svensson, E. (1998). On the adaptive significance of stress-induced immunosuppression. *Proceedings of the Royal Society B: Biological Sciences, 265*, 1637–1641.

Ramachandran, V. S. (2004). *A brief tour of consciousness: From impostor poodles to purple numbers.* New York: Pearson Education.

Ramachandran, V. S., & Blakeslee, S. (1998). *Phantoms in the brain: Probing the mysteries of the human mind.* New York: HarperCollins.

Rasmussen, N., & Niles, S. (2005). *Modular systems: The evolution of reliability.* American Power Conversion, white paper 76.

Rawls, J. (1971). *A Theory of Justice.* Cambridge, MA: Harvard University Press.

Riess, M., Rosenfeld, P., Melburg, V., & Tedeschi, J. T. (1981). Self-serving attributions: Biased private perceptions and distorted public perceptions. *Journal of Personality and Social Psychology, 41*, 224–231.

Reynolds, C., & Tymann, P. (2008). *Schaum's outline of principles of computer science.* [N.p.] McGraw-Hill.

Robinson, P. H., & Kurzban, R. (2007). Concordance and conflict in intuitions of justice. *Minnesota Law Review, 91*, 1829–1907.

Robinson, P. H., Kurzban, R., & Jones, O. D. (2008). The origins of shared intuitions of justice. *Vanderbilt Law Review, 60,* 1633–1688.

Rorty, A. O. (1985). Self-deception, akrasia and irrationality. In J. Elster (ed.), *The multiple self* (pp. 115–132). Cambridge: Cambridge University Press.

Rose, H., & Rose, S. (2000). *Alas poor Darwin: Arguments against evolutionary psychology.* New York: Harmony Books.

Ross, D. (2005). *Economic theory and cognitive science: Microexplanation.* Cambridge, MA: Bradford.

Roth, E. A. (2007). Repugnance as a constraint on markets. *Journal of Economic Perspectives, 21*, 37–58.

Rothman, A. J., Klein, W. M., & Weinstein, N. D. (1996). Absolute and relative biases in estimations of personal risk. *Journal of Applied Social Psychology, 26*, 1213–1236.

Samuelson, P. A. (1948). Consumption theory in terms of revealed preference. *Economica, 15*, 243–253.

Schacter, D. L. (2001). *The seven sins of memory: How the mind forgets and remembers.* New York: Houghton Mifflin.

Scheff, T. J., & Fearon, D. S., Jr. (2004). Cognition and emotion? The dead end in self-esteem research. *Journal for the Theory of Social Behaviour, 34*, 73–90.

Schelling, T. (1960). *The strategy of conflict.* Cambridge, MA: Harvard University Press.

———— (1980). The intimate context for self-command. *The Public Interest, 60*, 94–118.

———— (1984). Self-command in practice, in policy, and in a theory of rational choice. *American Economic Review, 74*, 1–11.

Schlenker, B. R., & Leary, M. R. (1982). Audiences' reactions to self-enhancing, self-denigrating, and accurate self-presentations. *Journal of Experimental Social Psychology, 18*, 89–104.

Schlenker, B. R., & Pontari, B. A. (2000). The strategic control of information: impression management and self-presentation in daily life. In A. Tesser, R. B. Felson, & J. Suls (eds.), *Psychological perspectives on self and identity* (pp. 199–232). Washington, DC: American Psychological Association.

Schmeichel, B. J., & Zell, A. (2007). Trait self-control predicts performance on behavioral tests of self-control. *Journal of Personality, 75*, 743–756.

Schwartz, B. (2004). *The paradox of choice: Why more is less.* New York: Ecco.

Sedikides, C., Gaertner, L., & Vevea, J. L. (2005). Pancultural self-enhancement reloaded: A meta-analytic reply to Heine (2005). *Journal of Personality and Social Psychology, 89*, 539–551.

Sedikides, C., & Gregg, A. (2008). Self-enhancement, food for thought. *Perspectives on Psychological Science, 3*, 102–116.

Sedikides, C., Herbst, K. C., Hardin, D. P., & Dardis, G. J. (2002). Accountability as a deterrent to self-enhancement: The search for mechanisms. *Journal of Personality and Social Psychology, 83*, 592–605.

Sedikides, C., & Luke, M. (2007). On when self-enhancement and self-criticism function adaptively and maladaptively. In E. C. Chang (ed.), *Self-criticism and self-enhancement: Theory, research and clinical implications* (pp. 181–198). Washington, DC: American Psychological Association.

Sen, A. (1997). Maximization and the act of choice. *Econometrica, 65*, 745–779.

Shafir, E., Simonson, I., & Tversky, A. (1993). Reason-based choice. *Cognition, 49*, 11–36.

Sheppard, J. A., Carroll, P., Grace, J., & Terry, M. (2002). Exploring the causes of comparative optimism. Special issue on self-other asymmetries in social cognition. *Psychological Belgica, 42*, 65–98.

Shoda, Y., Mischel, W., & Peake, P. K. (1990). Predicting adolescent cognitive and social competence from preschool delay of gratification: Identifying diagnostic conditions. *Developmental Psychology, 26*, 978–986.

Sidanius, J., & Kurzban, R. (2003). Evolutionary approaches to political psychology. In D. O. Sears, L. Huddy, and R. Jervis (eds.), *Handbook of Political Psychology* (pp. 146–181). Oxford: Oxford University Press.

Simonson, I. (1989). Choice based on reasons: The case of attraction and compromise effects. *Journal of Consumer Research, 16*, 158–174.

Simonson, I., & Tversky, Amos (1992). Choice in context: Tradeoff contrast and extremeness aversion. *Journal of Marketing Research, 29*, 281–295.

Slovic, P. (1975). Choice between equally-valued alternatives. *Journal of Experimental Psychology: Human Perception and Performance, 1,* 280–287.

——— (1995). The construction of preference. *American Psychologist, 5,* 364–371.

Slovic, P., & Lichtenstein, S. (1968). Relative importance of probabilities and payoffs in risk-taking. *Journal of Experimental Psychology Monographs, 78,* 1–18.

Sosis, R., & Bressler, E. (2003). Cooperation and commune longevity: A test of the costly signaling theory of religion. *Cross-Cultural Research, 37,* 211–239.

Sperber, D. (2000). Metarepresentations in an evolutionary perspective. In D. Sperber (ed.), *Metarepresentations: A multidisciplinary perspective* (pp. 117–138). New York: Oxford University Press.

——— (2005). Modularity and relevance: How can a massively modular mind be flexible and context-sensitive? In P. Carruthers, S. Laurence, & S. Stich (eds.), *The innate mind: Structure and content* (pp. 53–68). New York: Oxford University Press.

Steedman, I., & Krause, U. (1985). Goethe's Faust, Arrow's possibility theorem and the individual decision-taker. In J. Elster (ed.), *The Multiple Self* (197–232). Cambridge University Press.

Stephens, D. W., & John, R. K. (1986). *Foraging theory.* Princeton, NJ: Princeton University Press.

Stevens, J. R., Hallinan, E. V., & Hauser, M. D. (2005). The ecology and evolution of patience in two New World monkeys. *Biology Letters, 1,* 223–226.

Stewart, R. (2006). *The places in between.* Orlando, FL: Harcourt.

Stigler, G. J., & Becker, G. S. (1977). De gustibus non est disputandum. *American Economic Review, 67,* 76–90.

Stitch, S. (1983). *From folk psychology to cognitive science: The case against belief.* Cambridge, MA: Bradford.

Streufert, S., & Streufert, S. C. (1969). The effects of conceptual structure, failure, and success on attributions of causality and interpersonal attitudes. *Journal of Personality and Social Psychology, 11,* 138–147.

Surbey, M. K. (2004). Self-deception: Helping and hindering public and personal decision making. In C. Crawford & C. Salmon (eds.), *Evolutionary psychology, public policy, and personal decisions* (pp. 117–144). Mahwah, NJ: Elrbaum.

Symons, D. (1979). *The evolution of human sexuality.* New York: Oxford University Press.

Taleb, N. N. (2001). *Fooled by randomness: The hidden role of chance in the markets and in life.* New York: Texere LLC.

Tangney, J. P., Baumeister, R. F., & Boone, A. L. (2004). High self-control predicts good adjustment, less pathology, better grades, and interpersonal success. *Journal of Personality, 72,* 271–324.

Tavris, C., & Aronson, E. (2007). *Mistakes were made (but not by me): Why we justify foolish beliefs, bad decisions, and hurtful acts.* Orlando, FL: Harcourt.

Taylor, S. E. (1989*). Positive illusions: Creative self-deception and the healthy mind.* New York: Basic Books.

Tedeschi, J. T., & Norman, N. (1985). Social power, self-presentation, and the self. In B. R. Schlenker (ed.), *The self and social life* (pp. 293–322). New York: McGraw-Hill.

Tesser, A., & Smith, J. (1980). Some effects of task relevance and friendship on the helping: You don't always help the one you like. *Journal of Experimental Social Psychology, 16,* 582–590.

Tetlock, P. E., & Manstead, A. S. R. (1985). Impression management versus intrapsychic explanations in social psychology: A useful dichotomy? *Psychological Review, 92,* 59–77.

Thaler, R., & Sunstein, C. (2008). *Nudge: Improving decisions about health, wealth, and happiness.* New Haven, CT: Yale University Press.

Tice, D. M. (1992). Self-presentation and self-concept change: The looking-glass self is also a magnifying glass. *Journal of Personality and Social Psychology, 63,* 435–451.

Tice, D. M., & Baumeister, R. F. (2001). The primacy of the interpersonal self. In M. B. Brewer & C. Sedikides (eds.), *Individual self, relational self, collective self* (pp. 71–88). Philadelphia: Psychology Press.

Tice, D.M., Baumeister, R.F., Shmueli, D., & Muraven, M. (2007), Restoring the self: Positive affect helps improve self-regulation following ego depletion. *Journal of Experimental Social Psychology, 43,* 379–384.

Todd, P. M. (1997). Searching for the next best mate. In R. Conte, R. Hegselmann, & P. Terna (eds.), *Lecture notes in economics and mathematical systems* (pp. 419–436). Berlin: Springer-Verlag.

Todd, P. M., & Miller, G. (1999). From Pride and Prejudice to persuasion: Realistic heuristics for mate search. In G. Gigerenzer, P. M. Todd, & ABC Research Group (eds.), *Simple heuristics that make us smart* (pp. 287–308). New York: Oxford University Press.

Tooby, J., & Cosmides, L. (1990). The past explains the present: Emotional adaptations and the structure of ancestral environments. *Ethology and Sociobiology, 11,* 375–424.

———— (1992). The psychological foundations of culture. In J. H. Barkow, L. Cosmides & J. Tooby (eds.), *The adapted mind* (pp. 19–136). New York: Oxford University Press.

Tooby, J., & Cosmides, L. (1995). Mapping the evolved functional organization of mind and brain. In M. Gazzaniga (ed.), *The cognitive neurosciences* (pp. 1185–1197). Cambridge, MA: MIT Press.

———— (1996). Friendship and the banker's paradox: Other pathways to the evolution of adaptations for altruism. In W. G. Runciman, J. Maynard Smith, & R.I.M. Dunbar (eds.), *Evolution of social behaviour patterns in primates and man. Proceedings of the British Academy, 88*, 119–143.

———— (2005). Conceptual foundations of evolutionary psychology. In D. M. Buss (ed.), *The Handbook of Evolutionary Psychology* (pp. 5–67). Hoboken, NJ: Wiley.

———— (2008). The evolutionary psychology of the emotions and their relationship to internal regulatory variables. In M. Lewis, J. M. Haviland-Jones & L. F. Barrett (eds.), *Handbook of Emotions*, 3rd ed. (pp. 114–137.) New York: Guilford Press.

Tooby, J., Cosmides, L., Sell, A., Lieberman, D. & Sznycer, D. (2008). Internal regulatory variables and the design of human motivation: A computational and evolutionary approach. In Andrew J. Elliot (ed.), *Handbook of approach and avoidance motivation.* (pp. 251–271). Mahwah, NJ: Lawrence Erlbaum Associates.

Tomporowski, P. D. (2003). Effects of acute bouts of exercise on cognition. *Acta Psychologica, 112,* 297–324.

Trivers, R. L. (2000). The elements of a scientific theory of self-deception. *Annals of the New York Academy of Sciences, 907,* 114–131.

Trzesniewski, K. H., Donnellan, M. B., Moffitt, T. E., Robins, R. W., Poulton, R., & Caspi, A. (2006). Low self-esteem during adolescence predicts poor health, criminal behavior, and limited economic prospects during adulthood. *Developmental Psychology, 42,* 381–390.

Tversky, A., Slovic, P., & Kahneman, D. (1990). The causes of preference reversals. *American Economic Review, 80,* 204–217.

Tversky, A., & Thaler, R. H. (1990). Anomalies: Preference reversals. *Journal of Economic Perspectives, 4,* 201–211.

Uchino, B. N., Cacioppo, J. T., & Kiecolt-Glaser, J. K. (1996). The relationship between social support and physiological processes: A review with emphasis on underlying mechanisms and implications for health. *Psychological Bulletin, 119,* 488–531.

Uhlmann, E. L., Pizarro, D. A., Tannenbaum, D., & Ditto, P. H. (2009). The motivated use of moral principles. *Judgment and Decision Making, 4,* 476–491.

Van den Berg, C. J. (1986). On the relation between energy transformation in the brain and mental activities. In R. Hockey, A. Gaillard, & M. Coles (eds.),

Energetics and Human Information Processing (pp. 131–135). Dordrecht, Netherlands: Martinus Nijhoff.

van der Velde, F. W., van der Pligt, J., & Hooykaas, C. (1994). Perceiving AIDS-related risk: Accuracy as a function of differences in actual risk. *Health Psychology, 13,* 25–33.

Van Leeuwen, D.S.N. (2007). The spandrels of self-deception: Prospects for a biological theory of a mental phenomenon. *Philosophical Psychology, 20,* 329–348.

Vanderbilt, T. (2008). *Traffic: Why we drive the way we do (and what it says about us).* New York: Knopf.

Vogel. S. (1998). *Cat's paws and catapults : Mechanical worlds of nature and people.* New York: W.W. Norton.

Vokey, J. R., & Read, J. D. (1985). Subliminal messages: Between the Devil and the media. *American Psychologist, 40,* 1231–1239.

Walton, D. (1999). The fallacy of many questions: On the notions of complexity, loadedness and unfair entrapment in interrogative theory, *Argumentation, 13,* 379–383.

Wang, X. T., & Dvorak, R. D. (2010). Sweet future: Fluctuating blood glucose levels affect future discounting. *Psychological Science, 21,* 183–188.

Webber, D. W. (1997). *AIDS and the law.* [N.p.] Aspen Publishers.

Wedekind, C., & Følstad, I. (1994). Adaptive or nonadaptive immunosuppression by sex hormones? *American Naturalist, 143,* 936–938.

Weeden, J. (2003). Genetic interests, life histories, and attitudes towards abortion. Unpublished doctoral dissertation, University of Pennsylvania.

⁑ Wegner, D. M. (2002). *The illusion of conscious will.* Cambridge, MA: MIT Press.
——— (2003). The mind's best trick: How we experience conscious will. *Trends in Cognitive Sciences, 7,* 65–69.
——— (2005). Who is the controller of controlled processes? In R. Hassin, J. S. Uleman, & J. A. Bargh (eds.), *The new unconscious* (pp. 19–36). New York: Oxford University Press.

Weiner, B., Frieze, I., Kukla, A., Reed, L., Rest, S., & Rosenbaum, R. M. (1971). Perceiving the causes of success and failure. In E. E. Jones, D. E. Kanouse, H.H. Kelley, R. E. Nisbett, S. Valins, & B. Weiner (eds.), *Attribution: Perceiving the causes of behavior* (pp. 95–120). Morristown, NJ: General Learning Press.

Weiner, J. (1994). *The beak of the finch.* New York: Random House.

Weinstein, N. D. (1980). Unrealistic optimism about future life events. *Journal of Personality and Social Psychology, 39,* 806–820.

Weinstein, N. D. (1982). Unrealistic optimism about susceptibility to health problems. *Journal of Behavioural Medicine, 5,* 441–460.

Weisberg, D. S., Keil, F. C., Goodstein, J., Rawson, E., & Gray, J. (2008). The seductive allure of neuroscience explanations. *Journal of Cognitive Neuroscience, 20,* 470–477.

Westen, D. (2007). *The political brain: The role of emotion in deciding the fate of the nation.* New York: PublicAffairs.

Whiten, A., & Byrne, R. W. (1997). *Machiavellian intelligence II.* Cambridge: Cambridge University Press.

Wiley, H. R. (1994). Errors, exaggeration, and deception in animal communication. In L. Real (ed.), *Behavioral mechanisms in evolutionary ecology* (pp. 157–189). Chicago: University of Chicago Press.

Williams, E., & Gilovich, T. (2008). Do people really believe they are above average? *Journal of Experimental Social Psychology, 44,* 1121–1128.

Williams, G. C. (1966). *Adaptation and natural selection.* Princeton, NJ: Princeton University Press.

Williams, K. D. (2001). *Ostracism: The power of silence.* New York: Guilford Press.

———— (2007). Ostracism. *Annual Review of Psychology, 58,* 425–452.

Wilson, D. S. (2002). *Darwin's cathedral: Evolution, religion, and the nature of society,* Chicago: University of Chicago Press.

Wilson, T. D. (2002). *Strangers to ourselves: Discovering the adaptive unconscious.* Cambridge, MA: Harvard University Press.

Windschitl, P. D., Kruger, J., & Simms, E. N. (2003). The influence of egocentrism and focalism on people's optimism in competitions: When what affects us equally affects me more. *Journal of Personality and Social Psychology, 85,* 389–408.

Winston, G. C. (1980). Addiction and backsliding: A theory of compulsive consumption. *Journal of Economic and Behavioral Organization, 1,* 295–324.

Wolfers, J., & Zitzewitz, E. (2006). Interpreting prediction market prices as probabilities. Working paper.

Yamagishi, T., Hashimoto, H., & Schug, J. (2008). Preferences versus strategies as explanations for culture-specific behavior. *Psychological Science, 19,* 579–584.

index

The letter *n* following a page number indicates a note on that page.
The figure following the *n* indicates the number of the note cited.